ADVANCE PRAISE for **Rainbow Theology**

"This is a landmark book. It not only brings to the center of theological reflection the silenced but vibrant voices of LGBTIQ persons of color, but it charts ground-breaking directions for religious thought, church practices, and social and political analysis. This book is innovative, passionate, and challenging. With his rainbow theology Patrick Cheng provides for us piercing insights into God, the world, and ourselves that have been hidden from us because of our monochromatic views of the world and God. It is a must read for anyone committed to a more just world."

—Kelly Brown Douglas, Goucher College

Author of *Sexuality and the Black Church: A Womanist Perspective*

"With characteristic grace, Cheng not only turns the complex categories of race and sexuality into accessible speech, he links them to spirit without missing a beat. Tracing commonalities while deeply respecting differences, he challenges readers to allow queer of color lived experiences of multiplicity, middle spaces, and mediation to form a more viable framework for constructive theology."

—Laurel C. Schneider, Vanderbilt University

Author of *Beyond Monotheism: A Theology of Multiplicity*

"Patrick Cheng is one of the first theologians to substantively engage queer of color critique, thus fundamentally challenging the parameters of not only queer theology, but theology as a whole. This amazing book combines reader accessibility with theoretical sophistication. Cheng does not homogenize queer of color theology, but provides a comprehensive analysis of its multiple strands. The book is truly groundbreaking."

—Andrea Smith, University of California, Riverside

Author of *Native Americans and the Christian Right: The Gendered Politics of Unlikely Alliances*

"In a world dominated by a binary, either-or, monochromatic approach to diversity, Rainbow Theology challenges us to recover and reclaim a theological framework that has been there from the beginning of Christianity – a place where a multiplicity of experiences and identities are held in creative tension. A place where we can create a truly inclusive beloved community of Christ."

—Eric H.F. Law, Kaleidoscope Institute

Author of *Holy Currencies: Six Blessings for Sustainable Missional Ministries*

RAINBOW THEOLOGY

Bridging Race, Sexuality, and Spirit

PATRICK S. CHENG

Seabury Books
NEW YORK

Library of Congress Cataloging-in-Publication Data

Cheng, Patrick S.

Rainbow theology : bridging race, sexuality, and spirit / Patrick S. Cheng.
pages cm

  Includes bibliographical references and index.

  ISBN 978-1-59627-241-5 (pbk.) -- ISBN 978-1-59627-242-2 (ebook) 1. Church and minorities. 2. Homosexuality--Religious aspects--Christianity. 3. Multiculturalism--Religious aspects--Christianity. 4. Ethnicity--Religious aspects--Christianity 5. Race--Religious aspects--Christianity. I. Title.

  BV639.M56C44 2013
  230.08--dc23

                          2013000911

Cover design by Laurie Klein Westhafer
Typeset by Denise Hoff

Seabury Books
445 Fifth Avenue
New York, New York 10016

www.churchpublishing.org

An imprint of Church Publishing Incorporated

*To queer of color theologians,
past, present, and future.*

Contents

Acknowledgments

This book would not have been possible without the support of the Episcopal Divinity School community, including my faculty colleagues Angela Bauer-Levesque, Stephen Burns, Christopher Duraisingh, Suzanne Ehly, Miriam Gelfer, Bill Kondrath, Joan Martin, Kwok Pui-lan, Katherine Hancock Ragsdale, Ed Rodman, Susie Snyder, Fredrica Harris Thompsett, Larry Wills, and Gale Yee. Special thanks goes to the EDS and Sherrill Library staff, especially Chris Carr, Aura Fluett, Jamie Glass, Scott Kinkade, Jeffrey Perkins, and Stephanie Nelson.

I am grateful to those who have commented on the draft manuscript in whole or in part, including Darren Arquero, Mike Campos, Vincent Cervantes, Hugo Córdova Quero, Thomas Eoyang, Joe Goh, Robyn Henderson-Espinoza, Pamela Lightsey, Catherine Owens, Andy Smith, Lai Shan Yip, and Nikki Young. I am also grateful to those people who have given me feedback about the ideas in this book, including individuals from the following communities: Center for Lesbian and Gay Studies in Religion and Ministry; Chicago Theological Seminary; Episcopal Divinity School; Human Rights Campaign Summer Institute; Pacific School of Religion; Union Theological Seminary in the City of New York; Wabash Center for Teaching and Learning; and Wellesley College. Of course, all errors in the book are my responsibility alone.

During the writing of this book, I have been sustained by my friends in the following communities: American Academy of Religion Asian North American Religion, Culture, and Society Group; American Academy of Religion Committee on the Status of LGBTIQ Persons in the Profession; American

Academy of Religion Gay Men and Religion Group; Boston Queer Theology Forum; Christ Church Cambridge; Emerging Queer Asian Religion Scholars; Emmanuel Church in the City of Boston; Episcopal Diocese of Massachusetts; Metropolitan Community Churches Theologies Team; National Queer Asian Pacific Islander Alliance; Queer Asian Spirit; and Society of Christian Ethics. I am grateful for a 2012 summer fellowship awarded by the Wabash Center for Teaching and Learning that partially funded my work on this book.

In addition to the persons and communities mentioned above, I am grateful for the friendship, support, and inspiration of the following queer of color theologians, religion scholars, and allies: Victor Anderson, Margaret Aymer Oget, Rudy Busto, Monica Coleman, James Cone, Shawn Copeland, Miguel De La Torre, Aman De Sondy, Kelly Brown Douglas, Orlando Espín, Ibrahim Abdurrahman Farajajé, Horace Griffin, Jen Harvey, Renée Hill, Zayn Kassam, Eric Law, Benny Liew, Leng Lim, Irene Monroe, Su Pak, Laurel Schneider, Roger Sneed, Emilie Townes, and Traci West. I am also thankful for the ongoing friendship and wisdom of Faith Cantor, Kitt Cherry, Jessica Greenleaf, Kim Leary, Mary McKinney, Christine Pao, Amy Revell, Joe Robinson, Tom Shaw, Bob Shore-Goss, Geoffrey Tristram, Renee Ward, and Pam Werntz.

As always, I am grateful to the wonderful folks at Seabury Books, including my editor, Davis Perkins, and his colleagues Nancy Bryan, Mark Dazzo, Bill Falvey, Ryan Masteller, Deirdre Morrissey, Lillian Ort, Lorraine Simonello, and Laurie Westhafer.

I give thanks to my family, including Deanna Cheng, Andrew Cheng, Abi Karlin-Resnick, Jordan Cheng, and Noah Cheng. Last but not least, I could not have written this book—let alone pursued my vocation as a theologian, seminary professor, and ordained minister—without the steadfast love and support of my husband, Michael Boothroyd, and our dog, Chartres.

Introduction

When I was growing up in the San Francisco Bay Area in the 1970s and 80s, I looked forward each year to the annual network television broadcast of *The Wizard of Oz*. My favorite part of the movie was when it transitioned from black and white to dazzling Technicolor. The first part of the movie, when Dorothy and Toto are in Kansas, was shot in black and white. After Dorothy and Toto are transported over the rainbow, however, they step out of their monochromatic house into the multicolored hues of Munchkinland. Dorothy is greeted by Glinda, the Good Witch of the South, and Glinda urges the Munchkins to "come out, come out, wherever you are."[1]

Somehow I imagined that my own coming out process as a gay man would be just like Dorothy and Toto's transition from black and white into Technicolor. After all, gay men loved *The Wizard of Oz* and even called themselves "friends of Dorothy." That is, I would be transported from the closet—a monochromatic black and white space—into a fabulous rainbow-colored space that was the lesbian, gay, bisexual, transgender, intersex, and queer ("LGBTIQ" or "queer") community.[2]

Unfortunately, my coming out process as a gay man was far less fabulous than I had imagined. This was due in large part to the fact that I am also an Asian American man. I quickly found

---

[1] *The Wizard of Oz*, directed by Victor Fleming (1939).

[2] For more information about definitions relating to the LGBTIQ community, see chapter 1 below. See also Timothy Palmer and Debra W. Haffner, *A Time to Seek: Study Guide on Sexual and Gender Diversity* (Westport, CT: Religious Institute, 2006), 7–11; Patrick S. Cheng, *From Sin to Amazing Grace: Discovering the Queer Christ* (New York: Seabury Books, 2012), xvi–xviii; Patrick S. Cheng, *Radical Love: An Introduction to Queer Theology* (New York: Seabury Books, 2011), 2–8.

out that to be a person of color within the LGBTIQ community posed its own set of challenges. When I came out of the closet in the mid-1980s in college, I thought I was a unicorn. That is, I thought that I was a one-of-a-kind mythical creature because everyone I knew in the gay and lesbian community was white, and everyone I knew in the Asian American community was straight.[3]

Not only did I not know other LGBTIQ people of color, but I was actively excluded from parts of gay culture. When I went to a gay bar in Washington, D.C., with my white gay friends from college, I was asked to show several forms of identification, whereas my friends were not.[4] And once I was allowed inside the bar, I felt completely invisible. Nobody talked to me or said hello. So much for being "somewhere over the rainbow." I was stuck in a monochromatic world.

1. Never Quite Getting to Oz

In some ways, the experience of LGBTIQ people of color can be characterized as never quite getting to Oz. That is, those of us who identify as queer people of color are often stuck in the liminal space between Dorothy and Toto's monochromatic house from Kansas and the Technicolor hues of the Land of Oz. Although we may have been transported over the rainbow as a result of coming out of the closet, we are never able to walk out of the black and white doorway into a truly rainbow space—that is, a space in which the multicolored hues of our bodies, sexualities, and spiritualities are appreciated and seen as beautiful.

First, queer people of color never quite get to Oz because of the racism that we face from the predominantly white LGBTIQ

---

[3] See Patrick S. Cheng, "A Unicorn at the White House," *Huffington Post* (July 30, 2012), accessed January 3, 2013, http://huff.to/Phq3d2.

[4] The gay historian Allan Bérubé has written about the practice of "triple-carding" by gay bars to dissuade people of color from entering. This was done because a bar could lose its popularity if it was perceived to have been "taken over" by gay men of color. Allan Bérubé, *My Desire for History: Essays in Gay, Community, and Labor History* (Chapel Hill: University of North Carolina Press, 2011), 206.

community. In addition to experiencing the historical practices of exclusion such as multiple carding by gay bars, we are often rendered virtually invisible by the LGBTIQ media. For example, in 2011, *Out Magazine* released its fifth annual "Power 50 List" of the fifty most powerful people in the LGBTIQ community.[5] Of the fifty names on the list, only two persons were identifiably people of color. Furthermore, both were Latino men, which means that there were no African Americans, Asian Americans, people of Indigenous descent, or women of color on the list.

Second, queer people of color never quite get to Oz because of the queerphobia[6] that we experience from predominantly non-queer communities of color. For example, many of us are rejected by our biological families because of our sexualities and/or gender identities. Unlike our straight and cisgender[7] siblings of color, LGBTIQ people of color are often unable to turn to our families of origin for support when we face issues of racism either inside or outside of the LGBTIQ community.

Third, queer people of color never quite get to Oz because of both the racism *and* the queerphobia that we experience from many religious—and especially Christian—communities. That is, many conservative Christian communities are toxic sites for LGBTIQ people of color in which the mutually-reinforcing oppressions of racism and queerphobia converge. In particular, this dynamic can be seen in the context of the marriage equality debate in which the religious right has actively used racism and queerphobia to prevent the enactment of same-sex marriage laws.

With respect to racism, predominantly white religious groups such as the so-called National Organization for Marriage (NOM) intentionally exploit racial tensions by pitting people of color against LGBTIQ people. For example, a confidential report

---

[5] "Fifth Annual Power 50," Out.com, accessed January 3, 2013, http://bit.ly/yyesrL.

[6] "Queerphobia" is an umbrella term that refers collectively to the fears that certain straight and/or non-transgender people have of lesbians and gay men ("homophobia"), bisexuals ("biphobia"), and transgender people ("transphobia").

[7] "Cisgender" refers to people who do not identify as transgender.

by NOM was leaked in March 2012 that explicitly argued for a strategy to "drive a wedge between gays and blacks" as well as Latina/os.[8]

With respect to queerphobia, religious leaders such as Bishop Harry Jackson, an outspoken African American pastor from Maryland who is vehemently opposed to same-sex marriage rights, have articulated a false dichotomy of race on the one hand vs. sexuality on the other hand. For example, Jackson told a conference of the religious right in Texas in July 2012: "We need to steal back the rainbow. We can't let the gays have it." Jackson continued by proclaiming: "We're the rainbow coalition. We're the army of God."[9] According to Jackson, people of color are the "true" children of the rainbow. However, this ignores the fact that there are LGBTIQ people of color who are both queer *and* of color.

These divide-and-conquer strategies of the religious right are particularly reprehensible because not only do they exploit racism and queerphobia for political purposes, but they ignore the existence of LGBTIQ people of color. Contrary to what Harry Jackson and NOM may think, there are in fact millions of people in this country—not to mention around the world—who are queers of color.[10] And queers of color are *already* members of the very "rainbow coalition" that Jackson and NOM are trying to appropriate for their own goals.

In sum, LGBTIQ people of color never quite get to Oz. We are excluded from both the LGBTIQ community (because of racism) as well as communities of color (because of queerphobia). And

---

[8] John Becker, "Secret NOM Documents Reveal Race-Baiting Strategy," *Huffington Post* (March 27, 2012), accessed January 3, 2013, http://huff.to/HbkIUL.

[9] "Harry Jackson, Maryland Bishop, Claims Gays Are 'Trying to Recruit' Children, Wants to 'Steal Back' Rainbow," *Huffington Post* (August 3, 2012), accessed January 3, 2013, http://huff.to/QMrx3q. On November 6, 2012, Maryland voters approved same-sex marriage by popular vote, and the first same-sex marriages occurred in that state on January 1, 2013.

[10] Assuming that there are some 8.7 million LGBTIQ people in the United States, and approximately 37 percent of the population consists of racial and ethnic minorities, then there are some 3.2 million queers of color in the United States. See "How Many LGBT's Live in America?," *Advocate* (April 6, 2011), accessed January 3, 2013, http://bit.ly/JRLwKZ; Doris Nhan, "Census: Minorities Constitute 37 Percent of U.S. Population," *National Journal* (May 17, 2012), accessed January 3, 2013, http://bit.ly/QvPLLG.

we are caught in the middle when the religious right pits the LGBTIQ community against communities of color (because of both racism *and* queerphobia).

2. Goals of the Book

This book is written within the larger context of the exclusion and silencing of LGBTIQ people of color. Accordingly, the goals of this book are twofold. The first goal is to lift up the writings by LGBTIQ theologians of color and to break the silence with respect to such writings. The second goal is to rethink the enterprise of Christian theology by moving the experiences of LGBTIQ people of color from the margins to the center.

a. Lifting Up Queer of Color Theologies

The first goal of this book is to lift up the writings by LGBTIQ theologians of color. Although queer theologians of color have been writing about their experiences for at least the last two decades, these writings remain largely unknown within the broader queer theological world. My hope is that this book, by bringing together and organizing these writings, will begin to break the silence with respect to the work of LGBTIQ theologians of color.

For example, an important anthology of queer theological writings published in 2007, *Queer Theology: Rethinking the Western Body*, includes (as far as I can tell) no contributions from LGBTIQ theologians of color.[11] Other than a brief discussion about homophobia and the Black Church by the queer ethicist Kathy Rudy,[12] the anthology contains no discussion (again, as far as I can tell) relating to the experiences of LGBTIQ people of color. Sadly, the *Queer Theology* anthology is true to its subtitle; it is indeed a rethinking of the "western body," but bodies of African, Asian, Latin American, or Indigenous descent are not mentioned.

---

[11] See Gerard Loughlin, ed., *Queer Theology: Rethinking the Western Body* (Malden, MA: Blackwell Publishing, 2007), vii–viii.

[12] See Kathy Rudy, "Subjectivity and Belief," in Loughlin, *Queer Theology*, 46–48.

This is particularly problematic because queer theologies of color have been around for at least two decades. Two pioneering works of queer Black theology appeared in 1993: one about the silence of the Black Church with respect to gay and bisexual men and the HIV/AIDS pandemic;[13] and another about the silence of womanist theologians with respect to Black lesbians and issues of heterosexism and homophobia.[14]

These two works were followed in 1996 with a groundbreaking essay about the queer Asian American Christian experience.[15] The following year, 1997, saw the publication of a theological reflection about the Latina lesbian experience.[16] In 2000, a revolutionary book-length work on "indecent theology" was published by a Latin American bisexual theologian.[17] Since the mid-2000s, there has been a proliferation of writings by LGBTIQ theologians of color, including a book-length treatment about homophobia and the Black Church (2006),[18] a queer Black critique of Black liberation theology (2010),[19] and a rethinking of the Christian doctrines of sin and grace from a queer Asian American perspective (2012).[20]

To be sure, things are changing. The U.K. queer theologian Susannah Cornwall, in her 2011 introductory text on queer theology, *Controversies in Queer Theology*, included a chapter

---

[13] See Elias Farajaje-Jones, "Breaking Silence: Toward an In-the-Life Theology," in *Black Theology: A Documentary History, Volume II, 1980–1992*, ed. James H. Cone and Gayraud S. Wilmore (Maryknoll, NY: Orbis Books, 1993), 139–59.

[14] See Renee L. Hill, "Who Are We for Each Other?: Sexism, Sexuality and Womanist Theology," in Cone and Wilmore, *Black Theology II*, 345–51.

[15] See Leng Leroy Lim, "The Gay Erotics of My Stuttering Mother Tongue," *Amerasia Journal* 22, no. 1 (1996): 172–77.

[16] See Margarita Suárez, "Reflections on Being Latina and Lesbian," in *Que(e)rying Religion: A Critical Anthology*, ed. Gary David Comstock and Susan E. Henking (New York: Continuum, 1997), 347–50.

[17] See Marcella Althaus-Reid, *Indecent Theology: Theological Perversions in Sex, Gender and Politics* (London: Routledge, 2000).

[18] See Horace L. Griffin, *Their Own Receive Them Not: African American Lesbians and Gays in Black Churches* (Cleveland, OH: Pilgrim Press, 2006).

[19] See Roger A. Sneed, *Representations of Homosexuality: Black Liberation Theology and Cultural Criticism* (New York: Palgrave Macmillan, 2010).

[20] See Cheng, *From Sin to Amazing Grace*.

entitled "Is Queer Theology Inherently White or Western?" In that chapter, Cornwall addressed the critiques of theologians of color, including myself, that queer theologies have "failed to engage adequately with questions of ethnicity and 'race.'"[21] And the 2012 two-volume anthology *Queer Religion*, edited by Donald L. Boisvert and Jay Emerson Johnson, included a number of contributions from African American, Asian American, and Latina/o theologians and religious studies scholars.[22]

Nevertheless, to date, there has been no book-length treatment about the writings of LGBTIQ theologians of color, nor has there been any book-length work about the experiences of LGBTIQ people of color from a theological perspective. It is my hope that this book will begin to fill the gap in the literature.

b. From the Margins to the Center

The second goal of this book is to rethink the enterprise of Christian theology by moving the experiences of LGBTIQ people of color from the margins to the center. That is, this book asks what a queer of color theology can contribute to the larger theological enterprise. What does the unique position of LGBTIQ people of color—that is, those individuals who are both fully queer and fully of color—have to say about the Gospel? Where is God in the experiences of LGBTIQ people of color?

To date, LGBTIQ people have been relegated to the margins with respect to theological and ecclesial debates about sexuality. Whether it is the debates in the Anglican Communion over

---

[21] Susannah Cornwall, *Controversies in Queer Theology* (London: SCM Press, 2011), 73.

[22] See, e.g., Michael Sepidoza Campos, "The *Baklâ*: Gendered Religious Performance in Filipino Cultural Spaces," in *Queer Religion: Volume II, LGBT Movements and Queering Religion*, ed. Donald L. Boisvert and Jay Emerson Johnson (Santa Barbara, CA: Praeger, 2012), 167–91; Jojo (Kenneth Hamilton), "Searching for Gender-Variant East African Spiritual Leaders, From Missionary Discourse to Middle Course," in *Queer Religion: Volume I, Homosexuality in Modern Religious History*, ed. Donald L. Boisvert and Jay Emerson Johnson (Santa Barbara, CA: Praeger, 2012), 127–45; Juan A. Herrero-Brasas, "Whitman's Church of Comradeship: Same-Sex Love, Religion, and the Marginality of Friendship," in Boisvert and Johnson, *Queer Religion I*, 169–89; Roland Stringfellow, "Soul Work: Developing a Black LGBT Liberation Theology," in Boisvert and Johnson, *Queer Religion I*, 113–25; Ruth Vanita, "Hinduism and Homosexuality," in Boisvert and Johnson, *Queer Religion I*, 1–23; Lai-shan Yip, "Listening to the Passion of Catholic *nu-tongzhi*: Developing a Catholic Lesbian Feminist Theology in Hong Kong," in Boisvert and Johnson, *Queer Religion II*, 63–80; Kuukua Dzigbordi Yomekpe, "Not Just a Phase: Single Black Women in the Black Church," in Boisvert and Johnson, *Queer Religion II*, 109–23.

the 2003 consecration of the Right Reverend V. Gene Robinson as the first openly-gay partnered person to be consecrated a bishop,[23] or the debates in the United States over civil marriage equality, the lines of debate are usually divided between straight and cisgender communities of color on the one hand, and white LGBTIQ communities on the other. LGBTIQ people of color are often rendered invisible in these debates.

By contrast, this book will argue that the experiences of LGBTIQ people are central to the theological enterprise. Specifically, this book will propose a "rainbow theology," which is, simply put, a theology that celebrates the experiences of queer people of color. The book will explore the three rainbow themes of (1) multiplicity, (2) middle spaces, and (3) mediation. The book will also argue that these rainbow themes are not only central to the queer of color experience, but they are also central to Christian theology itself.

These three rainbow themes are contrasted with what this book will call "monochromatic theology," which is characterized by the opposing themes of (1) singularity, (2) staying home, and (3) selecting sides. Many progressive theologies—including early liberation theologies—are actually monochromatic theologies. That is, monochromatic theologies focus primarily on liberation from a singular oppression, as opposed to challenging the interplay of multiple oppressions. Monochromatic theologies also assume that there is a single, metaphorical "home" that consists of others who experience this singular oppression. Finally, monochromatic theologies urge those who are oppressed by this singular oppression to "choose" the side of the oppressed (as opposed to the oppressors). In reality, however, LGBTIQ people of color experience complicated dynamics of oppression that call into question the monochromatic themes of singularity, staying home, and selecting sides. By contrast, rainbow theology—with its themes of multiplicity, middle spaces, and mediation—can be a helpful corrective to monochromatic theologies.[24]

---

[23] See Miranda K. Hassett, *Anglican Communion in Crisis: How Episcopal Dissidents and Their African Allies Are Reshaping Anglicanism* (Princeton, NJ: Princeton University Press, 2007).

[24] It should be noted that I am not setting up a binary between rainbow and monochromatic theologies here. Rather, I am suggesting that the themes of rainbow theology can be used to enrich the analysis of traditional liberation theologies.

In sum, rainbow theology arises out of the specific experiences of LGBTIQ people of color, but it is not limited to such individuals. Rather, it is a new way of doing theology. Rainbow theology takes seriously the unique position of queers of color with respect to the LGBTIQ community and communities of color, and it challenges *all* theologies to reflect upon the intersections of race, sexuality, and spirit.

3. Overview of the Book

This book is divided into two parts. Part I of the book focuses on "queer of color theologies"—that is, theologies written by theologians who identify as both queer and of color. Chapter one introduces some of the definitions and key theoretical issues relating to such queer of color theologies.

Chapters two through five each provide a survey of the main subgroups of queer of color theology. Instead of covering the theologies chronologically, I have chosen to organize them by racial and ethnic groups. I do this not to reinforce traditional racial and ethnic categories, but rather to explore certain shared themes—and differences—within each subgroup.

Specifically, chapter two looks at queer Black theologies with its themes of Black Church exclusion, reclaiming Black lesbian voices, and challenging Black liberation theologies. Chapter three looks at queer Asian American theologies with its themes of Asian and Asian American church exclusion, critiquing LGBTIQ racism, and highlighting transnational perspectives. Chapter four looks at queer Latina/o theologies with its themes of living on the borderlands, challenging *machismo*, and crossing literary and religious borders. Chapter five looks at Two-Spirit Indigenous scholarship with its themes of resisting settler colonialism, recognizing Two-Spirit identities, and doing the work of allies.

Part II of the book focuses on the construction of a rainbow theology. Chapter six introduces the concept of rainbow theology and provides an overview to the three rainbow themes of (1) multiplicity, (2) middle spaces, and (3) mediation. As noted above, these three themes are contrasted with the mono-chromatic themes of (1) singularity, (2) staying home, and (3) selecting sides. Chapters seven, eight, and nine examine each of the above three rainbow themes in greater detail. Chapter ten concludes Part II of the book by illustrating how a rainbow theology might work in the specific context of christology.

Having mapped out the main themes and outline of the book, let us now turn to Part I of the book, which focuses on queer of color theologies.

Study Questions

1. Have you ever experienced "never quite getting to Oz"? That is, have you been in situations in which you have not felt completely welcomed because of your race, sexuality, and/or spirituality?

2. How do you describe your own social location with respect to race, sexuality, and spirituality? How fluid have these identities been throughout your life?

3. When did the first works of queer of color theology appear? How have such works been treated within mainstream queer theology?

4. What are the three "rainbow" themes covered by this book? How do they compare and contrast with the three "monochromatic" themes?

5. How might Part I of this book be useful in your own theological work and reflections? Part II?

For Further Study

Definitions
- Cheng, *From Sin to Amazing Grace*, xvi–xviii
- Cheng, *Radical Love*, 2–8
- Palmer and Haffner, *A Time to Seek*, 7–11

Queer of Color Theologies
- Cheng, *From Sin to Amazing Grace*, 133–45
- Cheng, *Radical Love*, 74–77
- Cornwall, *Controversies in Queer Theology*, 72–113
- Goss, *Queering Christ*, 253
- Schippert, "Implications of Queer Theory for the Study of Religion and Gender," 74–77

Part I

Race, Sexuality, and Spirit

Chapter 1

Queer of Color Theologies

For the last three years, I've had the privilege of serving as a mentor at the Human Rights Campaign Summer Institute at the Vanderbilt University Divinity School in Nashville, Tennessee. Each summer, the HRC Summer Institute brings together fifteen talented doctoral and advanced master's degree students who do work in LGBTIQ theology and religious studies. The students live and study together for a week, and they have a chance to network among themselves as well as with prominent scholars from across the country who are doing similar work in LGBTIQ theology and religious studies.

For me, one of the most rewarding aspects of serving as a mentor at the HRC Summer Institute has been working with queer students of color who are interested in the intersections of race, sexuality, and spirituality. Over the years, I've had the chance to work closely with many LGBTIQ and allied Black, Asian American, and Latina/o students, and it's been interesting to observe how many similarities—and differences—there are in terms of our research agendas.

For example, in 2012 the LGBTIQ and allied scholars of color at the HRC Summer Institute worked on a dizzying variety of projects, including the reclaiming of queer Black voices in the Civil Rights Movement, examining how LGBTIQ Asian Americans use religion as a means for decolonization and healing, studying the religious lives of LGBTIQ Muslims, examining methods of Latin American queer biblical interpretation, rethinking sexual ethics in Korean American churches, recording and archiving oral histories from queer spiritual leaders, analyzing the practices of radically welcoming spiritual communities with respect to race and sexuality, studying the work of North American Two-Spirit activists, and examining notions of sexual purity in the context of global sex trafficking.

This experience of working with younger queer scholars of color across different racial and ethnic groups has led me to think deeply about whether it is possible—or even desirable—to construct a queer of color theology.[1] On the one hand, all of us share an acute awareness of the ways in which issues of race and sexuality mutually reinforce each other with respect to oppression. On the other hand, these scholars each have very different research topics, methodologies, faith traditions, and communities of accountability. So is it possible to construct a queer of color theology? It is to this question that we now turn.

1. Is "Queer of Color" a Valid Category?

Is it even possible to talk about a queer of color theology? On the one hand, the very notion of queer is to "denaturalize or de-essentialize formerly stable identities such as homosexuality, heterosexuality, race, nationality, woman, and man."[2] In other words, the term "queer"—at least in the academic discipline

---

[1] As I have written elsewhere, "queer theology" can be defined in a number of different ways. First, queer theology is LGBTIQ people "talking about God." Second, queer theology is talking about God in a "self-consciously transgressive manner, especially in terms of challenging societal norms about sexuality and gender." Third, queer theology is talking about God in a way that "challenges and deconstructs the natural binary categories of sexual and gender identity." Cheng, *Radical Love*, 9–11. For overviews of queer theology and/or queer religious studies, see Mary Elise Lowe, "Gay, Lesbian, and Queer Theologies: Origins, Contributions, and Challenges," *Dialog: A Journal of Theology* 48, no. 1 (Spring 2009): 49–61; Claudia Schippert, "Implications of Queer Theory for the Study of Religion and Gender: Entering the Third Decade," *Religion and Gender* 1, no. 1 (2011): 66–84; Claudia Schippert, "Queer Theory and the Study of Religion," *Rever: Revista de Estudios da Religião* 5, no. 4 (2005): 90–99; Melissa M. Wilcox, "Queer Theory and the Study of Religion," in Boisvert and Johnson, *Queer Religion II*, 227–51.

[2] Laurel C. Schneider, "Queer Theory," in *Handbook of Postmodern Biblical Interpretation*, ed. A. K. M. Adam (St. Louis, MO: Chalice Press, 2000), 206.

of queer theory—challenges notions of fixed identity. It would seem, therefore, that using a term such as "queer of color" is to reinforce "natural" identity categories, and *not* to further the understanding that such categories are socially constructed. As such, it would seem that the term "queer of color" is highly problematic.

Furthermore, it could be argued that the use of the term "queer of color" as an umbrella term for LGBTIQ people of color does violence—metaphorically speaking—to the particular social contexts for each subgroup (for example, queer Asian Americans) within the umbrella. That is, it is important for any given marginalized group to name itself and come to voice about its own particular experiences. Take, for example, the parallel example of womanist theology. Womanist theology arose out of the fact that neither Black (male) liberation theology nor (white) feminist theology spoke to the experiences of African American women. Thus, to use the broader categories of "Black theology" or "feminist theology" would fail to honor the womanist experience.

In my view, the "queer of color" category is an important one, and I believe that the above objections to its use can be addressed in a number of ways. First, Gayatri Spivak's notion of strategic essentialism can be helpful with respect to the issue of fixed identity. That is, it is possible to speak about "queers of color" for strategic purposes—such as in the context of "struggles for liberation from the effects of colonial and neocolonial oppression"—without reinscribing essentialist notions of identity.[3] For example, an April 2012 report by the Center for American Progress shows that LGBTIQ people of color are often the very ones who are "left behind" with respect to educational attainment, economic insecurity, and health disparities.[4]

---

[3] Bill Ashcroft, Gareth Griffiths, and Helen Tiffin, eds., *Post-Colonial Studies: The Key Concepts* (London: Routledge, 2000), 79. See also Serene Jones, *Feminist Theory and Christian Theology: Cartographies of Grace* (Minneapolis, MN: Fortress Press, 2000), 42–48.

[4] Melissa Dunn and Aisha Moodie-Mills, "The State of Gay and Transgender Communities of Color in 2012" (April 13, 2012), Center for American Progress, accessed January 3, 2013, http://bit.ly/IhiwY6.

Thus, it is vitally important to speak about "queers of color," as long as we do so in a strategic manner.

Second, with respect to the umbrella term issue (that is, whether the category of "queer of color" does violence to its subgroups), it can be argued that "queer of color" does in fact serve a useful function while also honoring the experiences of its various subgroups. There are in fact important similarities among the work done by LGBTIQ scholars of color across racial and ethnic boundaries. For example, there is a deep "family resemblance," to cite the philosopher Ludwig Wittgenstein's work on language theory, with respect to this scholarship.[5] This can be seen in the secular academy in which a "queer of color critique" movement has arisen among LGBTIQ scholars of color. This movement has recognized the importance of bringing together similar voices while also preserving their differences.[6] Thus, it makes sense to look more closely at queer of color work as its own category.

Third, it may be the case that "queer of color" is less about an identity—that is, constructing yet another identity-based theology—and more about positionality. That is, LGBTIQ people of color share a unique "in between" position with respect to both the queer community and communities of color, and thus may actually require a unique signifier that discusses the specific issues that arise out of this social location. For all of these reasons, I believe that "queer of color" is a valid category that can—and must—be used.

2. Shared Scholarly Heritage

In addition to the above theoretical issues, LGBTIQ people of color also share a common genealogy, or heritage, with respect to scholarly writings about living at the intersections

---

[5] According to Wittgenstein, linguistic concepts need not, in general, have an essence. For example, there are many activities that fit within the concept of a "game," but there is no "one, essential characteristic" that ties all of such activities together beyond that of "family resemblance." See Chon Tejedor, *Starting with Wittgenstein* (London: Continuum, 2011), 111–14.

[6] See Grace Kyungwon Hong and Roderick A. Ferguson, "Introduction," in *Strange Affinities: The Gender and Sexual Politics of Comparative Racialization*, ed. Grace Kyungwon Hong and Roderick A. Ferguson (Durham, NC: Duke University Press, 2011), 1–22.

of race and sexuality. Although this genealogy is not as widely known as the more "canonical" works in queer theory by Michel Foucault, Judith Butler, Eve Kosofsky Sedgwick, and David M. Halperin, this history of queer of color scholarship does in fact exist and can help LGBTIQ people of color find a sense of community and belonging.

In the 1970s, there were few, if any, writings by LGBTIQ people of color about their experiences. As Barbara Smith wrote in her groundbreaking 1977 essay, "Toward a Black Feminist Criticism," it was "unprecedented" and "dangerous" to write about the Black lesbian experience because "these things have not been done" by Black men, by white feminists, or even by Black women.[7] Smith writes poignantly: "I finally want to express how much easier both my waking and my sleeping hours would be if there were one book in existence that would tell me something specific about my life."[8]

In the thirty-five years following the publication of Smith's essay, however, there have been many books written about the queer of color experience. These books include anthologies on the queer Asian American experience such as *Q&A: Queer in Asian America* (1998);[9] the queer Black experience such as *The Greatest Taboo: Homosexuality in Black Communities* (2000);[10] the queer Latina/o experience such as *Gay Latino Studies: A Critical Reader* (2011);[11] and the Two-Spirit Indigenous experience such as *Queer Indigenous Studies: Critical Interventions in Theory, Politics, and Literature* (2011).[12]

In addition to the above anthologies, there have also been works written by key queer of color theorists such as Audre

---

[7] Barbara Smith, "Toward a Black Feminist Criticism," in *The New Feminist Criticism: Essays on Women, Literature, and Theory*, ed. Elaine Showalter (New York: Pantheon Books, 1985), 168.

[8] Ibid., 183.

[9] David L. Eng and Alice Y. Hom, *Q&A: Queer in Asian America* (Philadelphia, PA: Temple University Press, 1998).

[10] Delroy Constantine-Simms, *The Greatest Taboo: Homosexuality in Black Communities* (Los Angeles, CA: Alyson Books, 2000).

[11] Michael Hames-García and Ernesto Javier Martínez, eds., *Gay Latino Studies: A Critical Reader* (Durham, NC: Duke University Press, 2011).

[12] Qwo-Li Driskill et al., eds., *Queer Indigenous Studies: Critical Interventions in Theory, Politics, and Literature* (Tuscon: University of Arizona Press, 2011).

Lorde[13] and Gloria Anzaldúa.[14] In fact, writings about the LGBTIQ of color experience—including spiritual experiences— can be traced back at least a *half-century*, with the publication of *Another Country* by the gay Black writer James Baldwin in 1962. The gay Latino scholar Michael Hames-García has assembled a remarkable timeline of key works by queer writers of color from the 1960s through the 1980s, including Barbara Smith, Audre Lorde, the Combahee River Collective, Cherríe Moraga, and Glora Anzaldúa, that predate the appearance of canonical queer theory in the early 1990s by several decades.[15]

As noted above, there is now an entire movement within academic queer studies—"queer of color critique"—that is dedicated to the work of LGBTIQ scholars of color on the intersections between race and queer theory. In a special 2005 issue of the journal *Social Text* entitled "What's Queer About Queer Studies Now?," the editors noted that queer studies have moved beyond issues of sexuality and now cover issues "on theories of race, on problems of transnationalism, on conflicts between global capital and labor, on issues of diaspora and immigration, and on questions of citizenship, national belonging, and necropolitics."[16] In sum, LGBTIQ people of color share a common scholarly heritage, and it is important to recognize and honor this history in constructing a queer of color theology.

3. Some Definitions

Concepts relating to race, sexuality, and spirituality are often more complicated than they initially seem. As such, it may be helpful to set out a few definitions of key terms that are used in this book.

---

[13] See, e.g., Audre Lorde, *Sister Outsider: Essays and Speeches*, rev. ed. (Berkeley, CA: Crossing Press, 2007).

[14] See, e.g., Gloria Anzaldúa, *Borderlands/La Frontera: The New Mestiza*, 3rd ed. (San Francisco, CA: Aunt Lute Books, 2007).

[15] See Michael Hames-García, "Queer Theory Revisited," in Hames-García and Martínez, *Gay Latino Studies*, 26–27.

[16] David L. Eng, Judith Halberstam, and José Esteban Muñoz, "What's Queer About Queer Studies Now?," *Social Text* nos. 84–85 (2005): 2.

First, the term "race" as used in this book is taken from Michael Omi and Howard Winant's seminal text, *Racial Formation in the United States: From the 1960s to the 1990s*. In that text, Omi and Winant define race as "a concept which signifies and symbolizes social conflicts and interests by referring to different types of human bodies." Although this definition refers to "biologically based human characteristics" or "phenotypes," Omni and Winant remind us that the "selection of these particular human features for purposes of racial signification is always and necessarily a social and historical process."[17]

Indeed, contemporary racial categories have their roots in the colonial expansion of western Europe starting in the fifteenth century. As Roger Sanjek has argued, race is a socially-constructed "framework of ranked categories segmenting the human population" that was developed during the 1400s and that "imputed racial quanta of intelligence, attractiveness, cultural potential, and worth."[18] Although none of this scaling is "real" from an anthropological perspective, Sanjek notes that race has "become all too real in its social ordering of perceptions and policies" and in the "pervasive racism that has plagued the globe."[19]

Thus, it is fair to understand the term "race" as referring to categories (for example, "Asian American") that are based upon "physical characteristics, such as skin color or hair type" as well as the "generalizations and stereotypes" that arise out of such racial categories. By contrast, the term "ethnicity" (for example, "Chinese American") refers to a group that shares "common experiences" such as language, culture, national origin, religious affiliation, or other factors that over time comes

---

[17] Michael Omi and Howard Winant, *Racial Formation in the United States: From the 1960s to the 1990s*, 2nd ed. (New York: Routledge, 1994), 55. A new anthology of essays was published in 2012 to mark the twenty-fifth anniversary of the Omi and Winant's work. See Daniel HoSang et al., eds., *Racial Formation in the Twenty-First Century* (Berkeley: University of California Press, 2012).

[18] Roger Sanjek, "The Enduring Inequalities of Race," in *Race*, ed. Steven Gregory and Roger Sanjek (New Brunswick, NJ: Rutgers University Press, 1994), 1.

[19] Ibid.

to "distinguish one group from another."[20] The term "people of color" refers collectively to those persons—including, but not limited to, African Americans, Asian Americans, Latina/os, and Indigenous people—who belong to racial and ethnic groups that have been historically marginalized within the United States and/or colonized by European and North American powers around the world.[21]

Second, the term "sexuality" as used in this book is very broad and refers to, on a societal level, "the bundle of social phenomena that shape erotic life: laws, religion, norms and values, beliefs and ideologies, the social organization of reproduction, family life, identities, domestic arrangements, diseases, violence and love" as well as to, on an individual level, the related "pleasures and pains that can shape our lives for good or ill."[22] As with race, sexuality is very much a social construct that changes with place and time.

As noted above, the term "LGBTIQ" is used in this book as a collective term to refer to lesbian, gay, bisexual, transgender, intersex, and queer persons. This book also uses "queer" interchangeably with "LGBTIQ." ("Queer" is also a catch-all term that includes those individuals who identify themselves as pansexual, asexual, questioning, allied, and Two-Spirit.)[23] And, as I have discussed elsewhere, the term "queer" also has other more specialized meanings within the realm of queer theology, including transgression as well as the dissolution of binaries with respect to sexuality and gender.[24]

As it may be fairly obvious by now, the subcategories that make up the terms "LGBTIQ" or "queer" are actually quite

---

[20] William Ming Liu and William R. Concepcion, "Redefining Asian American Identity and Masculinity," in *Culturally Responsive Counseling with Asian American Men*, ed. William Ming Liu, Derek Kenji Iwamoto, and Mark H. Chae (New York: Routledge, 2010), 129.

[21] As my Argentinian friend Hugo Córdova Quero has reminded me, the term "people of color" is used primarily in the United States. That is, former colonial subjects become "people of color" when they arrive in the United States and are classified into pre-existing racial categories.

[22] Jeffrey Weeks, "The Social Construction of Sexuality," in *Introducing the New Sexuality Studies*, ed. Steven Seidman, Nancy Fischer, and Chet Meeks, 2nd ed. (Abingdon, UK: Routledge, 2011), 19.

[23] For a discussion of the term "Two-Spirit," see chapter five below.

[24] See Cheng, *Radical Love*, 2–8.

different from one another. That is, the terms "lesbian," "gay," and "bisexual" refer to sexual orientation (that is, the object of one's attraction on a physical and emotional level). By contrast, "transgender" refers to gender identity and expression (that is, the gender(s) with which one identifies and/or expresses to the world). "Intersex" refers to biological sex (that is, one's sexual organs, hormones, and chromosomes). What binds these various terms together, ultimately, is a sense of marginalization with respect to dominant societal norms with respect to sexual orientation, gender identity and expression, and/or biological sex.[25]

Third, the term "spirituality" is used broadly in this book to describe "those attitudes, beliefs and practices which animate people's lives and help them to reach out toward super-sensible realities."[26] That is, spirituality refers to one's engagement with an ultimate reality that is beyond the realm of senses. This can include organized religions—whether the Abrahamic faiths of Judaism, Christianity, and Islam, or Eastern philosophies such as Hinduism, Buddhism, and Daoism—or it can involve more personal or individual spiritual practices.

It should be noted that these definitions are not intended to reinforce essentialist thinking about racial, sexual, and spiritual categories. That is, rather than pointing to something "essentialist" about a person (for example, a person's inherent "Asianness" or "queerness"), the categories of race, sexuality, and spirituality are actually fluid and highly dependent upon social context such as "time, place, and situation."[27] Although racial, sexual, and spiritual traits may be grounded in physical

---

[25] For some helpful definitions relating to issues of sexuality and gender identity, see Palmer and Haffner, "A Time to Seek," 7–11.

[26] Gordon S. Wakefield, "Spirituality," in *The Westminster Dictionary of Christian Theology*, ed. Alan Richardson and John Bowden (Philadelphia, PA: Westminster Press, 1983), 549.

[27] Laina Y. Bay-Cheng, "The Social Construction of Sexuality: Religion, Medicine, Media, Schools, and Families," in *Sex and Sexuality, Volume 1: Sexuality Today—Trends and Controversies*, ed. Richard D. McAnulty and M. Michele Burnette (Westport, CT: Praeger, 2006), 204. Indeed, given the fluidity of categories, one queer theorist has posed the question: "Must identity movements self-destruct?" Joshua Gamson, "Must Identity Movements Self-Destruct?: A Queer Dilemma," in *Queer Cultures*, ed. Deborah Carlin and Jennifer DiGrazia (Upper Saddle River, NJ: Pearson Prentice Hall, 2004), 279.

characteristics or experiences, the *significance* of such characteristics is socially constructed and changes over time.[28]

4. Scope and Limitations

Having discussed definitional issues, I believe that it is also important to describe the scope and limitations of this book. First and foremost, although this book does cover a number of very broad issues such as race, sexuality, and spirituality, it is ultimately a work of Christian theology. That is, this book is ultimately grounded in my own identity as a follower of Jesus Christ, which has shaped my vocation as a systematic theologian, a seminary professor, and an ordained minister.

That being said, I am deeply committed to bringing interfaith perspectives and sources into my work. Although I cannot speak on behalf of persons from non-Christian faith communities, I grew up in the San Francisco Bay Area with my maternal grandparents who had spent much of their adult lives in China, Taiwan, and Hong Kong. They never converted to Christianity and maintained a hybridized view of religion as a blend of Confucianism, Buddhism, and Daoism. My brother, as I have written elsewhere, is a convert to Judaism.[29] Accordingly, I am sensitive to interfaith issues, and I discuss them in greater detail in the second part of this book.

Second, I write from my own social location as an openly-gay, cisgender (that is, non-transgender), Gen X, and able-bodied Chinese American man in academia. I realize that within the hierarchy of power within communities of color, I occupy a relatively privileged position with respect to my sexual orientation, sex, gender identity, age, ability, ethnicity, class, and occupation. Although I have tried my best to step outside of my own

---

[28] Furthermore, instead of being mutually exclusive categories, such categories are actually deeply interrelated and ultimately cannot be separated from each other. See chapter seven below; see also Ian Barnard, *Queer Race: Cultural Interventions in the Racial Politics of Queer Theory* (New York: Peter Lang, 2004); Linwood J. Lewis, "Sexuality, Race, and Ethnicity," in McAnulty and Burnette, *Sex and Sexuality, Volume 1*, 229–64; Joane Nagel, *Race, Ethnicity, and Sexuality: Intimate Intersections, Forbidden Frontiers* (New York: Oxford University Press, 2003).

[29] See Cheng, *From Sin to Amazing Grace*, xviii.

social location and include perspectives other than my own in this book, I will inevitably fall short in terms of my sources and examples. For that I ask for your patience and understanding, and I invite you to contact me with comments and additional perspectives that I may have overlooked.

Third, the examples in this book will focus primarily on communities of color within the United States. One of the reasons for this focus is that most of the writings by LGBTIQ theologians of color have been produced within the United States. Another reason for this focus is that I have spent virtually all of my life living within the United States, and thus my own experiences are limited with respect to transnational issues. That being said, Part II of this book discusses the importance of cross-border issues for queer theologians of color. It also acknowledges that the United States vs. international divide is not so easy to draw, particularly in the case of queer Asian American and Latina/o theologians.

Having addressed a number of theoretical issues, definitions, and limitations of this book, particularly relating to LGBTIQ people of color, we now turn to a survey of queer of color theologies. In the remaining four chapters of Part I of this book, we will explore queer Black, queer Asian American, queer Latina/o, and Two-Spirit Indigenous theologies and religious scholarship.[30]

---

[30] I recognize that these racial and ethnic categories can serve to marginalize the experiences of mixed-heritage and multiracial people. As Ibrahim Abdurrahman Farajajé has noted, such categories require such people to "have to make the choice to identify with only one group as opposed to being able to define ourselves as we choose, acknowledging our place within the people-of-color communities." See Elias Farajaje-Jones, "Loving 'Queer': We're All a Big Mix of Possibilities of Desire Just Waiting to Happen," *In the Family* 6, no. 1 (Summer 2000): 17. It is my hope that the discussion of rainbow theology in Part II of this book will ultimately transcend these socially-constructed categories and honor the experiences of mixed-heritage and multiracial people.

Study Questions

1. What are your reasons for reading this book? What do you hope to learn from queer of color theologies?

2. It might be argued that the concept of "queer of color" is not a valid conceptual category. Do you agree or disagree? What are some reasons in favor of using this category?

3. Name some key scholarly works relating to the experiences of LGBTIQ people of color. Which of these works, if any, have you read in the past?

4. Explain, in your own words, how the terms "race," "sexuality," and "spirituality" are used in this book.

5. What are some limitations of this book as described by the author? Which of these limitations concern you the most?

For Further Study

Queer Theology and Religious Studies
- Cheng, *Radical Love*, 9–11
- Lowe, "Gay, Lesbian, and Queer Theologies"
- Schippert, "Implications of Queer Theory for the Study of Religion and Gender"
- Schippert, "Queer Theory and the Study of Religion"
- Schneider, "Queer Theory"
- Wilcox, "Queer Theory and the Study of Religion"

Queer of Color Scholarship
- Anzaldúa, *Borderlands/La Frontera*
- Constantine-Simms, *The Greatest Taboo*
- Driskill et al., *Queer Indigenous Studies*
- Eng, Halberstam, and Muñoz, "What's Queer about Queer Studies Now?"
- Eng and Hom, *Q&A*
- Hames-García, "Queer Theory Revisited," 26–27
- Hames-García and Martínez, *Gay Latino Studies*
- Lorde, *Sister Outsider*
- Smith, "Toward a Black Feminist Criticism"

Race
- Gregory and Sanjek, *Race*
- HoSang, LaBennett, and Pulido, *Racial Formation in the Twenty-First Century*
- Omni and Winant, *Racial Formation in the United States*
- Sanjek, "The Enduring Inequalities of Race"

Sexuality
- Cheng, *From Sin to Amazing Grace*, xvi–xviii
- Cheng, *Radical Love*, 2–8
- Farajaje-Jones, "Loving 'Queer'"
- Palmer and Haffner, *A Time to Seek*
- Weeks, "The Social Construction of Sexuality"

Chapter 2

Queer Black Theologies

S ince at least the early 1990s, queer Black[1] theologians have written about the ways in which they have wrestled with issues of race, sexuality, and spirituality. Specifically, LGBTIQ African Americans are caught between the hetero-sexism and homophobia of the Black Church on the one hand, and the racism of white queer religious communities on the other. As Irene Monroe, an African American lesbian minister and theologian, has written: "The task has always been to develop a theological language that speaks truth to our unique spirituality." According to Monroe, "Housing our spirituality in both religious cultures—white queer, and black—has been one of tenuous residency, that of spiritual wanderers and resident aliens."[2]

This chapter will examine key writings from LGBTIQ Black theologians. It will focus on three main themes that have emerged in these writings: (1) Black Church exclusion; (2) reclaiming Black lesbian voices; and (3) challenging Black liberation theologies. This chapter will serve as a roadmap of the terrain, but it will not attempt to cover everything that has been written on queer Black theology during the last two

---

[1] In this book, I use the terms "Black" and "African American" interchangeably.

[2] Irene Monroe, "Lifting Our Voices," in *Spirited: Affirming the Soul and Black Gay/Lesbian Identity*, ed. G. Winston James and Lisa C. Moore (Washington, DC: RedBone Press, 2006), xii.

decades. Rather, it will focus on key texts and provide additional study resources at the end of the chapter. Also, the discussion in this chapter will focus on self-identified LGBTIQ Black theologians. Allies such as Kelly Brown Douglas—and her highly influential text *Sexuality and the Black Church: A Womanist Perspective*[3]—will be cited, but the main focus will be on the voices of queer Black people.

1. Historical Background

Before turning to the writings of LGBTIQ Black theologians, we begin with a brief survey of the hidden history of queer African Americans. Although a number of works on LGBTIQ history have been written in recent years,[4] no historical text to date has focused primarily on the history of queer people of color in North America. As such, a comprehensive history of same-gender-loving and gender-variant African Americans has yet to be written. What is discussed in this chapter, therefore, is collected from a variety of different sources.

African Americans have been in North America since at least 1619, when a colonial resident of Virginia recorded the sale of "twenty Negars" by a Dutch trader.[5] The horrific slave trade from the fifteenth century through the nineteenth centuries resulted in nearly 10 million persons being "kidnapped out of Africa, all but about 350,000 of them for sale in the Americas."[6]

As early as 1630, a colonial court in Virginia wrote about the intersections of race, sexuality, and religion. In that year, a white man, Hugh Davis, was sentenced to be whipped as a result of his "defiling his body in lying with a [female] negro."

---

[3] Kelly Brown Douglas, *Sexuality and the Black Church: A Womanist Perspective* (Maryknoll, NY: Orbis Books, 1999).

[4] See, e.g., Robert Aldrich, ed., *Gay Life and Culture: A World History* (New York: Universe Publishing, 2006); Michael Bronski, *A Queer History of the United States* (Boston, MA: Beacon Press, 2011); Neil Miller, *Out of the Past: Gay and Lesbian History from 1869 to the Present*, rev. and updated ed. (New York: Alyson Books, 2006).

[5] Ronald Takaki, *A Different Mirror: A History of Multicultural America*, rev. ed. (New York: Back Bay Books, 2008), 51.

[6] Roger Daniels, *Coming to America: A History of Immigration and Ethnicity in American Life*, 2nd ed. (New York: Harper Perennial, 2002), 61.

This, according to the court, resulted in the "dishonor of God and the shame of Christianity." A decade later, another white man, Robert Sweat, was convicted for impregnating an unnamed "negro woman servant" who belonged to a military officer. The woman was sentenced to be whipped, but Sweat was required to do "public penance for his offence at James city church in the time of divine service."[7]

The earliest known documentation of a same-gender-loving African American dates back to the seventeenth century. Jan Creoli, a "negro," was convicted of sodomy in court proceedings dated June 25, 1646, from New Netherland Colony (that is, Manhattan Island). The court described the act as a "crime being condemned of God . . . as an abomination" and cited Genesis as well as Leviticus. Creoli was sentenced to be "choked to death" and then "burnt to ashes."[8]

Not much is known about consensual same-gender-loving relationships among African American slaves, but there is evidence that such relationships did occur among working-class African Americans in the nineteenth century. For example, two African American women—Rebecca Primus, a teacher, and Addie Brown, a servant—lived in Hartford, Connecticut, in the 1860s and had an "intense, deeply passionate relationship."[9]

The Harlem Renaissance in the 1920s attracted many same-gender-loving African Americans because of the neighborhood's "combination of license and sexual ambiguity."[10] Some of these individuals included the poet Langston Hughes, the singer Bessie Smith, and the playwright Wallace Thurman. This tradition of prominent LGBTIQ African American writers continued during the twentieth century with writers such as James Baldwin, Audre Lorde, and Alice Walker.[11]

---

[7] Takaki, *A Different Mirror*, 54.

[8] elias farajajé-jones, "Holy Fuck," in *Male Lust: Pleasure, Power, and Transformation*, ed. Kerwin Kay, Jill Nagle, and Baruch Gould (Binghamton, NY: Harrington Park Press, 2000), 327.

[9] Brett Genny Beemyn, "The Americas: From Colonial Times to the 20th Century," in Aldrich, *Gay Life and Culture*, 153.

[10] Miller, *Out of the Past*, 135.

[11] See generally Devon W. Carbado, Dwight A. McBride, and Donald Weise, eds., *Black Like Us: A Century of Lesbian, Gay, and Bisexual African American Fiction* (Berkeley, CA: Cleis Press, 2002).

A number of same-gender-loving African Americans were involved with the civil rights and other justice movements. These included Bayard Rustin, who was a close adviser to Martin Luther King, Jr. Despite having been arrested on a "morals charge" for having sex with two men in a car, Rustin was involved with the Montgomery bus boycott and served as the chief organizer of the March on Washington.[12] Other same-gender-loving African American leaders included Pauli Murray, the first African American woman who was ordained a priest in the Episcopal Church and a co-founder of the National Organization of Women.[13]

There were also same-gender-loving African Americans at the Stonewall Riots of June 1969, which many consider to be the beginning of the contemporary LGBTIQ rights movement. Miss Marsha P. Johnson, a well-known "black queen" and sex worker, climbed to the top of a lamppost and "dropped a bag with something heavy in it" on a police squad car below and shattered its windshield.[14]

Since the 1970s, a number of LGBTIQ Black writers have reflected openly about their experiences of race and sexuality. In 1977, the Black lesbian writer Barbara Smith published an important essay, "Toward a Black Feminist Criticism," that examined the interconnections of race, gender, and sexuality. In 1978, Audre Lorde published her influential essay "Uses of the Erotic," and in 1979 the Combahee River Collective, a self-described Black feminist collective in Boston, published "A Black Feminist Statement."[15]

In recent years, works such as Keith Boykin's *One More River to Cross: Black and Gay in America*[16] and the anthology

---

[12] For a discussion of the relationship between Bayard Rustin and Martin Luther King, Jr., see Michael G. Long, *Martin Luther King Jr., Homosexuality, and the Early Gay Rights Movement: Keeping the Dream Straight?* (New York: Palgrave Macmillan, 2012).

[13] See Bronski, *Queer History*, 203.

[14] Martin Duberman, *Stonewall* (New York: Plume, 1993), 67, 204.

[15] Hames-García, "Queer Theory Revisited," 26.

[16] Keith Boykin, *One More River to Cross: Black and Gay in America* (New York: Anchor Books, 1996). See also Keith Boykin, ed., *For Colored Boys Who Have Considered Suicide When the Rainbow Is Still Not Enough: Coming of Age, Coming Out, and Coming Home* (New York: Magnus Books, 2012), 153–81 ("Faith Under Fire").

The Greatest Taboo: Homosexuality in Black Communities[17] have continued the conversation on race, sexuality, and spirituality in the African American community.

2. Genealogy of Queer Black Theologies

For at least two decades, queer Black theologians have been writing about the experiences of LGBTIQ African Americans from a theological perspective. To date, however, there has not been a systematic review of such writings. This chapter seeks to remedy this gap by articulating a genealogy of queer Black theologies from the early 1990s to today.

Specifically, this chapter will examine these writings through three thematic strands: (1) Black Church exclusion; (2) reclaiming Black lesbian voices; and (3) challenging Black liberation theologies. It should be noted that these themes are not intended to be mutually exclusive. Rather, they are ways of organizing the various writings into similar topics. It is my hope that these thematic strands will encourage additional discussions about not just the underlying theological works, but also about the thematic strands themselves.

a. Black Church Exclusion

The first thematic strand relates to the exclusion of LGBTIQ African Americans from the Black Church. According to Irene Monroe, the Black lesbian minister and theologian, the Black Church "muffles our queer spirituality by applauding us in its choir pews on the one hand, yet excoriating us from its pulpits on the other." She continues with a sharp critique of hetero-sexism and homophobia in the Black Church: "Our connections and contributions to the larger black religious cosmos are desecrated every time homophobic pronouncements go unchecked in these holy places of worship."[18]

One of the earliest works relating to LGBTIQ African Americans and the Black Church appeared in 1993 in the

---

[17] Constantine-Simms, *The Greatest Taboo*, 76–121 ("Sexuality and the Black Church").

[18] Monroe, "Lifting Our Voices," xi.

second volume of James H. Cone and Gayraud S. Wilmore's *Black Theology: A Documentary History*.[19] That essay, "Breaking Silence: Toward an In-the-Life Theology," was by Ibrahim Abdurrahman Farajajé, an "avowed gay-identified, bisexual Black theologian" who was then a professor at Howard University Divinity School.[20]

In that essay, Farajajé argues for an "in-the-life" theology that would liberate Black theologies from the "strictures of homophobia/biphobia" as well as the "power and privilege" of heterosexism.[21] He critiques the Black Church for its "suffocating silence" with respect to homosexualities and bisexualities, as well as the HIV/AIDS pandemic.[22] Farajajé urges the Black Church to "move beyond the heritage of Euro-Protestantism." According to him, that heritage, with its binary "either-or view of the world," is "quite literally killing us."[23]

The Farajajé essay was followed in 1999 by the publication of *Sexuality and the Black Church: A Womanist Perspective* by Kelly Brown Douglas. Douglas, an Episcopal priest and straight Black ally of the LGBTIQ community, was teaching at the time at Howard University Divinity School. In her book, Douglas makes the connections between white racism and Black homophobia. She argues that homophobia is a "sin and betrayal of black faith" because it has alienated LGBTIQ Black people from God and has prevented the Black Church from affirming the full humanity of such individuals.[24]

In 2001, Gary David Comstock, a white gay man and ally of the Black community, published *A Whosoever Church: Welcoming Lesbians and Gay Men into African American Congregations.*

---

[19] Cone and Wilmore, *Black Theology II*.

[20] Farajaje-Jones, "Breaking Silence," 139. As of January 2013, Farajajé is Provost and Professor of Cultural Studies and Islamic Studies at the Starr King School for the Ministry in Berkeley, California.

[21] Ibid., 141.

[22] Ibid., 146.

[23] Ibid., 158. Subsequent writings from Farajajé include farajajé-jones, "Holy Fuck"; and Farajaje-Jones, "Loving 'Queer.'"

[24] Douglas, *Sexuality and the Black Church*, 126. As of January 2013, Douglas is the Elizabeth Conolly Todd Distinguished Professor of Religion at Goucher College in Baltimore, Maryland.

That book was a collection of interviews with twenty African American religious leaders who spoke out against homophobia. These leaders included LGBTIQ Black ministers such as Irene Monroe, Renée L. Hill, and Emilie M. Townes, as well as straight Black allies such as Jacquelyn Grant, James A. Forbes, James H. Cone, and Kelly Brown Douglas.[25]

A key moment in the development of queer Black theologies occurred in 2006, when Horace Griffin published *Their Own Receive Them Not: African American Lesbians and Gays in Black Churches*.[26] Griffin's book was the first book-length work on this topic that was written by an openly-gay Black theologian. Griffin, an Episcopal priest who was teaching at the time at General Theological Seminary in New York City, argues that a "true black liberation theology" would lead heterosexual Black church leaders to affirm "all loving sexual relationships and commitments as reflecting God's purpose in creation."[27] By doing so, such pastors can offer "healing to lives that are broken by homophobia" and help African Americans to "love our bodies and sexuality as God's gift to us."[28]

In 2010, M. Shawn Copeland, a professor of theology at Boston College, published a radically inclusive Roman Catholic ecclesiology that speaks to LGBTIQ African Americans. In her book, *Enfleshing Freedom: Body, Race, and Being*, Copeland argues that the body of Christ—and the "flesh of his Church"— takes us "*all* in as we are with all our different body marks," whether in our "red, brown, yellow, white, and black bodies" and in our "homosexual and heterosexual bodies."[29]

---

[25] Gary David Comstock, *A Whosoever Church: Welcoming Lesbians and Gay Men into African American Congregations* (Louisville, KY: Westminster John Knox Press, 2001).

[26] Griffin, *Their Own Receive Them Not*. As of January 2013, Griffin is the Associate Professor of Pastoral Theology at the Pacific School of Religion in Berkeley, California.

[27] Ibid., 219.

[28] Ibid., 220, 223.

[29] M. Shawn Copeland, *Enfleshing Freedom: Body, Race, and Being* (Minneapolis, MN: Fortress Press, 2010), 83. Bryan N. Massingale, an African American Roman Catholic priest and professor at Marquette University, is also interested in the intersections between race and sexuality in Roman Catholicism. Massingale has contributed an essay to the forthcoming *More Than a Monologue* anthology on LGBTIQ issues and the Roman Catholic Church. See Christine Firer Hinze, J. Patrick Hornbeck, and Michael A. Norko, *More Than a Monologue: Sexual Diversity in the Catholic Church* (Bronx, NY: Fordham University Press, forthcoming).

One organization that seeks the "full inclusion" of LGBTIQ Black people in communities of faith though scholarship (and other means) is the African American Roundtable (AART) at the Center for Lesbian and Gay Studies in Religion and Ministry at the Pacific School of Religion. Founded in 2000, AART also seeks to mobilize African American communities of faith to support social justice for LGBTIQ people.[30]

b. Reclaiming Black Lesbian Voices

The second thematic strand in queer Black theologies relates to reclaiming of Black lesbian voices in womanist theologies—that is, theologies by and for African American women.

A foundational work in this area is another essay in the 1993 Cone and Wilmore volume entitled "Who Are We for Each Other?: Sexism, Sexuality and Womanist Theology." The essay was written by Renée L. Hill, a "self-identified lesbian" and doctoral student at Union Theological Seminary in New York City.[31] In contrast to Farajajé's essay (which focuses primarily on gay and bisexual men), Hill focuses on Black lesbians and their exclusion from womanist theological reflection.

Despite the fact that womanist theology was founded by Black women in response to the failure of Black liberation and white feminist theologies to address Black women's experiences, Hill argues that the "lesbian voice is silenced in Christian womanist theology."[32] For Hill, womanist theologies must confront and critique the homophobia and heterosexism within African American communities and listen to Black lesbian voices.

The debate about the inclusivity of womanist theologies with respect to issues of lesbianism and bisexuality has continued in

---

[30] See "African American Roundtable," The Center for Lesbian and Gay Studies in Religion and Ministry, accessed January 3, 2013, http://bit.ly/Qze7FR. Roland Stringfellow is on the staff of the AART, and he has also written about the need to challenge the queerphobia in the Black church. See Stringfellow, "Soul Work."

[31] Hill, "Who Are We for Each Other?," 345. Following her graduation from Union Theological Seminary, Hill served as an assistant professor at the Episcopal Divinity School in Cambridge, Massachusetts, and is now an Episcopal priest who lives in New York City.

[32] Ibid., 346.

the two decades since the publication of Hill's essay. In 2006, the *Journal of Feminist Studies in Religion* published an important roundtable discussion, "Must I Be Womanist?"[33] Among other things, the roundtable addressed whether Black feminism was more open and accepting than womanism with respect to issues of Black women's sexuality.

In that roundtable, a number of Black women theologians and ethicists responded to an essay by Monica A. Coleman, a professor at Claremont School of Theology,[34] that critiqued the "heteronormativity" of womanist theology and its failure to take seriously Alice Walker's definition of a womanist as one who "loves other women sexually and/or nonsexually."[35] At least two of the respondents in the roundtable—Irene Monroe and Traci C. West, a professor at Drew University Theological School—agreed with Coleman's position.[36]

Also in 2006, Traci West published her book *Disruptive Christian Ethics: When Racism and Women's Lives Matter*. In that book, West dedicated an entire chapter to Black Christian leaders who challenge heterosexism in church and society.[37] And in 2008, Monica Coleman published her book, *Making a Way Out of No Way: A Womanist Theology*, which also contained a section about GSN Ministries, an LGBTIQ-affirming ministry in Atlanta, Georgia, that has challenged homophobia in the Black Church.[38]

---

[33] "Roundtable Discussion: Must I Be Womanist?", *Journal of Feminist Studies in Religion* 22, no. 1 (Spring 2006).

[34] As of January 2013, Coleman is the Associate Professor of Constructive Theology and African American Religions at the Claremont School of Theology in Claremont, California.

[35] Monica A. Coleman, "Roundtable Discussion: Must I Be Womanist?", *Journal of Feminist Studies in Religion* 22, no. 1 (Spring 2006): 86.

[36] See Irene Monroe, "Roundtable Discussion: Must I Be Womanist?", *Journal of Feminist Studies in Religion* 22, no. 1 (Spring 2006): 107–13; Traci C. West, "Roundtable Discussion: Must I Be Womanist?," *Journal of Feminist Studies in Religion* 22, no. 1 (Spring 2006): 128–34.

[37] See Traci C. West, *Disruptive Christian Ethics: When Racism and Women's Lives Matter* (Louisville, KY: Westminster John Knox Press, 2006), 141–79 ("Leadership: Dissenting Leaders and Heterosexism"). West has also co-authored a resource guide for congregations on talking about homosexuality, see Karen P. Oliveto, Kelly D. Turney, and Traci C. West, *Talking About Homosexuality: A Congregational Resource* (Cleveland, OH: Pilgrim Press, 2005), and edited an anthology on defending same-sex marriage, see Traci C. West, *Defending Same-Sex Marriage*, vol. 2 of *Our Family Values: Same-Sex Marriage and Religion* (Westport, CT: Greenwood-Praeger, 2006).

[38] See also Monica A. Coleman, *Making a Way Out of No Way: A Womanist Theology* (Minneapolis, MN: Fortress Press, 2008), 147–67.

In 2009, at the annual meeting of the American Academy of Religion in Montreal, Canada, there was a groundbreaking panel on the intersections of lesbianism and womanist theologies called "Hidden and Invisible in Plain Sight: Queer and Lesbian in the Black Church and Community."[39] Five papers from lesbian womanist scholars Malu Fairley, Pamela Lightsey, Raedorah Stewart, Elonda Clay, and Thelathia "Nikki" Young were presented at the panel. The panel was jointly sponsored by the Womanist Approaches to Religion and Society Group and the Lesbian-Feminist Issues and Religion Group.[40] The panel was chaired by professor Joan M. Martin of the Episcopal Divinity School,[41] and Renée Hill served as the respondent.

Finally, in 2011, Emilie M. Townes, a lesbian womanist ethicist and the Academic Dean and Andrew W. Mellon Professor of African American Religion and Theology at Yale Divinity School, delivered the 2011 Gilberto Castañeda Lecture at Chicago Theological Seminary.[42] The lecture, entitled "The Dancing Mind: Queer Black Bodies in Academy and Church," critiqued the silences in the Black academy and church about LGBTIQ African Americans in general and Black lesbians in particular. Townes writes: "I am bone weary pissed at the way

---

[39] AAR 2009 Annual Meeting Online Program Book, Session A9-120, accessed January 3, 2013, http://bit.ly/LfiP8r. Prior to this panel, there was a 2008 AAR panel on "Gendered Conversations Between Black Females and Males" that was sponsored by the Men's Studies in Religion Group, the Black Theology Group, and the Womanist Approaches to Religion and Society Group.

[40] Since 2009, the Womanist Approaches to Religion and Society Group has been co-chaired by Pamela Lightsey, an out Black lesbian who, as of January 2013, is an associate dean at Boston University School of Theology. For some of Lightsey's writings, see Pamela R. Lightsey, "The Eddie Long Scandal: It *Is* About Anti-Homosexuality," *Religion Dispatches* (September 29, 2010), accessed January 3, 2013, http://bit.ly/SRiuNQ; and Pamela R. Lightsey, "Methodist Clergy Pledge to Defy Church in Blessing LGBT Unions," *Religion Dispatches* (June 11, 2011), accessed January 3, 2013, http://bit.ly/ksYH9j.

[41] For some of Martin's writings on the intersections of womanism and LGBTIQ issues, see Joan M. Martin, "Yes, There Is a God!," *99 Brattle* (May 11, 2011), accessed January 3, 2013, http://bit.ly/MnGPZF; and Joan M. Martin, "What I Don't Know About Brittney Griner, NCAA Women's Basketball Champion," *99 Brattle* (April 4, 2012), accessed January 3, 2013, http://bit.ly/HO9btF. Martin also has contributed an essay to the forthcoming *More Than a Monologue* anthology. See Hinze, Hornbeck, and Norko, *More Than a Monologue*.

[42] Townes has since been appointed the dean of Vanderbilt University Divinity School, effective as of July 1, 2013.

black folk continue to be pathologized, fetishized, hypersexualized, demonized and the fact that we are now getting comfortable with doing it to ourselves / and to make matters worse, religious institutions like churches and seminaries are often of little help in calling us to account on this."[43]

The conversation with respect to womanist theologies and Black lesbians continues with a new generation of lesbian womanist theologians. Thelathia "Nikki" Young, a participant on the 2009 AAR panel and the Assistant Professor of Women's and Gender Studies and Religion at Bucknell University, has published a number of works on queer Black theology and ethics.[44] Young is the co-chair of the queer ethics group of the Society of Christian Ethics, and she is working on a book manuscript entitled *Imagining New Relationships: Black Queers and Family Values*.

c. Challenging Black Liberation Theologies

The third thematic strand relates to challenges by LGBTIQ Black theologians to the traditional Black liberation theology paradigm of the 1960s and 1970s. In that paradigm, African Americans—like the ancient Israelites—are liberated by God from the slavery of white racism through an Exodus moment.

One critique leveled by LGBTIQ Black theologians against the traditional Black liberation theology paradigm is that it does not go far enough with respect to sexuality issues. This point is made by a number of essays in the 2004 anthology *Loving the Body: Black Religious Studies and the Erotic*.[45] Irene Monroe—

---

[43] Emilie M. Townes, "The Dancing Mind: Queer Black Bodies in Academy and Church" (2011 Gilberto Castañeda Lecture, Chicago Theological Seminary, Chicago, IL, May 20, 2011). See also Emilie M. Townes, "Washed in the Grace of God," in *Violence Against Women and Children: A Christian Theological Sourcebook*, ed. Carol J. Adams and Marie M. Fortune (New York: Continuum, 1995), 60–70; Emilie M. Townes, "Roundtable Discussion: Same-Sex Marriage," *Journal of Feminist Studies in Religion* 20, no. 2 (Fall 2004): 100–103.

[44] See, for example, Thelathia "Nikki" Young, "De-Centering Religion as Queer Pedagogical Practice," *Bulletin for the Study of Religion* 39, no. 4 (November 2010): 13–18; Thelathia "Nikki" Young, "Queering 'The Human Situation,'" *Journal of Feminist Studies in Religion* 28, no. 1 (Spring 2012): 126–31; Thelathia "Nikki" Young, "'Uses of the Erotic' for Teaching Queer Studies," *WSQ* 40, nos. 3–4 (Fall/Winter 2012): 297–301.

[45] Anthony B. Pinn and Dwight N. Hopkins, eds., *Loving the Body: Black Religious Studies and the Erotic* (New York: Palgrave Macmillan, 2004).

the African American lesbian ordained minister—contributed an essay to that anthology entitled "When and Where I Enter, Then the Whole Race Enters with Me: Que(e)rying Exodus."[46] In that essay, Monroe writes: "The Exodus narrative calls us all to come out of whatever bondage enslaves us. For African Americans, our bodies and sexualities are in as much need for freedom as our skin color is."[47]

Horace Griffin—the gay Black seminary professor—made a similar point in his anthology contribution, "Toward a True Black Liberation Theology: Affirming Homoeroticism, Black Gay Christians, and Their Love Relationships."[48] In that essay, Griffin argues that African Americans must "engage seriously and critically the relationship between Christianity and homosexuality" in the same "faithful way" in which they have offered a "critical engagement" of Christianity and race in traditional Black liberation theologies.[49]

Some queer Black religious studies scholars have gone even further than Monroe and Griffin in their critique of the traditional Black liberation theology paradigm. In 2010, Roger A. Sneed, an openly-gay Black professor of religion at Furman University, published his book *Representations of Homosexuality: Black Liberation Theology and Cultural Criticism.*[50] This book is significant not only because it is the second book-length theological treatment of LGBTIQ African Americans by a gay Black person, but also because it critiques Black liberation theology for its failure to address adequately the complexities of queer Black lives.

Sneed argues that the focus of Black liberationist paradigms on homophobia and white supremacy leads to an "essentializing"

---

[46] Irene Monroe, "When and Where I Enter, Then the Whole Race Enters with Me: Que(e)rying Exodus," in Pinn and Hopkins, *Loving the Body*, 121–31.

[47] Ibid., 130.

[48] Horace Griffin, "Toward a True Black Liberation Theology: Affirming Homoeroticism, Black Gay Christians, and Their Love Relationships," in Pinn and Hopkins, *Loving the Body*, 133–53.

[49] Ibid., 150.

[50] Sneed, *Representations of Homosexuality*.

and "binary" notion of race that ignores the culpability of straight African Americans with respect to homophobic discourse.[51] Instead, Sneed proposes an "ethics of openness" and an affirmation of human flourishing as an alternative to the traditional liberation model.[52] For Sneed, the traditional liberation model of the oppressor vs. the oppressed requires gay Black men to be victims and does not recognize the complexity—including the joys—of the gay Black male experience.

Sneed uses a number of nontraditional sources in constructing his ethics, including queer Black literature and online personal ads. One such source is his use of Black gay men's writing. Specifically, Sneed cites the anthology *Black Like Us: A Century of Lesbian, Gay, and Bisexual African American Fiction*,[53] and he draws upon the works of Langston Hughes, Samuel R. Delany, Essex Hemphill, and E. Lynn Harris.[54] Sneed argues that Black queer literature not only serves to "retrieve black queer experience from the periphery of black existence," but also to "destabilize stable, steady readings of black identity."[55] Sneed's turn to literature makes sense in light of his critique of Black liberation and womanist theologies for their failure to adequately portray the complexity and fullness of the Black gay experience.

Another source used by Sneed is that of personal ads and internet profiles on gay hookup websites such as BGCLive. com. Sneed demonstrates that such ads and profiles are "snapshots" of how Black gay men use the internet "as a form of identity construction" in the "gay marketplace of desire."[56] For Sneed, these are examples of the diverse ways in which Black gay masculinities are performed. The divine is found in the *totality* of Black gay life. In sum, Sneed's work breaks from

---

[51] Ibid., 176.

[52] Ibid., 179–82.

[53] Carbado, McBride, and Weise, *Black Like Us*.

[54] Sneed, *Representations of Homosexuality*, 107–32.

[55] Ibid., 111. See also Roger A. Sneed, "Like Fire Shut Up in Our Bones: Religion and Spirituality in Black Gay Men's Literature," *Black Theology: An International Journal* 6, no. 2 (2008): 241–61.

[56] Sneed, *Representations of Homosexuality*, 167–68.

the traditional models that have largely defined the theological conversation about LGBTIQ African Americans to date.[57]

Other critiques of the traditional Black theology paradigm involve expanding the notion of Black religiosity beyond that of Christianity. In his essay "Feeling the Spirit in the Dark: Expanding Notions of the Sacred in the African American Gay Community," E. Patrick Johnson writes about finding the sacred in secular places like the nightclub as well as practices such as "house/club music, vogueing, dragging, snapping." According to Johnson, gay Black men "create new ways of understanding the linking of body and soul or sexuality and spirituality." By connecting sexuality with spirituality, such men transform a "supposedly solely secular, solely sexual, wholly sinful, utterly perverse club" into a spiritual space in which "the identities of African American, homosexual, and Christian no longer compete."[58]

Finally, a number of LGBTIQ African American theologians have written about the importance of reclaiming non-Christian faith traditions. For example, Renée Hill writes in her essay "Disrupted/Disruptive Movements: Black Theology and Black Power 1969/1999" that "Black Christian theologies cannot afford *not* to be in dialogue with other religious traditions."[59] She argues that Black theology must recognize the history of "Christian dominance" in relation with other faith traditions and be open in terms of learning from other traditions, including "African-derived traditional religions" such as Santeria, Akan, Yoruba, and Vodun.[60] Similarly, Monica Coleman in her 2006 roundtable essay argues that Black female religious scholars

---

[57] In a forthcoming essay, Sneed draws upon works of science fiction and music, thus continuing his use of innovative theological and ethical sources. See Roger A. Sneed, "Dark Matter: Liminality and Black Queer Bodies," in *Ain't I a Womanist Too?: Third Wave Womanist Religious Thought*, ed. Monica A. Coleman (Minneapolis, MN: Fortress Press, forthcoming).

[58] E. Patrick Johnson, "Feeling the Spirit in the Dark: Expanding Notions of the Sacred in the African American Gay Community," in Constantine-Simms, *The Greatest Taboo*, 106.

[59] Renée Leslie Hill, "Disrupted/Disruptive Movements: Black Theology and Black Power 1969/1999," in *Black Faith and Public Talk: Critical Essays on James H. Cone's* Black Theology and Black Power, ed. Dwight N. Hopkins (Maryknoll, NY: Orbis Books, 1999), 147.

[60] Ibid.

should be able to identify themselves not just as Christians, but also as "Muslim, pagan, new-thought, Buddhist, and Ifa."[61]

3. Conclusion

In sum, LGBTIQ theologians of color have been writing about the queer Black experience since at least the early 1990s. These writings can be organized into three thematic strands of (1) Black Church exclusion, (2) reclaiming Black lesbian voices, and (3) challenging Black liberation theologies. Additional work still needs to be done, however, with respect to developing these writings in a systematic manner. Queer Black theologies also need to address transgender and intersex issues within the African American community. As the recent report "Injustice at Every Turn" shows, Black transgender people face "particularly devastating levels of discrimination," including high rates of poverty, homelessness, HIV/AIDS, and attempted suicide.[62] Nevertheless, queer Black theologies provide an important perspective that is largely missing in mainstream queer theological reflection.

---

[61] Coleman, "Must I Be Womanist?," 95. For a holy union service in the tradition of Kwanzaa, see Darlene Garner, "A Sample Service of Holy Union Based on the Tradition of Kwanzaa," in *Equal Rites: Lesbian and Gay Worship, Ceremonies, and Celebrations*, ed. Kittredge Cherry and Zalmon Sherwood (Louisville, KY: Westminster John Knox Press, 1995), 94–100.

[62] National Gay and Lesbian Task Force, "Injustice at Every Turn: A Look at Black Respondents in the National Transgender Discrimination Survey" (September 15, 2011), accessed January 3, 2013, http://bit.ly/nLZBHX.

Study Questions

1. Which events from the history of queer African Americans surprised you the most? Troubled you the most? What would like to learn more about in terms of queer Black history?

2. What are some key writings by queer Black theologians about the exclusion of LGBTIQ African Americans from the Black Church?

3. What are some key writings by queer Black theologians about reclaiming the voices of Black lesbians and bisexual women in womanist theologies?

4. What are some key writings by queer Black theologians that challenge the traditional liberation theology paradigm?

5. How might you use nontraditional theological sources such as literature, online personal ads, or interfaith writings to enrich your own theological reflection and work?

For Further Study

Queer Black Experience
- Anderson, "Desiring to Be Together"
- Anderson, "Deadly Silence"
- Boykin, *For Colored Boys*
- Boykin, *One More River to Cross*
- Constantine-Simms, *The Greatest Taboo*

Black Church Exclusion
- Anderson, "African American Church Traditions"
- Comstock, *A Whosoever Church*
- Copeland, *Enfleshing Freedom*
- Crawley, "Circum-Religious Performance"
- Douglas, *Sexuality and the Black Church*
- Farajaje-Jones, "Breaking Silence"
- Griffin, *Their Own Receive Them Not*
- James and Moore, *Spirited*
- Monroe, "Between a Rock and a Hard Place"
- Stringfellow, "Soul Work"

Reclaiming Black Lesbian Voices
- Coleman, *Making a Way Out of No Way*, 147–67
- Coleman, "Must I Be Womanist?"
- Hill, "Who Are We for Each Other?"
- Lightsey, "The Eddie Long Scandal"
- Lightsey, "Methodist Clergy Pledge to Defy Church"
- Martin, "What I Don't Know About Britney Griner"
- Martin, "Yes, There Is a God!"
- Monroe, "Must I Be Womanist?"
- Townes, "The Dancing Mind"
- Townes, "Marcella Althaus-Reid's *Indecent Theology*"
- Townes, "Same-Sex Marriage"
- Townes, "Washed in the Grace of God"
- West, *Disruptive Christian Ethics*, 141–79
- West, "Must I Be Womanist?"
- Young, "De-centering Religion as Queer Pedagogical Practice"
- Young, "Queering 'The Human Situation'"
- Young, "'Uses of the Erotic' for Teaching Queer Studies"

Challenging Black Liberation Theologies
- Anderson, "The Black Church and the Curious Body of the Black Homosexual"
- Coleman, "Must I Be Womanist?"
- Garner, "A Sample Service of Holy Union"
- Griffin, "Toward a True Black Liberation Theology"
- Hill, "Disrupted/Disruptive Movements"
- Johnson, "Feeling the Spirit in the Dark"
- Jojo, "Searching for Gender-Variant East African Spiritual Leaders"
- Monroe, "When and Where I Enter"
- Sneed, "Dark Matter"
- Sneed, "Like Fire Shut Up in Our Bones"
- Sneed, *Representations of Homosexuality*
- Strongman, "Syncretic Religion and Dissident Sexualities"

Other Resources
- Baldwin, "To Crush a Serpent"
- Beckford, "Does Jesus Have a Penis?"
- farajajé-jones, "Holy Fuck"
- Hamilton, "'The Flames of Namugongo'"
- Kornegay, "Queering Black Homophobia"
- Moore, "Theorizing the 'Black Body' as a Site of Trauma"
- Schexnayder, *Setting the Table*, 37-38.
- West, *Defending Same-Sex Marriage*

Chapter 3

Queer Asian American Theologies

Since at least the mid-1990s, queer Asian American[1] theologians have written about the interplay of their racial, sexual, and spiritual identities. Although many of these theologians have experienced alienation from both the Asian American community (as a result of queerphobia) as well as the LGBTIQ community (as a result of racism), many of these individuals have also experienced a pathway to the divine as a result of their particular social location.

For example, Eric H. F. Law, a gay Chinese American Episcopal priest, has written about how his experiences of living "in between two cultures" and "[in] between the gay and straight worlds" have given him a "foretaste of what it felt like to be in between the divine and the human."[2] Similarly, I have written about how the "embattled gay Asian male body" might in fact serve an "atoning purpose" by "decolonizing the racism

---

[1] In this book, I use the term "Asian American" to describe people of Asian descent living in the United States. As I have noted elsewhere, there are many ways other ways of referring to such people, including "Asian," "Asian Pacific American," "Asian Pacific Islander," and "API." See Patrick S. Cheng, "Multiplicity and Judges 19: Constructing a Queer Asian Pacific American Biblical Hermeneutic," *Semeia* 90/91 (2002): 123.

[2] Eric H. F. Law, "A Spirituality of Creative Marginality," in Comstock and Henking, *Que(e)rying Religion*, 345.

and homophobia of contemporary Christian theologies."[3] I have also written about how the threefold interplay of race, sexuality, and spirituality in the lives of LGBTIQ Asian Americans can be understood as a reflection of the trinitarian nature of God.[4]

This chapter will examine key writings from LGBTIQ Asian American theologians. It will focus on three main themes that have emerged in the writings of queer Asian American theologians: (1) Asian and Asian American church exclusion; (2) critiquing LGBTIQ racism; and (3) highlighting transnational perspectives. Before discussing these themes, however, this chapter begins by providing a brief history of the LGBTIQ Asian American experience.

1. Historical Background

The history of LGBTIQ Asian Americans is still largely hidden and has yet to be written. Although a number of works have been written about the history of same-sex and gender-variant behaviors in Asian cultures (that is, in Asia),[5] far less has been written about the history of LGBTIQ Asian Americans. As a threshold matter, it should be noted that there is no such thing as a generic "Asian American" history. That is, the history of Asian Americans are very much dependent upon the migration stories of the different ethnic groups—that is, the people of Burmese, Chinese, Filipino, Hmong, Indian, Korean, Japanese, Malaysian, Pacific Islander, Pakistani, Thai, and Vietnamese descent—that make up the umbrella term "Asian American."[6]

---

[3] Patrick S. Cheng, "Gay Asian Masculinities and Christian Theologies," *CrossCurrents* 61, no. 4 (December 2011): 540.

[4] See Patrick S. Cheng, "A Three-Part Sinfonia: Queer Asian Reflections on the Trinity," in *New Overtures: Asian North American Theology in the 21st Century*, ed. Eleazar S. Fernandez (Upland, CA: Sopher Press, 2012), 173-91.

[5] See, for example, Adrian Carton, "Desire and Same-Sex Intimacies in Asia," in Aldrich, *Gay Life and Culture*, 303–31; Wayne R. Dynes and Stephen Donaldson, *Asian Homosexuality* (New York: Garland Publishing, 1992); Giti Thadani, *Sakhiyani: Lesbian Desire in Ancient and Modern India* (London: Cassell, 1996); Giovanni Vitiello, *The Libertine's Friend: Homosexuality and Masculinity in Late Imperial China* (Chicago, IL: University of Chicago Press, 2011); Tsuneo Watanabe and Jun'ichi Iwata, *The Love of the Samurai: A Thousand Years of Japanese Homosexuality* (London: GMP Publishers, 1989).

[6] For a history of Asian Americans, see Ronald Takaki, *Strangers from a Different Shore: A History of Asian Americans*, updated and rev. ed. (New York: Back Bay Books, 1998).

Although Asian Americans are often viewed as relatively recent arrivals to the United States, they have in fact lived in North America since the eighteenth century. For example, there is historical evidence that Filipino sailors reached Louisiana as early as 1765 as part of the Spanish galleon trade and established fishing villages near New Orleans.[7]

During the California gold rush of the mid-nineteenth century, tens of thousands of Chinese men migrated to the United States to work in the mining industry and on the railroads. They formed bachelor societies in Chinatowns, which were characterized by the dominant white ruling class as "perverse spaces" that were full of "deviant sexualities" and "peculiar domestic arrangements."[8] In some ways, these were the first queer Asian American spaces in the United States.

As Chinese immigrants entered the mining, railroad, manufacturing, and agricultural workforce in greater numbers, there was a backlash. The Chinese workers were characterized as "nagurs," and they were described as "heathen, morally inferior, savage, childlike, and lustful."[9] In 1854, the California Supreme Court ruled in *People v. Hall* that Chinese witnesses—like Blacks or Indigenous people—were not permitted to testify in court either in favor of, or against, white people.[10]

In 1882, the United States passed the Chinese Exclusionary Act, which prohibited Chinese people from entering the country (Chinese women had been effectively banned since 1875), and it denied citizenship to Chinese immigrants who were already in the country.[11] Despite this official ban (which was not fully repealed until the Immigration and Nationality Act of 1965), Asian Americans—and queer Asian Americans—continued to live in this country. For example, Amy Sueyoshi, a

---

[7] See Gary Y. Okihiro, *The Columbia Guide to Asian American History* (New York: Columbia University Press, 2001), 7.

[8] Nayan Shah, "Perversity, Contamination, and the Dangers of Queer Domesticity," in *Queer Studies: An Interdisciplinary Reader*, ed. Robert J. Corber and Stephen Valocchi (Malden, MA: Blackwell, 2003), 121.

[9] Takaki, *A Different Mirror*, 188.

[10] See ibid., 189.

[11] See ibid., 189-90.

professor of race and resistance studies and of sexuality studies at San Francisco State University, has published a biography of Yone Noguchi, a bisexual Japanese American man who had a passionate same-sex interracial affair during the turn of the twentieth century.[12]

Queer Asian Americans were even part of the pre-Stonewall homophile rights movement. One of the early gay rights Asian American activists was Kiyoshi Kuromiya, a third-generation Japanese American who was born in a Japanese American internment camp. Kuromiya took part in one of the first gay rights demonstrations in Philadelphia on July 4, 1965, and he continued his activism in the LGBTIQ community, including HIV/AIDS activism, until his death in 2000.[13]

The queer Asian American community started to organize in earnest in the 1970s and 1980s.[14] For example, the Asian American lesbian activist Michiyo Cornell addressed the 1979 March on Washington about the formation in October 1979 of the Lesbian and Gay Asian Collective, the first "network of support of, by, and for Asian American lesbians and gay men."[15] This history of LGBTIQ Asian Americans has been documented by a number of anthologies published in the 1990s, including *Asian American Sexualities: Dimensions of the Gay and Lesbian Experience*[16] and *Q&A: Queer in Asian America.*[17]

Today, the LGBTIQ Asian American community continues to thrive.[18] The National Queer Asian Pacific Islander Association

---

[12] See Amy Sueyoshi, *Queer Compulsions: Race, Nation, and Sexuality in the Affairs of Yone Noguchi* (Honolulu: University of Hawai'i Press, 2012).

[13] See Liz Highleyman, "Kiyoshi Kuromiya: Integrating the Issues," in *Smash the Church, Smash the State!: The Early Years of Gay Liberation*, ed. Tommi Avicolli Mecca (San Francisco, CA: City Lights Books, 2009), 17–21.

[14] See, for example, Eric C. Wat, *The Making of a Gay Asian Community: An Oral History of Pre-AIDS Los Angeles* (Lanham, MD: Rowman and Littlefield, 2002).

[15] Michiyo Cornell, "Living in Asian America: An Asian American Lesbian's Address Before the Washington Monument (1979)," in *Asian American Sexualities: Dimensions of the Gay and Lesbian Experience*, ed. Russell Leong (New York: Routledge, 1996), 83.

[16] Leong, *Asian American Sexualities*.

[17] Eng and Hom, *Q&A.*

[18] See, for example, J. R. Tungol, "The Most Influential LGBT Asian Icons," *Huffington Post* (October 29, 2012), accessed January 3, 2013, http://huff.to/SU4hQr.

(NQAPIA) is a federation of over forty LGBTIQ Asian American, South Asian, Southeast Asian, and Pacific Islander organizations across the country. In July 2012, NQAPIA held a conference in Washington, D.C., that included a briefing at the White House on issues of interest to this community.[19] In November 2012, Mark Takano, a gay Japanese American man, became the first openly-queer person of color to be elected to the United States Congress.[20]

2. Genealogy of Queer Asian American Theologies

Since the mid-1990s, queer Asian American theologians have written a number of works about the LGBTIQ Asian American experience. These works can be organized into three thematic strands: (1) Asian and Asian American church exclusion; (2) critiquing LGBTIQ racism; and (3) highlighting transnational perspectives.

a. Asian and Asian American Church Exclusion

The first thematic strand in queer Asian American theologies relates to the exclusion of LGBTIQ people from Asian and Asian American churches. This has been an important issue in recent years, particularly since many evangelical Asian American churches have actively opposed marriage equality for LGBTIQ people. For example, Chinese American churches played an important role in the passage of California Proposition 8 in 2008.[21] (Proposition 8 amended the California state constitution so as to eliminate the right to same-sex marriage in the state.)

One of the main queer Asian American theologians to write on this topic is Leng Lim, a gay Episcopal priest who grew up in Singapore and came to the United States for college and divinity school. Subsequent to his ordination, Lim earned an

---

[19] See Cheng, "A Unicorn at the White House."

[20] See Diane Anderson-Minshall, "Mark Takano Becomes First LGBT Person of Color in Congress," *Advocate.com* (November 7, 2012), accessed Janaury 3, 2013, http://bit.ly/RWal9L.

[21] See Cheng, "Gay Asian Masculinities and Christian Theologies," 543.

MBA from Harvard Business School and now divides his time between the United States and Asia.

Lim's writings have focused on the ways in which many Asian and Asian American churches have ostracized LGBTIQ people. In 1996, Lim wrote an essay, "The Gay Erotics of My Stuttering Mother Tongue," which was one of the earliest published works of queer Asian American theology. In that essay, Lim wrote about growing up with the shame of his homosexuality in Singapore and how his "mother tongue" did not give him the language to express his sexuality adequately.[22] Leng wrote about "struggling with God" while growing up, and also his amazement at the fact that he did not kill himself.[23]

In 1997, Lim wrote another essay about his growing up gay in Singapore. In that essay, "Webs of Betrayal, Webs of Blessing," Lim writes about his experiences of growing up gay in a fundamentalist Christian church in Singapore. In a particularly powerful passage, Lim writes about how his mother had an intensely negative reaction to his coming out and how she accused the devil of infiltrating his mind.[24]

Lim has also written about the pain that is experienced by many LGBTIQ Asian Americans here in the United States. In 2002, Lim published an article, "'The Bible Tells Me to Hate Myself': The Crisis in Asian American Spiritual Leadership," in a special issue of the biblical journal *Semeia* on the Bible in Asian America. In that article, Lim reflects upon his ministry as an Episcopal priest, and he notes how much pain the Bible has caused to LGBTIQ Asian Americans. In particular, Lim tells the story of a gay Asian American UCLA student who believed that being a "good Christian" required "hating himself" simply because "the Bible tells him to do so." Lim says that the student "has been told a lie" and that the student's spiritual teachers "*abused* him."[25]

---

[22] Lim, "Gay Erotics," 173.

[23] Ibid., 174.

[24] See Leng Leroy Lim, "Webs of Betrayal, Webs of Blessings," in *Our Families, Our Values: Snapshots of Queer Kinship*, ed. Robert E. Goss and Amy Adams Squire Strongheart (Binghamton, NY: Harrington Park Press, 1997), 227–41.

[25] Leng Leroy Lim, "'The Bible Tells Me to Hate Myself': The Crisis in Asian American Spiritual Leadership," *Semeia* 90/91 (2002): 320.

Finally, Lim has criticized church leaders in Asia for failing to accept LGBTIQ people fully. In 2006, Lim co-authored an essay, "The Mythic-Literalists in the Province of Southeast Asia," in which he criticizes the Anglican Province of Southeast Asia for its opposition to LGBTIQ people. Lim argued that the province had regressed to a "lower level of faith and conscious-ness development" as a result of its stance.[26] There are a number of other essays in the *Other Voices, Other Worlds* anthology (in which Lim's essay appears) about LGBTIQ issues in Anglican churches in Oceana, Hong Kong, India, and Japan.[27]

In sum, the central theme that runs through Lim's writings is how LGBTIQ people have been excluded from Asian and Asian American churches. Although over fifteen years have passed since the publication of Lim's first article, this is still an important issue for many LGBTIQ Asian Americans today.

For example, "Michael Kim"—the pseudonym for a young Korean American gay man who is unable to be fully out about his sexuality—wrote a powerful essay, "Out and About: Coming of Age in a Straight White World," in the *Asian American X* anthology about the overwhelming difficulties of coming out in a Korean American Christian community. Kim writes that to come out would be, "quite literally, the ultimate failure—moral, social, and personal all at once. It would nullify everything good that I have done and would stand as the single mark upon me."[28] Accordingly, much still needs to be done with respect to the issue of exclusion by Asian and Asian American churches.

Currently, the Asian Pacific Islander Roundtable at the Center for Lesbian and Gay Studies in Religion and Ministry

---

[26] Leng Lim with Kim-Hao Yap and Tuck-Leong Lee, "The Mythic-Literalists in the Province of Southeast Asia," in *Other Voices, Other Worlds: The Global Church Speaks Out on Homosexuality*, ed. Terry Brown (New York: Church Publishing, 2006), 59.

[27] Brown, *Other Voices, Other Worlds*.

[28] Michael Kim, "Out and About: Coming of Age in a Straight White World," in *Asian American X: An Intersection of 21st Century Asian American Voices*, ed. Arar Han and John Hsu (Ann Arbor: University of Michigan Press, 2004), 147. For a discussion of Korean immigrant Protestant churches and the issue of homosexuality, see Eunai Shrake, "Homosexuality and Korean Immigrant Protestant Churches," in *Embodying Asian/American Sexualities*, ed. Gina Masequesmay and Sean Metzger (Lanham, MD: Lexington Books, 2009), 145–56.

at the Pacific School of Religion is an organization that is dedicated to affirming the "dignity and spiritual wholeness" of LGBTIQ people of Asian descent through scholarship and other means.[29] Other organizations with similar goals include the Network on Religion and Justice[30] and Queer Asian Spirit.[31]

b. Critiquing LGBTIQ Racism

The second thematic strand in queer Asian American theologies relates to critiquing the racism of the white LGBTIQ community. A number of queer Asian American theologians, including Eric H. F. Law and myself, have written about this theme.

In 1997, Eric H. F. Law, a gay Chinese American Episcopal priest, wrote an article, "A Spirituality of Creative Marginality," which was published in the *Que(e)rying Religion* anthology. In that article, Law writes about coming out in college and his experience of profound exclusion from the gay community: "No one talked to me. No one even looked at me. No one invited me to dance. When another Asian came in, I felt competitive." For Law, his experiences of racism in the LGBTIQ community ultimately led him to articulate a spirituality of "creative marginality."[32] That is, Law affirmed his location of being "in between" both the Asian and the LGBTIQ worlds; like Jesus Christ's experience of divinity and humanity, Law was "part of both ends but not fully one or the other."[33]

In 2004, Law wrote an imaginary dialogue between an LGBTIQ person of color and a white LGBTIQ person in his book *The Word at the Crossings: Living the Good News in a Multicontextual Community*. The dialogue was about the racism

---

[29] "Asian and Pacific Islander Roundtable," Center for Lesbian and Gay Studies in Religion and Ministry, accessed January 3, 2013, http://bit.ly/Tqda91.

[30] Network on Religion and Justice for Asian Pacific Islander Lesbian, Gay, Bisexual, and Transgender People, accessed January 3, 2013, http://www.netrj.org.

[31] Queer Asian Spirit, accessed January 3, 2013, http://www.queerasianspirit.org.

[32] Law, "A Spirituality of Creative Marginality," 344.

[33] Ibid., 345–46. Law is currently the director of the Kaleidoscope Institute, which offers training programs to develop "competent leadership in a diverse, changing world." Kaleidoscope Institute, accessed January 3, 2013, http://www.kscopeinstitute.org.

that the LGBTIQ person of color had experienced at an ecumenical LGBTIQ-affirming conference for Christians. The LGBTIQ person of color said: "I thought that by coming here and being with all the gay and lesbian Christians, I would feel accepted. But judging from what I see, this so-called welcoming community is the same as any white community."[34]

I have also written extensively about racism and the LGBTIQ community. In 2002, I published an article, "Multiplicity and Judges 19: Constructing a Queer Asian Pacific American Biblical Heremeneutic," in the special issue of *Semeia*.[35] In that article, I argued that the queer Asian American person is a "radical sexual and geographical outsider," and her/his experience of racism is reflected in the narrative of the unnamed concubine in Judges 19 who is gang raped and dismembered. That is, both the queer Asian American person and the unnamed concubine experience oppression in the form of erasure as well as sexual objectification.[36]

One theme that I have explored in my scholarship is the need for spiritual healing in light of the racism that is experienced by LGBTIQ Asian Americans. In my 2006 article "Reclaiming Our Traditions, Rituals, and Spaces: Spirituality and the Queer Asian Pacific American Experience" in the journal *Spiritus*, I argue that queer Asian Americans experience metaphorical homelessness as well as bodily alienation because of the racism that we experience from the LGBTIQ community. In order to heal this homelessness and alienation, queer Asian Americans have sought to reclaim their own spiritual traditions, rituals, and spaces.[37]

Another theme that I have explored in my scholarship is the need to challenge an unspoken "code of conduct" that the dominant white queer culture imposes upon LGBTIQ Asian

---

[34] Eric H. F. Law, *The Word at the Crossings: Living the Good News in a Multicontextual Community* (St. Louis, MO: Chalice Press, 2004), 87.

[35] Cheng, "Multiplicity and Judges 19."

[36] Ibid., 125–27.

[37] Patrick S. Cheng, "Reclaiming Our Traditions, Rituals, and Spaces: Spirituality and the Queer Asian Pacific American Experience," *Spiritus* 6, no. 2 (Fall 2006): 234–40.

Americans. That is, white queer culture discourages LGBTIQ Asian Americans from being "too Asian" with respect to language, food, music, and even notions of beauty. In my 2006 commentary on Paul's Letter to the Galatians in *The Queer Bible Commentary*, I argue that Galatians can be read as freeing LGBTIQ Asian Americans from "the yoke of slavery to the implicit codes of conduct that are imposed by the dominant white queer community."[38]

I also have written a number of other articles that have addressed issues of sexual racism in gay male cyberculture. These include my 2011 article "'I Am Yellow and Beautiful': Reflections on Queer Asian Spirituality and Gay Male Cyberculture" in the *Journal of Technology, Theology, and Religion*, in which I explore how "gay male cyberculture inhibits the spiritual development of gay Asian men."[39] I have discussed similar themes in my 2011 article "Gay Asian Masculinities and Christian Theologies" in *CrossCurrents*, in which I note that the statement "No Asians" is routinely seen on gay online dating sites and hookup apps.[40]

Finally, I have addressed the issue of racism in the LGBTIQ community in my other books on queer theology. For example, in my 2011 book *Radical Love: An Introduction to Queer Theology*, I argue that the doctrine of sin can be understood as splitting off issues of sexuality from issues of race in theological discourse.[41] Similarly, in my 2012 book *From Sin to Amazing Grace: Discovering the Queer Christ*, I discuss the sin of singularity—that is, the failure of LGBTIQ people to address both racism *and* homophobia—in my chapter on the Hybrid Christ.[42]

---

[38] Patrick S. Cheng, "Galatians," in *The Queer Bible Commentary*, ed. Deryn Guest et al. (London: SCM Press, 2006), 629.

[39] Patrick S. Cheng, "'I Am Yellow and Beautiful': Reflections on Queer Asian Spirituality and Gay Male Cyberculture," *Journal of Technology, Theology, and Religion* 2, no. 3 (June 2011): 3, accessed January 3, 2013, http://bit.ly/jOCltG.

[40] Cheng, "Gay Asian Masculinities and Christian Theologies," 542; see also Indie Harper, "No Asians, Blacks, Fats, or Femmes," in Boykin, *For Colored Boys*, 129–35.

[41] See Cheng, *Radical Love*, 74–77.

[42] Cheng, *From Sin to Amazing Grace*, 133–45; see also Patrick S. Cheng, "Rethinking Sin and Grace for LGBT People Today," in *Sexuality and the Sacred: Sources for Theological Reflection*, ed. Marvin M. Ellison and Kelly Brown Douglas, 2nd ed. (Louisville, KY: Westminster John Knox Press, 2010), 114–15.

c. Highlighting Transnational Perspectives

The third and final thematic strand in queer Asian American theologies relates to the highlighting of transnational perspectives. In light of the complex migration and immigration histories of queer Asian American communities, the line between domestic and international theologies is often quite blurred. A number of queer Asian American theologians have crossed international borders in their writings.

For example, Michael Sepidoza Campos, a queer Filipino scholar with a doctorate in cultural studies from the Graduate Theological Union in Berkeley, California, crosses international borders in his essay "The *Baklâ*: Gendered Religious Performance in Filipino Cultural Spaces."[43] Campos writes about the *baklâ*, or the "effeminate gay man who personifies Filipino popular conceptions of homosexuality." Campos has argued that the *baklâ*'s body both affirms and challenges the "two-gendered conceptualization of human sexuality."[44] In his essay, Campos takes the reader around the globe, moving from Roman Catholic religious processions in the Philippines to a gay Filipino American Holy Cross procession in New York City.

Similarly, Lai-shan Yip, a queer Chinese doctoral student from Hong Kong at the Graduate Theological Union in Berkeley, California, engages in transnational border crossings in her essay "Listening to the Passion of Catholic *nu-tongzhi*: Developing a Catholic Lesbian Feminist Theology in Hong Kong."[45] Yip writes about the struggles that Chinese lesbians, or *nu-tongzhi*, face in coming out and being accepted by their parish communities. She writes about the need to form a "new Church community of liberation."[46]

Joseph N. Goh, a queer Malaysian doctoral student in gender, sexuality, and theology at Monash University, Malaysia, who also studied at the Graduate Theological Union, has published

---

[43] Campos, "The *Baklâ*."

[44] Ibid., 167–68.

[45] Yip, "Listening to the Passion."

[46] Ibid., 76.

a number of theological works relating to governmental antagonism toward queer Malaysians, including "The Word Was *Not* Made Flesh: Theological Reflections on the Banning of *Seksualiti Merdeka* 2011"[47] and "*Mak Nyah* Bodies as Sacred Sites: Uncovering the Queer Body-Sacramentality of Malaysian Male-to-Female Transsexuals."[48] Goh is also the editor of the *Queer Asian Spirit E-Zine*, an international online journal of spiritual writings by LGBTIQ Asians and Asian Americans.[49]

Campos, Yip, and Goh are members of EQARS, the Emerging Queer Asian Religion Scholars group, which is a group of LGBTIQ Asian and Asian American theologians from around the world who meet monthly via Skype to share their work.[50] The members of EQARS have given presentations at professional conferences such as the American Academy of Religion, and they have also contributed to a special issue of *Theology and Sexuality* on queer Asian theologies.[51]

There have been a number of recent queer theological developments in Asia, including the publication in 2010 of a special issue on queer theology in Hong Kong in the Asian feminist journal *In God's Image*.[52] Rose Wu, an ally of the LGBTIQ Asian community in Hong Kong, has documented the rise of the *tongzhi* movement in Hong Kong from an ecclesial perspective in her works, including *Liberating the Church from Fear: The Story of Hong Kong's Sexual Minorities*.[53]

---

[47] Joseph N. Goh, "The Word Was *Not* Made Flesh: Theological Reflections on the Banning of *Seksualiti Merdeka* 2011," *Dialog: A Journal of Theology* 51, no. 2 (Summer 2012): 145–54.

[48] Joseph N. Goh, "*Mak Nyah* Bodies as Sacred Sites: Uncovering the Queer Body-Sacramentality of Malaysian Male-to-Female Transsexuals," *CrossCurrents* 62, no. 4 (December 2012): 512–21.

[49] For the inaugural issue of the journal, see *Queer Asian Spirit E-Zine* 1 (December 2012), accessed January 3, 2013, http://bit.ly/YeGNM7.

[50] See Emerging Asian Pacific Islander Queer Religion Scholars, accessed January 3, 2013, http://www.eqars.org. Other members of EQARS include Hugo Córdova Quero, Elizabeth Leung, Miak Siew, and myself.

[51] See *Theology and Sexuality* 17, no. 3 (forthcoming).

[52] Rose Wu, ed., "Beyond Right and Wrong: Doing Queer Theology in Hong Kong," *In God's Image* 29, no. 3 (September 2010).

[53] Rose Wu, *Liberating the Church from Fear: The Story of Hong Kong's Sexual Minorities* (Kowloon, Hong Kong: Hong Kong Women Christian Council, 2000).

A closely related theme to transnational perspectives is that of interfaith reflection. Leng Lim has written about his experiences as a "Buddhist-raised Christian convert turning into a syncretist." That is, Lim insists upon drawing upon Asian religious traditions, "no matter which Christian accuses me of syncretism."[54] Indeed, Lim has proposed that Asian American Christian leaders can counter the dangers of spiritual abuse with the Bible by drawing upon the twin Buddhist traditions of (1) non-attachment to the truth and (2) the practice of mindfulness.[55] Perhaps future queer Asian theologians might also draw upon the research of scholars such as Ann-Marie Hsiung on same-sex relations in Confucianism and Taoism, as well as Yu-chen Li on reconstructing Buddhist perspectives on homosexuality.[56]

I have also written about how LGBTIQ Asian Americans have reclaimed the spiritual traditions of their ancestors. These practices can take the form of interfaith meditation groups, sacred drum rituals, reflection upon sacred texts such as the *Dao De Jing*, as well as other practices.[57] I have also written an essay on how the Buddhist bodhisattva Kuan Yin can be viewed as a queer Asian Christ. That is, Kuan Yin is *queer* because s/he has transitioned from male to female in moving from India to China. S/he is *Asian* because she is currently located in China. And s/he is a *christological* figure (soteriologically speaking) in that s/he refuses to enter Nirvana before bringing others there first.[58] By drawing upon the spiritual traditions of their ancestors, LGBTIQ Asian Americans—including those who are Christians—can deepen their own connections with the divine.

---

[54] Lim, "Gay Erotics," 176, 175.

[55] Lim, "'The Bible Tells Me to Hate Myself,'" 321–22.

[56] Ann-Marie Hsiung, "Gender and Same-Sex Relations in Confucianism and Taoism," in *Heterosexism in Contemporary World Religion: Problem and Prospect*, ed. Marvin M. Ellison and Judith Plaskow (Cleveland, OH: Pilgrim Press, 2007), 99–34; Yu-chen Li, "Reconstructing Buddhist Perspectives on Homosexuality: Enlightenment from the Study of the Body," in Ellison and Plaskow, *Heterosexism in Contemporary World Religion*, 135–53.

[57] Cheng, "Reclaiming Our Traditions, Rituals, and Spaces," 236–37.

[58] Patrick S. Cheng, "Kuan Yin: Mirror of the Queer Asian Christ" (unpublished paper, 2003), accessed January 3, 2013, http://bit.ly/qyvGtk.

In addition to interfaith reflections by Christians, there are also articles being written from non-Christian religious perspectives. For example, Yuenmei Wong, a doctoral student from Malaysia at the University of Maryland, has written an article about the *Pengkid*, who is a "masculine-looking Malay-Muslim lesbian who is outlawed in Malaysia through Islamic discourses."[59] Wong explores how female masculinities are constructed through the *Pengkid* identity and how this "growing social phenomenon" will continue to "challenge the emerging fundamentalist Islamic interpretations and sanctions."[60]

Finally, it is important to note the contributions of allies to the LGBTIQ Asian American community. One prominent ally is Kwok Pui-lan, the William F. Cole Professor of Christian Theology and Spirituality at the Episcopal Divinity School in Cambridge, Massachusetts, and a former president of the American Academy of Religion. Kwok has published a number of works relating to LGBTIQ Asian American issues, including one article about LGBTIQ-positive Asian American churches and another article that critiques the silence of white LGBTIQ theologians with respect to issues of race.[61] Another prominent ally is Tat-siong Benny Liew, who is the academic dean and a professor of New Testament studies at the Pacific School of Religion in Berkeley, California. Like Kwok, Liew has written about the intersections of LGBTIQ and Asian American issues, and he has also critiqued the silence of LGBTIQ biblical scholars with respect to issues of race.[62]

---

[59] Yuenmei Wong, "Islam, Sexuality, and the Marginal Positioning of *Pengkids* and Their Girlfriends in Malaysia," *Journal of Lesbian Studies* 16 (2012): 1.

[60] Ibid., 14.

[61] See Kwok Pui-lan, "Asian and Asian American Churches," in *Homosexuality and Religion: An Encyclopedia*, ed. Jeffrey S. Siker (Westport, CT: Greenwood Press, 2007), 59–61; Kwok Pui-lan, "Body and Pleasure in Postcoloniality," in *Dancing Theology in Fetish Boots: Essays in Honour of Marcella Althaus-Reid*, ed. Lisa Isherwood and Mark D. Jordan (London: SCM Press, 2010), 31–43; Kwok Pui-lan, *Postcolonial Imagination and Feminist Theology* (Louisville, KY: Westminster John Knox Press, 2005); Kwok Pui-lan, "Touching the Taboo: On the Sexuality of Jesus," in Ellison and Douglas, *Sexuality and the Sacred*, 119–34.

[62] See Tat-siong Benny Liew, "(Cor)Responding: A Letter to the Editor," in *Queer Commentary and the Hebrew Bible*, ed. Ken Stone (Cleveland, OH: Pilgrim Press, 2001), 182–92; Tat-siong Benny Liew, "Queering Closets and Perverting Desires: Cross-Examining John's Engendering and Transgendering Word Across Different Worlds," in *They Were All Together in One Place?: Toward Minority Biblical Criticism*, ed. Randall C. Bailey, Tat-siong Benny Liew, and Fernando F. Segovia (Atlanta, GA: Society of Biblical Literature, 2009), 251–88.

3. Conclusion

In conclusion, quite a number of works have been written on queer Asian theology since the mid-1990s. These articles have addressed a number of key themes, including (1) Asian and Asian American church exclusion, (2) critiquing LGBTIQ racism, and (3) highlighting transnational perspectives. There is still much work to be done in the future, however, with respect to queer Asian American theology. For example, there are presently very few works that address Asian American transgender voices.[63] There are also very few LGBTIQ voices doing Christian theology from South Asian (that is, Indian), Southeast Asian, and Pacific Islander contexts.[64] There are, however, an increasing number of voices that are addressing the transnational boundaries that separate queer Asia from queer Asian America,[65] and it will be exciting to see how these boundaries become even more fluid in the future.

---

[63] One such work is *Two Spirits, One Heart*, which tells the story of a Japanese American mother and her transgender son. See Marsha Aizumi with Aiden Aizumi, *Two Spirits, One Heart: A Mother, Her Transgender Son, and Their Journey to Love and Acceptance* (Arcadia, CA: Peony Press, 2012). For an overview of the challenges faced by many Asian American transgender people, see National Gay and Lesbian Task Force, "Injustice at Every Turn: A Look at Asian American, South Asian, Southeast Asian, and Pacific Islander Respondents in the National Transgender Discrimination Survey" (July 19, 2011), accessed January 3, 2013, http://bit.ly/MRTpTP.

[64] See Brown, *Other Voices, Other Worlds*.

[65] See Ramón A. Guitiérrez, ed., "Further Desire: Asian and Asian American Sexualities," *Amerasia Journal* 37, no. 2 (2011); see also Travis S. K. Kong, *Chinese Male Homosexualities: Memba, Tongzhi and Golden Boy* (London: Routledge, 2011); Martin F. Manalansan, *Global Divas: Filipino Gay Men in the Diaspora* (Durham, NC: Duke University Press, 2003); Fran Martin et al., eds., *AsiaPacifiQueer: Rethinking Genders and Sexualities* (Urbana: University of Illinois Press, 2008).

Study Questions

1. Which events from the history of queer Asian Americans surprised you the most? Troubled you the most? What would like to learn more about in terms of queer Asian American history?

2. What are some key writings by queer Asian American theologians about the exclusion of LGBTIQ Asians and Asian Americans from their churches?

3. What are some key writings by queer Asian American theologians about racism and the white LGBTIQ community?

4. What are some key writings by queer Asian American theologians on transnational issues?

5. How might you use transnational and interfaith perspectives to enrich your own theological reflection and work?

For Further Study

Queer Asian American Experience
* Eng and Hom, *Q&A*
* Guitiérrez, "Further Desire"
* Leong, *Asian American Sexualities*
* Lim-Hing, *The Very Inside*

Asian and Asian American Church Exclusion
* Brown, *Other Voices, Other Worlds*
* Kim, "Out and About"
* Kwok, "Asian and Asian American Churches"
* Lim, "'The Bible Tells Me to Hate Myself'"
* Lim, "Gay Erotics"
* Lim, "Webs of Betrayal"
* Lim, with Yap and Lee, "Mythic Literalists"
* Shrake, "Homosexuality and Korean Immigrant Protestant Churches"

Critiquing LGBTIQ Racism
* Harper, "No Asians, Blacks, Fats, or Femmes."
* Law, "A Spirituality of Creative Marginality"
* Law, *The Word at the Crossings*
* Liew, "(Co)Responding"
* Cheng, *From Sin to Amazing Grace*, 133–45
* Cheng, "Galatians"
* Cheng, "Gay Asian Masculinities and Christian Theologies"
* Cheng, "'I am Yellow and Beautiful'"
* Cheng, "Multiplicity and Judges 19"
* Cheng, *Radical Love*, 74–77
* Cheng, "Reclaiming Our Traditions, Rituals, and Spaces"
* Cheng, "Rethinking Sin and Grace for LGBT People Today"

Highlighting Transnational Perspectives
* Campos, "The *Baklâ*"
* Goh, "*Mak Nyah* Bodies as Sacred Sites"
* Goh, "The Word Was *Not* Made Flesh"
* Robinson, *In the Eye of the Storm*, 135–38
* Wong, "Islam, Sexuality, and the Marginal Positioning of *Pengkids*"
* Wu, *Beyond Right and Wrong*
* Wu, *Liberating the Church from Fear*
* Wu, "A Story of Its Own Name"
* Yip, "Listening to the Passion"

Other Resources
* Busto, "Normally Queer?"
* Cheng, "Roundtable Discussion: Same-Sex Marriage"
* Cheng, "A Three-Part Sinfonia"
* Consolacion, "Where I Am Today"
* Hsiung, "Gender and Same-Sex Relations in Confucianism and Taoism"
* Kwok, "Body and Pleasure in Postcoloniality"
* Kwok, *Postcolonial Imagination and Feminist Theology*, 100–121
* Law, "A Litany for Dialogue Among People with Different Sexual Orientations"
* Lee, "Queerly a Good Friday"
* Li, "Reconstructing Buddhist Perspectives on Homosexuality"
* Liew, "Queering Closets and Perverting Desires"
* Schexnayder, *Setting the Table*, 39-40.
* Tuaolo, *Alone in the Trenches*, 199–210

Chapter 4

Queer Latina/o Theologies

S ome of the newest voices to emerge in the realm of queer of color theologies are those of queer Latina/o theologians. One of the challenges that such theologians face is an overwhelming silence among non-LGBTIQ Latina/o theologians about issues of queer sexualities and gender identities. As Orlando O. Espín, a gay Latino professor of theology at the University of San Diego, writes: "The topic seems to be so untouchable that, in fact, we have not reflected on it at length . . . and mere inclusion in a passing phrase does not qualify as sustained reflection."[1]

Indeed, James B. Nickoloff, a gay theologian and white ally of the LGBTIQ Latina/o community, published an essay in 2003, "Sexuality: A Queer Omission in U.S. Latino/a Theology," about the silence in Latina/o theologies about queer sexualities. In that essay, Nickoloff proposed a conversation between Latina/o theologians and white LGBTIQ theologians—*una teología "homo" de conjunto*—to develop a theology around the themes of redemptive solitude, salvific self-sacrifice, and the rejection of "dangerous falsehoods."[2]

---

[1] Orlando O. Espín, *Grace and Humanness: Theological Reflections Because of Culture* (Maryknoll, NY: Orbis Books, 2007), 58.

[2] James B. Nickoloff, "Sexuality: A Queer Omission in U.S. Latino/a Theology," *Journal of Hispanic/ Latino Theology* 10, no. 3 (2003): 50–51.

This chapter, as with the previous two chapters about queer Black and queer Asian American theologies, will begin with some historical background about LGBTIQ Latina/os in the United States. It will then focus on three specific themes in developing a genealogy of queer Latina/o theologies: (1) living on the borderlands; (2) challenging *machismo*; and (3) crossing literary and religious borders. Although queer Latina/o theological voices have been in existence as far back as the mid-1990s, there is less writing on this topic than has been the case with queer Black and queer Asian American theologies. As such, this chapter will also focus on the newer queer Latina/o theological voices that are emerging in the academy.

1. Historical Background

The story of LGBTIQ Latina/os differs from that of their African American and Asian American siblings. Spain began the colonization of what is known today as California in 1769, when Father Junipero Serra founded the mission of San Diego de Alcalá.[3] However, it was not until the 1800s that Latina/os became official residents of the United States. This occurred not so much by their crossing national borders, but as a result of the borders shifting around them following conquest by the United States. The Treaty of Guadalupe Hidalgo, signed in 1848, ended the Mexican-American War and resulted in the United States acquiring over one million square miles from Mexico. This included parts of what we know today as Arizona, California, Colorado, Nevada, New Mexico, Texas, and Utah.[4]

As a result of the treaty, the citizens of Mexico who lived in the acquired territories were allowed to choose United States citizenship, and most of them did. However, they experienced an extreme sense of alienation. As one Mexican diplomat predicted: "Our race, our unfortunate people will have to wander in search of hospitality in a strange land, only to be

---

[3] See Takaki, *A Different Mirror*, 159–60.
[4] See ibid., 163.

ejected later." He said that "the North Americans hate us" and that "they consider us unworthy to form with them one nation and one society."[5] Mexicans continued to immigrate to the United States, particularly as refugees after the 1910 Mexican Revolution, but they were met with anti-immigrant sentiments, and many were repatriated back to Mexico during the Great Depression. The second half of the twentieth century saw an influx of Latina/os from other nations and territories, including Puerto Rico, Cuba, the Dominican Republic, and Central America.[6]

The term "Latina/o" has a complicated history. As the Latino theologian Benjamín Valentín explains, the term is a "panethnic umbrella term" that is used "in an attempt to coalesce the varied U.S. experiences and identities of peoples with Spanish-speaking ancestry." (That is, the term "Latina/o" refers to people who reside in the United States, as opposed to Latin Americans, who reside in Central and South America.) Although the term is often used interchangeably with the term "Hispanic," many people prefer "Latina/o" because it "better embraces all Latin American nationalities, some of which have no ties to Spain."[7] Because the term "Latina/o" focuses on a shared linguistic heritage, it is technically not a racial term (that is, to the extent that race is signified by biological markers), but rather an ethnic one.[8]

Queer Latina/o voices have appeared in print since at least the early 1960s. Manuel de Jesús Hernández-Gutiérrez, a professor of Latina/o literature at Arizona State University, has documented the writings of queer Latina/o writers within the three major Latina/o ethnic groups: Chicanas/os (Mexican Americans), AmeRícans (Puerto Ricans), and Cuban-Americans.

---

[5] Ibid., 165.

[6] See Daniels, *Coming to America*, 307–27, 371–84.

[7] Benjamín Valentín, "Introduction," in *New Horizons in Hispanic/Latino(a) Theology*, ed. Benjamín Valentín (Cleveland, OH: Pilgrim Press, 2003), 1n1. The term "Hispanic" was created by the United States Census Bureau to categorize people of Spanish culture or origin, regardless of race.

[8] For example, this is reflected in the United States 2010 census form, which states explicitly that "for this census, Hispanic origins are not races." See "United States 2010 Census Form," accessed January 3, 2013, http://1.usa.gov/6Pph2M.

According to Hernández-Gutiérrez, it took nearly a quarter century before LGBTIQ Latina/o writings were recognized by the academy. He writes that "it took over twenty-four years of conscious efforts—from *City of Night* by John Rechy in 1963 to *Borderlands/La Frontera* by Gloria Anzaldúa in 1987—to establish such a voice among U.S. Latinos, mainstream Americans in general, and academia."[9]

As with the case of the queer Black and queer Asian American communities, few materials are readily available with respect to the history of the queer Latina/o community. For example, one little-known historical fact is that a gay Latino man, José Sarria, was the first openly gay candidate to run for public office in the United States in 1961.[10]

Despite the general lack of historical materials, one helpful resource for queer Latina/o history is the essay "Borderlands, Diasporas, and Transnational Crossings: Teaching LGBT Latina and Latino Histories" by Horacio N. Roque Ramírez. The essay opens with an oral history of a 1950s lesbian love affair in New York City that was recounted by Julia, a "black-identified Puerto Rican lesbian." Julia recounts how her mother found her at her girlfriend María's house and dragged her through the streets, even as Julia was shouting, "María, I love you! I'm going to go with you, María!"[11]

The Roque Ramírez essay also discusses the central role played by Sylvia Ray Rivera, a Latina trans woman, in the Stonewall Riots of June 1969.[12] Toward the end of her life, Rivera was very involved with the Metropolitan Community Church of New York (MCCNY), and the MCCNY youth shelter is named in her memory. I served as the Assistant Pastor of

---

[9] Manuel de Jesús Hernández-Gutiérrez, "Building a Research Agenda on U.S. Latino Lesbigay Literature and Cultural Production: Texts, Writers, Performance Artists, and Critics," in *Chicano/Latino Homoerotic Identities*, ed. David William Foster (New York: Garland Publishing, 1999), 297.

[10] In 1961, Sarria ran as an openly gay man for a seat on the San Francisco Board of Supervisors. See "José Sarria: First Gay Man in History to Run for Public Office Was Latino," *Gay LAtino* (September 9, 2011), accessed January 3, 2013, http://bit.ly/P1UdqP.

[11] Horacio N. Roque Ramírez, "Borderlands, Diasporas, and Transnational Crossings: Teaching LGBT Latina and Latino Histories," *OAH Magazine of History* (March 2006): 39.

[12] See ibid., 40.

Congregational Life at MCCNY from 2000 to 2001, and I had the privilege of knowing Sylvia and learning about her many decades of queer activist work. In 2005, a corner in Greenwich Village was named Silvia Rivera Way in her honor.[13]

Following the Stonewall Riots, LGBTIQ Latina/os started to organize around their racial and sexual identities. In 1970, lesbian and gay Chicana/os (that is, Latina/os of Mexican descent) founded *Unidos* in Los Angeles. In 1979, LGBTIQ Latina/os were participants in the National Third World Lesbian and Gay Conference that coincided with the first National March on Washington for Lesbian and Gay Rights.[14] And in 1987, the National Latina/o Lesbian, Gay, Bisexual, and Transgender Organization (LLEGÓ) was founded after the second national march on Washington.[15] (Unfortunately, LLEGÓ ceased to exist in 2004.)

One of the longest-standing organizations of LGBTIQ Latina/os is ALLGO, which was founded in 1985 as the Austin Latina/o Lesbian and Gay Organization. It was originally founded out of frustration by "gay activist agendas that did not include farm workers, police brutality and racism and by Latino activists who told them to check their sexual identity at the door."[16] In the intervening decades, ALLGO has broadened its mandate and now serves queer people of color throughout the state of Texas.

No history of the LGBTIQ Latina/o movement would be complete without discussing the work of Gloria Anzaldúa. As a lesbian Latina writer, she coined the term "borderlands," or *la frontera*, as "a site for political, historical, and sexual consciousness for appreciating the coming together of different cultures." Anzaldúa's *mestiza* (or mixed-race) consciousness

---

[13] Vicki L. Eaklor, *Queer America: A People's GLBT History of the United States* (New York: New Press, 2008), 197. For an interview with Rivera about the Stonewall Riots, see Eric Marcus, *Making Gay History: The Half-Century Fight for Lesbian and Gay Equal Rights* (New York: Harper, 2002), 126–30.

[14] See Eaklor, *Queer America*, 151.

[15] See ibid., 188.

[16] "History & Future," ALLGO: A Statewide Queer People of Color Organization, accessed January 3, 2013, http://bit.ly/sjUd5F.

was an "in-between state" that reflected her borderland existence. As such, she had a tolerance for "ambiguity and seeming contradictions."[17] In 1981, Anzaldúa co-edited *This Bridge Called My Back: Writings By Radical Women of Color* with Cherríe Moraga, which contains a section of essays by lesbian and bisexual women of color called "Between the Lines: On Culture, Class, and Homophobia."[18] In 2009, an anthology of Anzaldúa's works, *The Gloria Anzaldúa Reader*, was published by Duke University Press.[19]

2. Genealogy of Queer Latina/o Theologies

Queer Latina/o theologians have been writing about their experiences of ethnicity, sexuality, and spirituality since the mid-1990s. However, as with the case of queer Black and queer Asian American theological voices, there has not been any systematic examination of such writings to date.[20] As such, this section will construct a genealogy of queer Latina/o theologies. This genealogy will focus on three main themes: (1) living on the borderlands; (2) challenging *machismo*; and (3) crossing literary and religious borders.

It should be noted that this chapter acknowledges, but does not focus on, the work of the late Argentinian queer theologian Marcella Althaus-Reid. As a Latin American theologian who taught at the University of Edinburgh in Scotland, Althaus-Reid's pioneering work in queer theology—including *Indecent Theology: Theological Perversions in Sex, Gender and Politics*[21]—

---

[17] Roque Ramírez, "Borderlands, Diasporas, and Transnational Crossings," 40.

[18] Cherríe Moraga and Gloria Anzaldúa, eds., *This Bridge Called My Back: Writings by Radical Women of Color* (New York: Kitchen Table: Women of Color Press, 1981), 105–59.

[19] See Gloria Anzaldúa, *The Gloria Anzaldúa Reader*, ed. AnaLouise Keating (Durham, NC: Duke University Press, 2009).

[20] Salvador Vidal-Ortiz has written an essay that surveys the existing scholarship on Latina/o sexuality and religion. However, that essay focuses more upon social science literatures than theology. See Salvador Vidal-Ortiz, "Religion/Spirituality, U.S. Latina/o Communities, and Sexuality Scholarship: A Thread of Current Works," in *Latina/o Sexualities: Probing Powers, Passions, Practices, and Policies*, ed. Marysol Asencio (New Brunswick, NJ: Rutgers University Press, 2010), 173–87.

[21] Althaus-Reid, *Indecent Theology*.

transformed the theological world by weaving together liberation theology, queer theory, and postcolonial thought. Although
this chapter focuses primarily on the contributions of queer
Latina/o theologians in the United States, we will return to
Althaus-Reid's thought in Part II of this book.

a. Living on the Borderlands

The first theme in queer Latina/o theologies is that of living
on the borderlands. This notion is indebted to the work of
Gloria Anzaldúa, who writes about how *la frontera*, or the
borderlands, is an important site for her, both physically and
metaphorically, as a Latina lesbian. She writes, "I am a border
woman. . . . I have been straddling that *tejas*-Mexican border,
and others, all my life." For Anzaldúa, the borderlands is "not
a comfortable territory to live on," and yet there is the joy of
"living on borders and in margins, keeping intact one's shifting
and multiple identity and integrity."[22]

One of the earliest works of queer Latina/o theology was
published in 1996 in the *Boundary Wars* anthology. That essay,
"Barriers Not Withstanding: A *Lesbianista* Perspective," was
written by Mari E. Castellanos, a Cuban American lesbian feminist activist, pastor, and theologian.[23] In that article, Castellanos
reflects upon her borderland existence as a *"lesbianista."* Because
of the "cultural reality" of her social location—that is, one in
which people do not do business with strangers—Castellanos
refuses to keep separate her multiple roles as friend and as
pastor. That is, she subscribes to the notion of "dual relations"
in which ministers are able to enter into professional pastoral
relationships with personal friends.[24]

A year later, in 1997, another pioneering work of queer
Latina/o theology was published in the *Que(e)rying Religion*
anthology. That essay, "Reflections on Being Latina and

---

[22] Anzaldúa, *Borderlands, La Frontera* 19.

[23] Mari E. Castellanos, "Barriers Not Withstanding: A *Lesbianista* Perspective," in *Boundary Wars: Intimacy and Distance in Healing Relationships*, ed. Katherine Hancock Ragsdale (Cleveland, OH: Pilgrim Press, 1996), 197-207.

[24] Ibid., 197–200.

Lesbian," was written by Margarita Suárez, a lesbian Latina and ordained United Church of Christ minister.[25] Suárez's essay was written in the form of a coming out letter to *"Popi,"* her recently deceased father. In the letter, she writes about the joys and challenges of integrating her sexuality with her cultural identity as a Cuban-American. She tells him that, at long last, she has been "able to accept [her]self enough to risk the rejection and/or acceptance of other Latin people in the church."[26] In other words, Suárez was able to bring together her Latina, lesbian, and Christian identities in the borderland space that she occupies.

The theme of borderlands is explicitly brought to the foreground in a 2011 article by the gay Latino biblical scholar Manuel Villalobos. The article, "Bodies *Del Otro Lado* Finding Life and Hope in the Boderland: Gloria Anzaldúa, the Ethiopian Eunuch of Acts 8:26-40, *y Yo,"* draws upon Anzaldúa's notion of the borderlands. Villalobos places three bodies in dialogue— Anzaldúa's, the Ethiopian eunuch's (of Acts 8), and his own—in order to see how "bodies find life and hope in the borderland," especially when they "cross borders, challenge institutions, and follow the Spirit who breathes new life into us."[27] Villalobos' work is a creative use of the notion of borderland space, particularly in the field of biblical studies.[28]

b. Challenging *Machismo*

The second theme in queer Latina/o theologies is that of *machismo*. Under traditional notions of *machismo*, it is important that the "man be the active penetrator in sexual encounters and not the one in the role of the passive recipient, as it would

---

[25] Suárez, "Reflections on Being Latina and Lesbian."

[26] Ibid., 350.

[27] Manuel Villalobos, "Bodies *Del Otro Lado* Finding Life and Hope in the Borderland: Gloria Anzaldúa, the Ethiopian Eunuch of Acts 8:26–40, *y Yo,"* in *Bible Trouble: Queer Reading at the Boundaries of Biblical Scholarship*, ed. Teresa J. Hornsby and Ken Stone (Atlanta, GA: Society of Biblical Literature, 2011), 192.

[28] Michael A. Diaz, a gay Latino man and ordained minister with the Metropolitan Community Churches, recently completed a doctor of ministry thesis on constructing a queer Latina/o biblical hermeneutic based upon the notion of *nepantla*, an indigenous term for middle space. See Michael A. Diaz, *"Nepantla* as Indigenous Middle Space: Developing Biblical Reading Strategies for Queer Latina/os" (DMin thesis, Episcopal Divinity School, 2012).

be degrading for men, in this traditional understanding, to play the role of a woman."[29] Much theological reflection relating to LGBTIQ Latina/os touches upon the issue of *machismo* and gender roles in Latina/o culture.

Orlando O. Espín, the gay Latino professor at the University of San Diego, has written about the silences within Latina/o theology about LGBTIQ issues and its relationship to cultural constructions of gender, including *machismo*. In the chapter "Humanitas, Identity, and Another Theological Anthropology of (Catholic) Tradition" in his book *Grace and Humanness: Theological Reflections Because of Culture*, Espín argues that the silences about LGBTIQ Latina/os arises out of gender stereotypes. According to Espín, "gender is not just biological, it is cultural too" and that is why queer Latina/os still suffer from the "very real consequences of the specific, living, historical intersections of cultural maleness and cultural womanness among our peoples."[30]

In their essay "Religion and Masculinity in Latino Gay Lives," published in 2000, Eric M. Rodriguez and Suzanne C. Ouellette write about a study they conducted of four Latino gay men who were involved with MCC New York, a gay-affirming church in Manhattan. They were interested in how traditional "machismo ideologies"—that is, theories that "typify Latino men as physically aggressive, sexually promiscuous, domineering toward women, and using alcohol excessively"—intersected with these gay men's feelings about sexuality, religion, and masculinity.[31] Rodriguez and Ouellette discovered that there was a striking transformation of *machismo* in a context where the men could be "caring and supportive of others while

---

[29] Jeffrey S. Siker, "Latin@ Church Traditions," in Siker, *Homosexuality and Religion*, 145.

[30] Espín, *Grace and Humanness*, 64–65. Espín is the co-convener of the Latino/a Roundtable at the Center for Lesbian and Gay Studies in Religion and Ministry. See "Latino/a Roundtable," Center for Lesbian and Gay Studies in Religion and Ministry, accessed January 3, 2013, http://bit.ly/gKAxfp. In 2012, Espín delivered the Fifth Annual John E. Boswell Lecture at the Pacific School of Religion. His lecture was entitled "Who Is Human?—The Subversive Question at the Heart of Christianity."

[31] Eric M. Rodriguez and Suzanne C. Ouellette, "Religion and Masculinity in Latino Gay Lives," in *Gay Masculinities*, ed. Peter Nardi (Thousand Oaks, CA: Sage Publications, 2000), 107.

at the same time taking on quite a bit of responsibility." In particular, the "feminine" components of *machismo*—that is, "pride, dignity, courage, perseverance in face of adversity, and selflessness"—were traits that were viewed as positive within the religious community.[32]

Miguel A. De La Torre, a professor of social ethics and Latina/o studies at Iliff School of Theology, is a strong ally of the LGBTIQ community. In his 2009 essay "Confessions of a Latino Macho: From Gay Basher to Gay Ally," he writes about his own journey of rethinking Latina/o notions of *machismo* from a theological and ethical perspective. De La Torre writes about how he was socialized to protect "the power and privilege of men made of steel, not feathers." To that end, the *macho* is "concerned with men who fail to live up to the *macho* construction of what it means to be a man."[33] In the end, however, De La Torre argues that both the macho and the non-macho are "alienated" from this "false construction of manliness," and they both suffer from an "obsessive neurotic orientation" that requires "liberation from their condition."[34]

c. Crossing Literary and Religious Borders

One of the most interesting recent developments in queer Latina/o theology is the crossing of literary and religious borders. That is, a number of powerful works that address queer Latina/o spirituality are not in the form of traditional

---

[32] Other scholars have explored the role of spirituality in the lives of Latino gay men. In 2010, Heriberto Vallescorbo wrote a doctoral dissertation on how Latino gay men "abandoned their original religions due to a conflict between their sexual orientation and the anti-homosexual stances of their churches." Vallescorbo found that ultimately these men were able to reintegrate spirituality into their lives. See Heriberto Vallescorbo, "Latino Gay Men's Experiences of Spiritual Reintegration: A Heuristic Study" (PsyD diss., California Institute of Integral Studies, 2010), UMI (No. 3432452).

[33] Miguel A. De La Torre, "Confessions of a Latino Macho: From Gay Basher to Gay Ally," in *Out of the Shadows into the Light: Christianity and Homosexuality*, ed. Miguel A. De La Torre (St. Louis, MO: Chalice Press, 2009), 63–64.

[34] Ibid., 74. De La Torre is a co-author of a bilingual resource published by the Human Rights Campaign Foundation for the Latina/o community on the Bible, sexual orientation, and gender identity. See Miguel A. De La Torre, Ignacio Castuera, and Lisbeth Meléndez Rivera, *A La Familia: Conversation About Our Families, the Bible, Sexual Orientation and Gender Identity*, ed. Sharon Groves and Rebecca Voelkel (Washington, DC: Human Rights Campaign Foundation, 2010).

Christian theological texts. Rather, they blur literary genres and religious boundaries. This crossing of literary and religious borders is the third and final theme to be discussed in this genealogy of queer Latina/o theologies.

For example, Emanuel Xavier is a gay Latino poet and has published a collection of poems called *If Jesus Were Gay and Other Poems*. Xavier weaves together powerfully the themes of ethnicity, sexuality, and religion. For example, in his 2010 poem "The Mexican," he writes about the excitement of encountering a Chicano man after a performance in Texas: "So when I walked out from backstage / and my Nuyorican eyes rested on your Xicano smile . . . / It was as if the Virgin de Guadalupe / and all the orishas / Had sanctioned this meeting." It turns out, however, that the man has a boyfriend, a "*vato*," and the poem abruptly ends. "*Estupida*, / This poem could have been epic," writes Xavier with profound disappointment.[35] Xavier's poetry is a brilliant expression of the amazingly transcendent—yet fleeting—nature of sexuality and religious ecstasy that is difficult to capture in traditional theological language.

Manuel Muñoz, a gay Latino writer, also addresses issues of ethnicity, sexuality, and religion in his work. In his 2003 short story "Zigzagger," Muñoz plays with the traditional Mexican American folk tale about a young woman who dances with a handsome stranger who turns out to be the devil. Here, Muñoz writes about a young gay man who is entranced by a handsome stranger at a dance. The stranger takes the young man outside. There, the young man "could see himself in the arms of the man who glowed in the darkness of the canopy of branches, his skin a dull red, the pants and boots gone." Suddenly the young man sees "a flash of the man's feet" as "long, hard hooves digging into the soil"—Satan's hooves! As the young man is penetrated, "he had no choice but to scream out."[36] Like Xavier, Muñoz uses language to convey the queer Latino spiritual experience in a powerful way.

---

[35] Emanuel Xavier, "The Mexican," in Emanuel Xavier, *If Jesus Were Gay and Other Poems* (Bar Harbor, ME: Queer Mojo, 2010), 21.

[36] Manuel Muñoz, "Zizgagger," in Manuel Muñoz, *Zizgagger* (Evanston, IL: Northwestern University Press, 2003), 17.

Laura E. Pérez, a Latina professor of ethnic studies at the University of California, Berkeley, has also crossed genres in her scholarship. Specifically, she has focused on Chicana feminist and queer art as a source for religious and theological reflection. In her essay "Decolonizing Sexuality and Spirituality in Chicana Feminist and Queer Art," Pérez includes a number of powerful images of Chicana feminist and queer art in her work, including a number of variations of the well-known Virgin of Guadalupe icon.[37] Pérez has argued that such works view "the dark, the female, [and] the queer body" as sacred. Such bodies manifest a "goddess or superheroine force being summoned in the battle against dehumanizing religiosities, social mores, and ideologies of the body and sexuality that are man-made rather than divine or natural and that are harmful rather than healing."[38]

Literary genres are not the only boundaries that are being crossed. There is also the issue of LGBTIQ Latina/os and multiple faith traditions (that is, beyond Christianity). Salvador Vidal-Ortiz, a gay Latino professor of sociology at American University, has written a number of essays about the role of Santería, the Afro-Cuban religion, in the lives of LGBTIQ Latina/os. One of the attractions of that tradition is that it allows for queer people to participate fully as sexual beings, but also does not require them to fall within a "very rigid" notion of gayness.[39] Interestingly, other factors—such as "the lineage of the *padrino* and *madrina*, their *costumbres*, or ways of being"—end up being more important to queer Santeros than the sexualities of the people in their houses (that is, their communities of worship).[40] This demonstrates

[37] Laura E. Pérez, "Decolonizing Sexuality and Spirituality in Chicana Feminist and Queer Art," *Tikkun Magazine* (July/August 2010), accessed January 3, 2013, http://bit.ly/ahPJiW.

[38] Ibid. Marietta Messmer has also written about lesbian forms of embodied spirituality in contemporary Chicana culture. See Marietta Messmer, "Transformations of the Sacred in Contemporary Chicana Culture," *Theology and Sexuality* 14, no. 3 (May 2008): 259–78.

[39] Salvador Vidal-Ortiz, "Sexuality and Gender in Santería: LGBT Identities at the Crossroads of Santería Religious Practices and Beliefs," in *Gay Religion*, ed. Scott Thumma and Edward R. Gray (Walnut Creek, CA: AltaMira Press, 2005), 117.

[40] Ibid., 124.

the fluidity of categories when religious practice intersects with sexuality.

In addition to literary and religious borders, there is also the issue of international border crossings. As noted above, the focus of this chapter is on queer Latina/o theologies. As such, the theologies of queer Latin American theologians are outside the scope of this book. However, the work of queer Latin American theologians such as Marcella Althaus-Reid,[41] Hugo Córdova Quero,[42] Tom Hanks,[43] and André S. Musskopf[44] are of critical importance for anyone who is interested in queer Latina/o theologies. There are also a number of chapters in the anthology *Other Voices, Other Worlds* that address LGBTIQ issues within the Anglican churches of Cuba, Brazil, Argentina, Paraguay, Uruguay, Chile, Bolivia, and Peru.[45]

3. Future Voices

In addition to the various voices mentioned above, there are a number of emerging scholars who are doing work in the field of queer Latina/o theology. Robyn Henderson-Espinoza, a doctoral student in ethics at Iliff School of Theology, has written an article about the body as borderland—that is, *la frontera*—space. In that article, Henderson-Espinoza reflects upon

---

[41] Althaus-Reid, *Indecent Theology*; Marcella Althaus-Reid, *The Queer God* (London: Routledge, 2003); Marcella Althaus-Reid, ed., *Liberation Theology and Sexuality* (Aldershot, UK: Ashgate, 2006); Marcella Althaus-Reid and Lisa Isherwood, eds., *The Sexual Theologian: Essays on Sex, God, and Politics* (London: T&T Clark, 2004).

[42] Hugo Córdova Quero, "Risky Affairs: Marcella Althaus-Reid Indecently Queering Juan Luis Segundo's Hermeneutical Circle Propositions," in Isherwood and Jordan, *Dancing Theology*, 207–18; Martín Hugo Córdova Quero, "Friendship with Benefits: A Queer Reading of Aelred of Rievaulx and His Theology of Friendship," in Althaus-Reid and Isherwood, *The Sexual Theologian*, 26–46; Martín Hugo Córdova Quero, "The Prostitutes Also Go into the Kingdom of God: A Queer Reading of Mary of Magdala," in Althaus-Reid, *Liberation Theology*, 81–110.

[43] Tom Hanks, *The Subversive Gospel: A New Testament Commentary of Liberation*, trans. John P. Doner (Cleveland, OH: Pilgrim Press, 2000).

[44] André S. Musskopf, "A Gap in the Closet: Gay Theology in the Latin American Context," in *Men and Masculinities in Christianity and Judaism: A Critical Reader*, ed. Björn Krondorfer (London: SCM Press, 2009), 460–71; André S. Musskopf, "Cruising (with) Marcella," in Isherwood and Jordan, *Dancing Theology*, 228–39.

[45] Brown, *Other Voices, Other Worlds*, viii.

the queer body as a "queermestizo" space in which knowledge is produced through connections with "multiple and constitutive contact zones."[46]

Vincent D. Cervantes, a doctoral student in comparative literature at the University of Southern California, has woven together theology with literary analysis. For example, Cervantes has engaged in a theological reading of *El vampiro de la colonia Roma*, a sexually explicit novel about a young Mexican man who is a prostitute in Mexico City. According to Cervantes—who is constructing a *jotería* theology[47]—such a reading can help us to "rethink certain theological categories of the body and the divine," including a theology of "promiscuous incarnation."[48]

Cervantes draws upon the work of Laurel Schneider, a lesbian theology professor at Chicago Theological Seminary.[49] Schneider argues that the incarnation is promiscuous because the divinity that is revealed by the flesh of Jesus Christ is "radically open to consorting with anyone." According to Schneider, Jesus Christ "simply does not seem to be attentive to identity classifications," whether they relate to centurians, politicians, the poor, the wealthy, children, prostitutes, fishermen, or women. For Schneider, the incarnation reveals God's "excess of intimacy and disregard for propriety," which is the very definition of promiscuity.[50] By describing a Mexican gay hustler in christological terms, Cervantes argues that a *jotería* theology

---

[46] See Robyn Henderson-Espinoza, "*El Cuerpo Como (un) Espacio de Frontera*: The Body as (a) Borderland Space," in *New Frontiers in Latin American Borderlands*, ed. Leslie Cecil (Newcastle Upon Tyne, UK: Cambridge Scholars Publishing, 2012), 41–48.

[47] According to Cervantes, the term *jotería* speaks to a sexual identity that is beyond the categories of "homosexuality" and "queer." For more information, see Cervante's blog, *jot(e)ología*, accessed January 3, 2013, http://joteologia.blogspot.com.

[48] Vincent D. Cervantes, "Hustling the Divine: Promiscuously Rethinking Sex, Flesh, and Incarnation in Luis Zapata's *El vampiro de la colonia Roma*" (unpublished paper, 2012), 2, 7; see also Vincent D. Cervantes, "Evolving Theologies: Rethinking Progressive Theology Along the Lines of Jotería Studies" (unpublished paper, 2012).

[49] As of fall 2013, Schneider will join the faculty of Vanderbilt University as a professor of religious studies, gender studies, and philosophy.

[50] Laurel C. Schneider, "Promiscuous Incarnation," in *The Embrace of Eros: Bodies, Desires, and Sexuality in Christianity*, ed. Margaret D. Kamitsuka (Minneapolis, MN: Fortress Press, 2010), 244.

can help us see God's "excess and indiscriminate divine love with the world."[51] The work of queer Latina/o scholars such as Henderson-Espinoza, Cervantes, and others[52] bodes well for the future of queer Latina/o theologies.

4. Conclusion

In sum, queer Latina/o theologies have been around since the mid-1990s, but this is still a relatively new field of writing. In this chapter, we examined three thematic strands: (1) living on the borderlands; (2) challenging *machismo*; and (3) crossing literary and religious borders. In addition to the promising voices that are emerging in this area, it is important for queer Latina/o theologies to address various silences, such as transgender issues, in the future.[53]

---

[51] Cervantes, "Hustling the Divine," 15.

[52] Jared Vázquez, a gay Latino doctoral student at Iliff School of Theology, has written about queering Pentacostalism and is interested in the intersections of Latina/o studies, sexuality, and religion. See Jared Vázquez, "Queer Tongues Confess, I Know That I Know That I Know: A Queer Reading of James K.A. Smith's *Thinking in Tongues*" (MDiv thesis, Phillips Theological Seminary, 2012).

[53] For example, a recent study of transgender Latina/os noted that 28 percent of that population live in extreme poverty—nearly five times the rate of the general Latina/o population—and 47 percent have attempted suicide. See National Gay and Lesbian Task Force, "Injustice at Every Turn: A Look at Latino/a Respondents in the National Transgender Discrimination Survey" (April 18, 2011), accessed January 3, 2013, http://bit.ly/QPEBGU.

Study Questions

1. Which events from the history of queer Latina/os surprised you the most? Troubled you the most? What would like to learn more about in terms of queer Latina/o history?

2. What are some key writings by queer Latina/o theologians about living on the borderlands?

3. What are some key writings by queer Latina/o theologians about challenging *machismo*?

4. What are some key writings by queer Latina/o theologians about crossing literary and religious borders?

5. How might you use the queer Latina/o and Latin American perspectives articulated in this chapter to enrich your own theological reflection and work?

For Further Study

Queer Latina/o Experience
- De La Torre, Castuera, and Meléndez Rivera, *A La Familia*
- Díaz, *Latino Gay Men and HIV*
- Foster, *Chicano/Latino Homoerotic Identities*
- Hames-García and Martínez, *Gay Latino Studies*
- Misa, "Where Have All the Queer Students of Color Gone?"
- Moraga and Anzaldúa, *This Bridge Called My Back*
- Ramirez-Valles, *Compañeros*
- Roque Ramírez, "Borderlands, Diasporas, and Transnational Crossings"

Living on the Borderlands
- Anzaldúa, *Borderlands/La Frontera*
- Castellanos, "Barriers Not Withstanding"
- Diaz, "*Nepantla* as Indigenous Middle Space"
- Henderson-Espinoza, "*El Cuerpo Como (un) Espacio de Frontera*"
- Suárez, "Reflections on Being Latina and Lesbian"
- Villalobos, "Bodies *Del Otro Lado*"

Challenging *Machismo*
- De La Torre, "Confessions of a Latin Macho"
- Espín, *Grace and Humanness*
- Girman, *Mucho Macho*
- Rodriguez and Ouellette, "Religion and Masculinity in Latino Gay Lives"
- Siker, "Latin@ Church Traditions"

Crossing Literary and Religious Borders
- Cervantes, "Evolving Theologies"
- Cervantes, "Hustling the Divine"
- Messmer, "Transformations of the Sacred"
- Moya, "Comment"
- Muñoz, *Zigzagger*
- Pérez, "Decolonizing Sexuality and Spirituality in Chicana Feminist and Queer Art"
- Vidal-Ortiz, "Sexuality and Gender in Santería"
- Xavier, *If Jesus Were Gay and Other Poems*

Latin American Queer Theologies
- Althaus-Reid, *Indecent Theology*
- Althaus-Reid, *Liberation Theology and Sexuality*
- Althaus-Reid, *The Queer God*
- Brown, *Other Voices, Other Worlds*
- Córdova Quero, "Friendship with Benefits"
- Córdova Quero, "The Prostitutes Also Go into the Kingdom of God"
- Córdova Quero, "Risky Affairs"
- Hanks, *The Subversive Gospel*
- Murray, *Latin American Male Homosexualities*
- Musskopf, "Cruising (with) Marcella"
- Musskopf, "A Gap in the Closet"
- Musskopf, "Ungraceful God"
- Petrella, "Queer Eye for the Straight Guy"

Other Resources
- Crowley, "An Ancient Catholic"
- García, "Priests"
- Nickoloff, "Sexuality"
- Oliver, "Why Gay Marriage?"
- Rodriguez, *Hunger of Memory*
- Schexnayder, *Setting the Table*, 39
- Vallescorbo, "Latino Gay Men's Experience of Spiritual Reintegration"
- Vazquez, "Presión Bajo Gracia"
- Vidal-Ortiz, "Religion/Spirituality, U.S. Latina/o Communities, and Sexuality Scholarship"

Chapter 5

Two-Spirit Indigenous Scholarship

We conclude Part I of this book with a discussion of Two-Spirit Indigenous (that is, queer Native American) scholarship. This chapter differs from the previous three chapters in that it does not focus exclusively—or even primarily—on writings by Christian theologians. Rather, the discussion focuses more generally on religious scholarship by LGBTIQ2 people of Indigenous descent.[1] It is important to have a separate chapter on this topic, not only because of the creative and important work that is being done in this area, but also to recognize the horrific legacy of settler colonialism (often in connection with Christian proselytizing) that has stripped Indigenous people of their sovereignty over their lands.

Since 2010, there have been a number of books written on Two-Spirit Indigenous scholarship. These works have highlighted the deep connections between heterosexuality, patriarchy, and the ideology of settler colonialism. These works include: *Sexuality, Nationality, Indigeneity* (2010);[2] *Queer Indigenous Studies: Critical Interventions in Theory, Politics, and*

---

[1] The "2" in "LGBTIQ2" recognizes and names the Two-Spirit tradition within Indigenous cultures. Although it has been my intent for the "Q" in "LGBTIQ" to include Two-Spirit identities, I believe it is particularly important to expressly name such identities in this chapter.

[2] Daniel Heath Justice, Mark Rifkin, and Bethany Schneider, eds., "Sexuality, Nationality, Indigeneity," *GLQ: A Journal of Lesbian and Gay Studies* 16, nos. 1–2 (2010).

Literature (2011);[3] *Spaces Between Us: Queer Settler Colonialism and Indigenous Decolonization* (2011);[4] *When Did Indians Become Straight?: Kinship, the History of Sexuality, and Native Sovereignty* (2011);[5] and *The Erotics of Sovereignty: Queer Native Writing in the Era of Self-Determination* (2012).[6] Although it is beyond the scope of this chapter to address each of these works, this chapter will provide some basic information that will help orient the reader to this area of scholarship.

This chapter will begin, as with the previous three chapters, with a brief history of Indigenous people in North America generally and LGBTIQ2 Native Americans specifically. It will then provide a genealogy of the recent queer Indigenous scholarship cited above. In particular, it will focus on three themes: (1) resisting settler colonialism; (2) recognizing Two-Spirit identities; and (3) doing the work of allies.

1. Historical Background

The story of Indigenous people in North America has been one of colonization and conquest. Christopher Columbus, who first arrived in the "New World" in 1492, kidnapped approximately 550 Indigenous people during his second voyage and brought them back to Spain (although around 200 died on the ship before arriving in Europe), as did English explorers in the early 1600s. Although relationships were initially cordial between the European settlers and Indigenous people, things turned increasingly violent as the colonizers seized Indigenous lands in order to grow tobacco for export.

Not surprisingly, religious language was used to justify the colonization of Indigenous lands and people. For example, John

---

[3] Driskill et al., *Queer Indigenous Studies*.

[4] Scott Lauria Morgensen, *Spaces Between Us: Queer Settler Colonialism and Indigenous Decolonization* (Minneapolis: University of Minnesota Press, 2011).

[5] Mark Rifkin, *When Did Indians Become Straight?: Kinship, the History of Sexuality, and Native Sovereignty* (New York: Oxford University Press, 2011).

[6] Mark Rifkin, *The Erotics of Sovereignty: Queer Native Writing in the Era of Self-Determination* (Minneapolis: University of Minnesota Press, 2012).

Winthrop proclaimed to his fellow English colonizers prior to embarking to America in 1629 that the "whole earth is the Lord's garden" and that God had given it to the "sons of men" to "subdue it."[7] When numerous Indigenous people died from smallpox in a horrific manner—dying like "rotten sheep" with their skin peeling off from their bodies—William Bradford said that "it pleased God to visit these Indians with a great sickness" and that "many of them did rot above ground for want of burial."[8]

One of the characteristics of Indigenous people that most disturbed the European explorers and missionaries were gender-variant, or Two-Spirit, individuals who took on gender roles that differed from their biological sexes.[9] Not only was there an official role in most Indigenous cultures for such Two-Spirit individuals, but many of them were also "shamans who commanded respect as having special spiritual powers."[10]

Beginning in the sixteenth century, European explorers and missionaries used religious language to condemn the same-sex and gender-variant practices of Indigenous people. There were also documented cases of violence against Two-Spirit Indigenous people. One case involved European explorers who had their dogs "tear apart" forty Indigenous gender-variant people whom they called "sodomites." Another case involved a European explorer burning alive a gender-variant Indigenous person. The European explorers called such gender-variant people "berdaches," which was a French adaptation of the Arabic word for male prostitute.[11]

The violence against Indigenous people continued into the nineteenth century, including the massacre of hundreds of people from the Sioux nation at Wounded Knee in 1890. In 1887, Congress sought to "break up the reservations and accelerate the transformation of Indians into property holders and U.S.

---

[7] Takaki, *A Different Mirror*, 26.

[8] Ibid., 39.

[9] Bronski, *Queer History*, 3.

[10] Eaklor, *Queer America*, 17.

[11] Beemyn, "The Americas," 145–49.

citizens." This policy of "allotment" to individual landowners was intended to be a "blow, meant to be fatal, at Indian tribal existence."[12] In 1934, Congress reversed its allotment policy and returned to a program of reservations and self-government for those tribes who voted to participate.

The voices of LGBTIQ2 Indigenous people began to emerge in the 1990s as a result of criticism over the term "berdache" and the desire to find a replacement term that would name "at once, their diverse lives and their sense of relationship to Indigenous traditions of gender/sexual diversity and spirituality."[13] A number of communities began to use the term "Two-Spirit" during this time. An important marker with respect to these discussions was the publication in 1997 of *Two-Spirit People: Native American Gender Identity, Sexuality, and Spirituality*,[14] which was the first academic anthology to focus on the "historical Indigenous gender/sexual diversity or Indigenous GLBTQ2 people today."[15]

Since 2010, there have been a number of writings by LGBTIQ2 Indigenous people that focus on the intersections of Two-Spirit and Indigenous scholarship, and it is to these writings that we now turn.

2. Genealogy of Two-Spirit Indigenous Scholarship

As noted above, much of the body of Two-Spirit Indigenous scholarship has appeared just in the last few years. This differs from queer Black, queer Asian American, and queer Latina/o scholarship in that there has not yet been an archive of Two-Spirit Indigenous scholarship spanning fifteen to twenty years. As such, this genealogy will focus less on the historical development of these writings, and more on three themes

---

[12] Takaki, *A Different Mirror*, 221, 225.

[13] Qwo-Li Driskill et al., "Introduction," in Driskill et al., *Queer Indigenous Studies*, 12.

[14] Sue-Ellen Jacobs, Wesley Thomas, and Sabine Lang, eds., *Two-Spirit People: Native American Gender Identity, Sexuality, and Spirituality* (Urbana: University of Illinois Press, 1997).

[15] Driskill et al., "Introduction," 13.

in this recent scholarship: (1) resisting settler colonialism; (2) recognizing Two-Spirit identities; and (3) doing the work of allies.

a. Resisting Settler Colonialism

The first theme in our genealogy of queer Indigenous studies is that of resisting settler colonialism. Settler colonialism is the ideology that historically enabled and perpetuated the conquest and settling of Native lands by European colonizers. As one queer Indigenous scholar defines it, settler colonialism is the attempt to erase indigeneity as a "marker of national difference." Non-natives—that is, most people in the United States today—live "as though Native lands, societies, or cultures were theirs to inherit, control, or enjoy."[16]

One of the most prominent voices in contemporary queer Indigenous scholarship is Andrea Smith, a Cherokee scholar and activist who is a professor of media studies at the University of California, Riverside. Smith, who is a graduate of Union Theological Seminary in New York City, has written two books: *Conquest: Sexual Violence and American Indian Genocide*; and *Native Americans and the Christian Right: The Gendered Politics of Unlikely Alliances.*[17]

In a recent essay, "Queer Theory and Native Studies: The Heteronormativity of Settler Colonialism," Smith argues that queer Indigenous studies must be liberated from the narrow project of only studying Natives, a project that she describes as "ethnographic entrapment." That is, instead of focusing just on LGBTIQ2 Indigenous people, Smith argues for a broader project of "intellectual sovereignty" in which Indigenous people are not simply "objects of analysis," but rather "producers of theory."[18]

---

[16] Morgensen, *Spaces Between Us*, 1.

[17] Andrea Smith, *Conquest: Sexual Violence and American Indian Genocide* (Cambridge, MA: South End Press, 2005); Andrea Smith, *Native Americans and the Christian Right: The Gendered Politics of Unlikely Alliances* (Durham, NC: Duke University Press, 2008).

[18] Andrea Smith, "Queer Theory and Native Studies: The Heteronormativity of Settler Colonialism," in Driskill et al., *Queer Indigenous Studies*, 45.

In other words, Smith asks what queer theory would look like if the Indigenous critique of settler colonialism was incorporated as a central concern of queer theory. Smith suggests that queer theory presumes "the givenness of the nation-state in general, and the United States in particular." That is, rather than understanding Native people as "colonized people struggling against a settler state," the queer theorist often "collapses Native peoples into the category of racial minority."[19]

By contrast, Smith argues for a vision of indigeneity that goes beyond simply "representing the interests of Indigenous people." This broader vision would serve to "deconstruct western epistemology and global state and economic structures in the interests of building another world that could sustain all peoples." It would also challenge the "heteronormativity of national belonging."[20] If achieved, Smith's vision of resisting settler colonialism would have a profound effect on changing the goals of queer theory as well as queer theology.

b. Recognizing Two-Spirit Identities

The second theme in our genealogy of queer Indigenous studies is recognizing the term "Two-Spirit" as a way of describing LGBTIQ2 Indigenous people. As we have seen, the question of terminology is an important issue for marginalized groups. In particular, Indigenous people have rejected the term "berdache" that was originally coined by the European colonizers. Many, however, have also rejected using the terms "queer" or "LGBTIQ" as a synonym for Indigenous people who engage in same-sex or gender-variant acts. Instead, they have embraced the term "Two-Spirit."

In their introductory essay, the editors to the anthology *Queer Indigenous Studies* use the history of the term "Two-Spirit" as a case study for "illustrating the challenges and promises of Indigenous GLBTQ2 criticism." Originally, the term Two-Spirit arose out of a critique of the use of "berdache" in anthropological studies. Initially that term was used to write about "sexual

---

[19] Ibid., 56–57.

[20] Ibid., 61.

and gender 'deviants,' notably among gender-transitive males who had sexual and domestic relations with men in tribal societies."[21]

Later, the term "berdache" was used by anthropologists in a positive manner to "praise American Indian tolerance of same-sex relations." That use was also problematic, however, because even though it used Indigenous culture to critique a settler society (that is, the United States), the critique still ultimately benefited the members of that settler society (that is, non-Indigenous LGBTIQ people). Furthermore, it did nothing to change the power dynamics between that society and Indigenous people. The focus was still on sexual identity, and not an honoring of the "cultural categories of Indigenous communities."[22]

In the 1990s, a consensus emerged within LGBTIQ2 communities that the term "Two-Spirit" was the best way not only to displace the term "berdache," but also to name "their diverse lives" as well as their "relationship to Indigenous traditions of gender/sexual diversity and spirituality."[23] That is, the term "Two-Spirit" honors the ways in which LGBTIQ2 people were an integral part of Indigenous cultures. Unlike the term "queer," which suggests marginality and transgressivity, the term "Two-Spirit" acknowledges how LGBTIQ2 people were a central part of the daily life of many Indigenous cultures. It should be noted, however, that not all Indigenous people like the term "Two-Spirit." As such, it is an important but not exclusive signifier for queer Native people.[24]

Although the term "Two-Spirit" had largely shifted from academic discourse to community-based organizing and activism during the first decade of the 2000s, the editors of the *Queer Indigenous Studies* anthology have argued in favor of reclaiming the term because it is grounded in "community-based usage"

---

[21] Driskill et al., "Introduction," 11.

[22] Ibid., 11–12.

[23] Ibid., 12.

[24] I am grateful to my friend Andy Smith for reminding me of this point.

and it also critiques heteropatriarchy—that is, the linking of "gender, sexuality, spirituality, and social roles"—both inside and outside of Native communities.[25]

c. Doing the Work of Allies

The third and final theme in our genealogy of queer Indigenous studies is doing the work of allies. Specifically, in light of the corrosive dynamics and history of settler colonialism, how can non-Indigenous allies—for example, non-Indigenous queer people of color—engage in queer Indigenous studies? How can we draw from queer Indigenous studies without running into issues of appropriation or to reinforce the dynamics of settler colonialism from an intellectual perspective?

In his essay "Unsettling Queer Politics: What Can Non-Natives Learn from Two-Spirit Organizing?" Scott Lauria Morgensen addresses many of these questions. Morgensen, a co-editor of the *Queer Indigenous Studies* anthology and professor at Queen's University in Canada, is a white queer ally of the Indigenous community. Morgensen notes that most non-Indigenous queer people are interested in the "histories of gender and sexual diversity in Native societies." However, such people were not interested in the work of Two-Spirit activists to "critique settler colonialism and decolonize Native communities."[26]

From Morgensen's perspective, if non-Indigenous people want to learn about Two-Spirit people, then they should learn about settler colonialism "as a condition of their own and Two-Spirit people's lives."[27] In his essay, Morgensen mentions three lessons learned, and I believe that these lessons can be helpful with respect to the broader context of theological reflection about Two-Spirit Indigenous people.

The first lesson for Morgensen is that "Two-Spirit is not a Native sexual minority." As we have seen in the previous part of this chapter, Two-Spirit is not merely a synonym for

---

[25] Driskill et al., "Introduction," 17.

[26] Scott Lauria Morgensen, "Unsettling Queer Politics: What Can Non-Natives Learn from Two-Spirit Organizing?," in Driskill et al., *Queer Indigenous Studies*, 132.

[27] Ibid.

"LGBTIQ." Rather, the term "calls into question the colonial origin and logic of sexual minority identity for non-Natives." That is, instead of understanding Two-Spirit identity as a minority position defined against majority sexuality or gender norms, Two-Spirit people were actually in an "integral location" that "through kinship, economics, social life, or religion linked all Native people in relationship."[28] As a result, Two-Spirit organizing challenges both white and non-Native identities in queer politics.

The second lesson for Morgensen is that "Non-Native narratives of Two-Spirit have reflected non-Native desires." That is, Morgensen critiques the ways in which many non-Indigneous people have appropriated cultural manifestations of Two-Spirit existence, but they have failed to challenge the underlying ideology of settler colonization that makes this appropriation possible in the first place. By contrast, Morgensen notes how lesbian Chicana writers such as Gloria Anzaldúa and Cherríe Moraga explored their ethnic heritage by looking at Two-Spirit histories. Although Anzaldúa and Moraga affirmed their own indigenous identity, they "did not claim to be identical to Native American Two Spirit people."[29] Anzaldúa and Moraga might serve as helpful models for non-Indigenous queer people who wish to engage in dialogue with Two-Spirit traditions.[30]

The third and final lesson for Morgensen is that "Two-Spirit organizing challenges power relations in settler society." Morgensen highlights the need for non-Indigenous queer people to be aware of how the LGBTIQ civil rights discourse of gender or sexual liberation in fact "makes the settler state the horizon of freedom and reinforces settler authority on Native

---

[28] Ibid., 134–35.

[29] Ibid., 141.

[30] It should be noted, however, that some Indigenous scholars, including Andrea Smith, have critiqued Anzaldúa for creating a binary of the "primitive Native" on the one hand and a more mature "mestizaje consciousness" on the other. That is, Anzaldúa relegates her indigenous identity to a "primitive past" that is contrasted with a "more modern, sophisticated mestizo identity." Smith, "Queer Theory and Native Studies," 49.

land."[31] That is, non-Indigenous queer people need to acknowledge their complicity with settler colonialism. Perhaps that is one of the gifts that non-Indigenous queer people of color—including immigrants of color—can bring to the conversation, particularly those who do work with "anticolonialism, antiracism, and anti-imperialism" strategies.[32]

Perhaps it may be helpful—particularly in the theological context—for queer people of color to reflect upon Morgensen's three lessons and see how they might be applied with respect to interrogating white queer theologies. That is, how do queer of color ancestral sexualities and gender identities differ from the "sexual minority" discourse of white queer theologians? How do white queer theological narratives about queer people of color reflect white desires? And how does queer of color spiritual or religious organizing challenge power relations in the white queer world?[33]

3. Summary

It seems appropriate to end Part I of this book with a chapter on Two-Spirit Indigenous scholarship. First, it is important to bear witness to—and honor—the horrific experiences of LGBTIQ2 Indigenous people, particularly in light of the ugly role that Christian theological discourse played in the colonization and conquest of their lands. As such, this chapter has not tried to force the writings of Two-Spirit Indigenous people into the same identity categories that were articulated in the previous three chapters. Nor has this chapter focused

---

[31] Morgensen, "Unsettling Queer Politics," 145.

[32] Ibid., 146.

[33] It is also important for queer people of color to address transgender issues in the Two-Spirit Indigenous community. For example, a recent study noted that transgender American Indian and Alaskan Native people live in extreme poverty at a rate that is about three times that of the general American Indian and Alaskan Native population, and nearly six times that of the general United States population. See National Gay and Lesbian Task Force, "Injustice at Every Turn: A Look at American Indian and Alaskan Native Respondents in the National Transgender Discrimination Survey" (October 8, 2012), accessed January 3, 2013, http://bit.ly/RM31A6.

on constructing a Christian theology from the perspective of LGBTIQ2 Indigenous people.

Second, it is important to recall that, notwithstanding the oppression of people of color in America, the United States remains a settler nation state. This raises an important critique with respect to the stated focus of this book, which is on people of color in the United States. That is, this book presumes the existence of the settler nation state—as opposed to challenging it on a broader level. It is my hope, however, that Part II of this book will raise certain themes that transgress and break down our traditional nation-state boundaries.

Third, the remainder of this book will build upon Andrea Smith's notion of intellectual sovereignty. That is, rather than being subject to "ethnographic entrapment" with respect to queer people of color, the rest of the book will draw upon queer theologies of color to construct a broader theology that challenges the current state of theological discourse. In other words, the rainbow theology to be constructed in Part II of this book will propose a *methodology* of doing theology, as opposed to just focusing on content relating to LGBTIQ2 people of color. And so we now turn to constructing a rainbow theology.

Study Questions

1. Which events from the history of Two-Spirit Indigenous people surprised you the most? Troubled you the most? What would like to learn more about in terms of Two-Spirit Indigenous history?

2. What are some key writings by Two-Spirit Indigenous scholars on resisting settler colonialism?

3. What are some key writings by Two-Spirit Indigenous scholars about recognizing Two-Spirit identities?

4. What are some key writings about doing the work of allies to Two-Spirit Indigenous people?

5. How might you use the notion of intellectual sovereignty to enrich your own theological reflection and work?

For Further Study

Two-Spirit Indigenous Experience
- Driskill et al., *Queer Indigenous Studies*
- Justice, Rifkin, and Schneider, "Sexuality, Nationality, Indigeneity"
- Morgensen, *Spaces Between Us*
- Rifkin, *The Erotics of Sovereignty*
- Rifkin, *When Did Indians Become Straight?*

Resisting Settler Colonialism
- Smith, *Conquest*
- Smith, *Native Americans and the Christian Right*
- Smith, "Queer Theory and Native Studies"

Recognizing Two-Spirit Identities
- Driskill et al., "Introduction"

Doing the Work of Allies
- Morgensen, "Unsettling Queer Politics"

Part II

___

Rainbow Theology

Chapter 6

Introducing Rainbow Theology

In Part I of this book, we examined the writings of LGBTIQ theologians of color. Specifically, we looked at writings by queer Black, queer Asian American, queer Latina/o, and Two-Spirit Indigenous theologians and religion scholars. Although these writings have been around since at least the early 1990s, there has been little to no systematic analysis of such works to date. In so doing, we examined the often hidden histories of such groups, as well as the themes that were common to each group.

In Part II of this book, we will introduce the concept of "rainbow theology." Rainbow theology is a new way of doing theology that arises out of the experiences of LGBTIQ people of color.[1] It is important to note that rainbow theology is not just theology about queer people of color (that is, theology with queer people of color as its subject). Rather, rainbow theology is a broader methodology and critique that can be applied to all forms of theological reflection.

Andrea Smith, a professor at the University of California at Riverside, has argued that the Indigenous critique of settler colonialism is not just about the lives of Indigenous peoples.

---

[1] For an earlier articulation of rainbow theology, see Patrick S. Cheng, *The Rainbow Connection: Bridging Asian American and Queer Theologies* (Berkeley, CA: Center for Lesbian and Gay Studies in Religion and Ministry, 2011).

Rather, as a means of escaping "ethnographic entrapment," the Indigenous critique is about a broader task "to uncover and analyze the logics of settler colonialism as they affect all areas of life."[2] In the same way, rainbow theology is not just about LGBTIQ people of color, but it is a "subjectless critique" that challenges all theologies to rethink the relationships between race, sexuality, and spirituality.

In this chapter, we will first examine the symbol of the rainbow and how it represents the convergence of race, sexuality, and spirit. We will then examine the ways in which rainbows reflect the experiences of queer people of color with respect to the three rainbow themes of (1) multiplicity, (2) middle spaces, and (3) mediation. Finally, we will examine how rainbow theology critiques monochromatic theology and its three diametrically opposed characteristics of (1) singularity, (2) staying home, and (3) selecting sides.

1. Rainbows and the Convergence of Race, Sexuality, and Spirit

The rainbow is an ideal metaphor for the experiences of LGBTIQ people of color. Like queer people of color, rainbows exist within a space where race, sexuality, and spirit converge or come together. In other words, rainbows are fluid symbols that have racial, sexual, and spiritual significance.

First, the rainbow is a symbol of *race*. It has been used by groups to signify coalition-building across different racial and ethnic groups. For example, the National Rainbow Coalition was an organization founded in 1984 by the Reverend Jesse Jackson to bring together diverse racial and ethnic groups for political power. Similarly, the Most Reverend Desmond Tutu, the retired Anglican archbishop of South Africa and Nobel Prize laureate, included the symbol of the rainbow in the title of *The Rainbow People of God: The Making of a Peaceful Revolution*, his 1994 book about post-apartheid South Africa.[3]

---

[2] Smith, "Queer Theory and Native Studies," 44–46, 61.

[3] Desmond Tutu, *The Rainbow People of God: The Making of a Peaceful Revolution*, ed. John Allen (New York: Image Books, 1994).

In some instances, however, the association between rainbows and racial and ethnic coalition building can become too exclusive. As noted in Part I of the book, Bishop Harry Jackson, the outspoken African American pastor from Maryland who is vehemently opposed to same-sex marriage rights, insisted during a conference of the religious right in Texas in July 2012 that *"we're"* the rainbow coalition. By "we," Jackson presumably meant only heterosexual and cisgender people of color. He continued by urging people of color to "steal back the rainbow" from "the gays."[4] In other words, Jackson wanted to keep the rainbow "pure"—as a racial symbol and nothing else. This is problematic, of course, because he assumes that there are no people of color who are also queer.

Second, the rainbow is a symbol of *sexuality*. As Harry Jackson has noted, rainbows are in fact closely associated with the LGBTIQ communities. The multicolored rainbow flag, created by the San Francisco artist Gilbert Baker in 1978, has become synonymous with LGBTIQ pride celebrations around the world.[5] Indeed, rainbow flags—with their red, orange, yellow, green, blue, and violet stripes—can be found year-round within LGBTIQ communities across the United States from the crosswalks of West Hollywood to the Chelsea neighborhood of New York City.

For an older generation of gay men in the United States who experienced the tyranny of growing up in the closet, rainbows are closely associated with the 1939 movie *The Wizard of Oz*.[6] In the song "Somewhere Over the Rainbow" from that movie, Judy Garland (who plays the character Dorothy) sings longingly for a land "way up high" in which "dreams that you dare to dream / really do come true."[7] Indeed, a code name for gay

---

[4] "Harry Jackson, Maryland Bishop, Claims Gays Are 'Trying to Recruit' Children, Wants to 'Steal Back' Rainbow," *Huffington Post* (August 3, 2012), accessed January 3, 2013, http://huff.to/QMrx3q.

[5] See Randy P. Conner, David Hatfield Sparks, and Mariya Sparks, *Cassell's Encyclopedia of Queer Myth, Symbol and Spirit* (London: Cassell, 1997), 279.

[6] *The Wizard of Oz*, directed by Victor Fleming (1939).

[7] Harold Arlen and E. Y. Harburg, "Somewhere Over the Rainbow," 1939.

men (dating at least as far back as the 1940s) was a "Friend of Dorothy," and the Stonewall Riots—the start of the modern-day LGBTIQ rights movement—occurred shortly after Garland's death in June of 1969.

For a younger generation of LGBTIQ people, rainbows evoke Kermit the Frog's song "The Rainbow Connection," a tribute to the magical power of rainbows for "lovers, the dreamers, and me."[8] The ties between the Muppets and the queer community were considerably strengthened in July 2012 after the Jim Henson Company ended its relationship with the Chick-fil-A fast-food chain, which had donated millions of dollars to antigay causes.[9]

Third, the rainbow is a symbol of *spirit*. From a Judeo-Christian perspective, the rainbow appears several times in both the Hebrew Bible and the New Testament. For example, the rainbow, or *qeshet* in Hebrew, first appears in Genesis 9:13–16 as a "sign of the covenant" between God and the earth. Through that sign, God promises that "the waters shall never again become a flood to destroy all flesh."[10] Later the rainbow appears in Ezekiel 1:28; it surrounds the divine throne and is part of the "likeness of the glory of the Lord."[11] In the New Testament, the rainbow, or *iris* in Greek, appears in Revelation 4:3, where it surrounds the divine throne. The rainbow is also seen in Revelation 10:1, where it is above the head of a "mighty angel."[12]

The rainbow is also a symbol of spirit in many religious traditions outside of Christianity. For example, in Greek and Roman

---

[8] Paul Williams and Kenneth Ascher, "The Rainbow Connection," 1979.

[9] See Timothy Stenovec, "Chick-Fil-A President's Anti-Gay Comments Continue To Inspire Movements Across The Country," *Huffington Post* (July 27, 2012), accessed January 3, 2013, http://huff.to/P7bOYb.

[10] Genesis 9:13–16 (New Revised Standard Version). Unless otherwise noted, all biblical quotations are from the New Revised Standard Version.

[11] Ezekiel 1:28.

[12] Revelation 4:3, 10:1. The rainbow also appears in the apocryphal/deuterocanonical books. See Sirach 43:11–12: "Look at the rainbow, and praise him who made it; it is exceedingly beautiful in its brightness. / It encircles the sky with its glorious arc; the hands of the Most High have stretched it out."

mythology, the messenger goddess Iris used the rainbow as a path upon which to travel. By contrast, some Indigenous people from the Americas believe that the rainbow is the garment of the Great Spirit. Still others believe that the rainbow is a giant serpent. Tibetan Buddhists believe that a person who is freed from all desire attains a rainbow body that ultimately dissolves into light.[13] These are just some of the many ways in which the rainbow has been a symbol of spirit across different cultures.

In sum, the rainbow—like LGBTIQ people of color—exists at a place where race, sexuality, and spirit converge. As such, it is an ideal symbol for constructing a theology that speaks to the experiences of LGBTIQ people of color.

2. Rainbows and LGBTIQ People of Color

The similarities between rainbows and LGBTIQ people of color do not end with the fact that they both share the three-fold themes of race, sexuality, and spirit. Rainbows also reflect the experiences of queer people of color, particularly with respect to three "rainbow themes" of (1) multiplicity, (2) middle spaces, and (3) mediation. Although the next three chapters will describe each of these three themes in greater detail, this section will discuss briefly the ways in which rainbows and LGBTIQ people of color share these themes.

First, rainbows and queer people of color share the characteristic of *multiplicity*. Multiplicity refers to a state of having multiple co-existing and overlapping identities, as opposed to a singular dominant identity. Rainbows are defined by multiplicity because they have been understood in many different ways throughout history. As we have already seen, the rainbow has multiple meanings in different cultures, whether it symbolizes a covenant, a pathway, a garment, a serpent, or an enlightened body. Even within the Christian scriptures, there is not just one meaning for the rainbow—it is both a symbol of God's

---

[13] For more about these examples, and many others, see Richard Whelan, *The Book of Rainbows: Art, Literature, Science, and Mythology* (Cobb, CA: First Glance Books, 1997), 104–21 ("The Mythology of Rainbows").

promise never to wipe out the human race by flood, as well as a symbol of God's divine glory that surrounds a throne or an angel. Even the word in the Hebrew scriptures for rainbow, *qeshet*, has multiple meanings in that it is also signifies the word for a hunter's bow.

In the case of LGBTIQ people of color, they also experience multiple co-existing and overlapping identities. Because queer people of color are both racial *and* sexual minorities or subalterns,[14] no single identity (that is, either race or sexuality) can be dominant over the other. Furthermore, these identities are not mutually exclusive and cannot be separated from each other. Rather, these identities are mutually co-constituted. That is, as many scholars have argued, one cannot think about race without also thinking—either explicitly or implicitly—about its sexual dimension (and vice versa).[15] Even the racial and sexual subcategories themselves involve multiplicity. In the case of Asian Americans, for example, there are many different ethnicities and nationalities (for example, Chinese American, Japanese American, Korean American, Vietnamese American).[16] It is precisely through this experience of multiplicity that queer people of color have a window into the innermost workings of the triune God.

Second, rainbows and queer people of color share the characteristic of *middle spaces*. A middle-space existence is never quite being at "home"; it is a state of being perpetually suspended in a third space in between two poles. This is the case with rainbows, since they occupy the middle space between the two poles of the heavenly and earthly realms. For example, the Japanese god Izanagi and the goddess Izanami stood in the

---

[14] In postcolonial discourse, the "subaltern" means persons "of inferior rank" who are subject to the "hegemony of the ruling classes." Ashcroft, Griffiths, and Tiffin, *Post-Colonial Studies*, 215.

[15] See, e.g., Nagel, *Race, Ethnicity, and Sexuality*.

[16] I do recognize that *all* people—and not just LGBTIQ people of color—experience multiplicity to some degree or another in their lives. For example, a working mother may experience the tension of multiplicity in terms of her identity as an employee and as a parent. That being said, I also believe that racism and homophobia are particularly painful oppressions because both send a message that the person is intrinsically worthless based upon a core characteristic of herself or himself (that is, race and sexuality).

middle space of a rainbow bridge and created the islands of Japan by dipping a jeweled spear into the waters of the Pacific Ocean.[17] Rainbows also occupy a middle space to the extent that certain societies have associated them with fluidity of sex. Specifically, certain cultures—including Bohemian, Hungarian, Serbian, French, and Albanian cultures—have thought that a person's or animal's sex could change if s/he crossed underneath a rainbow.[18]

In the case of LGBTIQ people of color, they also experience a state of metaphorical homelessness, or being caught in a middle space. They are caught in between the binary poles of race and sexuality. In other words, they are never fully at home within their racial and ethnic communities of origin (which are often heterosexist and homophobic), nor are they fully home within the LGBTIQ community (which is often racist). Queer people of color may also experience a sense of profound homelessness with respect to their bodies. Drawing upon the work of Asian American theologians such as Sang Hyun Lee and Jung Young Lee,[19] it can be argued that queer people of color exist in a liminal or interstitial space. Although this space may at times be incredibly painful, it can ultimately help those of us who identify as Christians to recognize that only in God can they find their true homes.

Third, rainbows and queer people of color share the characteristic of *mediation*. Mediation refers to a bridging function of bringing together disparate identities and ideas that would not normally belong together. Rather than picking sides or reinforcing false binaries, a mediator finds common ground upon which both sides can co-exist. It is precisely through this mediating function that the disparate identities and ideas are woven

---

[17] See Whelan, *Book of Rainbows*, 108.

[18] See Raymond L. Lee and Alistair B. Fraser, *The Rainbow Bridge: Rainbows in Art, Myth, and Science* (University Park: Pennsylvania State University Press, 2001), 27–28; Carl B. Boyer, *The Rainbow: From Myth to Mathematics* (Princeton, NJ: Princeton University Press, 1987), 29.

[19] See Sang Hyun Lee, *From a Liminal Place: An Asian American Theology* (Minneapolis, MN: Fortress Press, 2010); Jung Young Lee, *Marginality: The Key to Multicultural Theology* (Minneapolis, MN: Fortress Press, 1995).

together, and the mediator becomes a transformative agent. As we have seen, rainbows serve a bridging function that bring together the divine and human realms. In so doing, the rainbows allow for both realms to be transformed. Similarly, in the Christian context, the rainbow brings together the divine and human in terms of God's covenant with Noah and all of humanity. It is through this covenant that both God and humanity are transformed.

In the case of LGBTIQ people of color, they also play a mediating role between communities of color on the one hand, and LGBTIQ communities on the other. Paradoxically, the fact that they do not exist solely in either community actually means that they are able to participate in both. Queer people of color are also able to weave together experiences that cross transnational borders, interdisciplinary work, and interfaith traditions. It is precisely this mediating function that allows queer people of color to be transformed as well as transform those whom they encounter. In other words, rather than remaining in a state of stasis, queer people of color are able to cross physical and metaphorical borders and also help to transform others through the gift of mediation.[20]

3. Resisting Monochromatic Theology

Before taking a closer look at each of the three rainbow themes in the following chapters, let us examine a brief example of monochromatic theology, which is in many ways the antithesis of rainbow theology. The purpose of this example is not so much to create yet another dichotomy (that is, rainbow vs. monochromatic modes of thinking), but rather to show how the three rainbow themes of multiplicity, middle spaces, and mediation might help us to resist a theology that, on its face, seems liberative for LGBTIQ people.

---

[20] Indeed, the mediating function of queer people of color recalls the postcolonial notion of hybridity in which binary poles (for example, the colonizer and the colonized) are mutually transformed within the hybrid space through a process of mediation.

Monochromatic theology is characterized by the three themes of (1) singularity, (2) staying home, and (3) selecting sides. With respect to *singularity*, monochromatic theology focuses on a single form of oppression. That is, even though an individual may experience multiple forms of oppression, monochromatic theology contends that there is a single oppression that rises above all others. With respect to *staying home*, monochromatic theology contends that oppressed people can find a metaphorical "home" by being in solidarity with others who also experience that singular oppression. Finally, with respect to *selecting sides*, monochromatic theology sees the world in binary terms (for example, oppressor vs. oppressed, bondage vs. liberation). That is, it is the job of the oppressed individual to choose sides and to select liberation over oppression. Although monochromatic theology is well-meaning, it ultimately fails to address the complexity of the queer of color experience.

One example of a monochromatic theology is Richard Cleaver's *Know My Name: A Gay Liberation Theology*.[21] In this book, which was published in 1995, Cleaver draws from Latin American liberation theology to construct a liberation theology for lesbians and gay men. Cleaver argues for a theological revolution that will liberate lesbians and gay men—and presumably, by extension, other queer folk—from oppression by the church and society.

While Cleaver's work is well-intentioned and seeks to liberate lesbians and gay men (and presumably other LGBTIQ people as well) from ecclesial and societal oppression, it is *not* characterized by the three rainbow themes of multiplicity, middle spaces, and mediation. Rather, it is characterized by the opposing monochromatic themes of singularity, staying home, and selecting sides.

For example, with respect to *singularity*, Cleaver focuses upon a single category of oppression: that of gayness.[22] He does not

---

[21] Richard Cleaver, *Know My Name: A Gay Liberation Theology* (Louisville, KY: Westminster John Knox Press, 1995).

[22] See ibid., 1 (noting that the "whole book" is focused on the question of "lesbians and gay men").

address the complexities of the category of "gay" with respect to multiple intersecting identities such as race, ethnicity, and class. As noted earlier, Black feminists have written about these issues since at least the 1970s, and so these ideas would not have been unknown in the mid-1990s. The singular focus of Cleaver's book is liberation from gay oppression, and Cleaver does not examine how LGBTIQ people may very well experience more than one oppression based upon other factors.

With respect to *staying home*, Cleaver assumes for the sake of his analysis that there is in fact a "home" for gay people. Just like the ancient Israelites, gay people are a tribe; their task is simply to come together and find a way from the bondage of slavery into a new home that is the promised land.[23] For Cleaver, there is no questioning of one's belonging as a "gay" person. That is, there is no sense of living in a middle space that continually resists the notion of being "home" within the LGBTIQ community, whether that is due to one's race, ethnicity, or other factors.

Finally, with respect to *selecting sides*, Cleaver sets up a clear binary of the oppressor vs. the oppressed.[24] He sets up a challenge for the reader to choose sides instead of bringing together disparate ideas and theological sources that might result in a surprising transformation of all involved. Furthermore, Cleaver only uses traditional theological sources; he does not draw upon interdisciplinary sources (for example, literature), transnational examples (for example, the experiences of LGBTIQ people in the two-thirds world), or interfaith ideas (for example, non-Christian religious experiences) in his book.

To be fair, Cleaver's work was written at a time when the postmodern discourses of queer theory and postcolonial thought had not yet significantly influenced LGBTIQ theological reflection. Nevertheless, it is still helpful to look at *Know My Name* through the lens of rainbow theology and examine

---

[23] See ibid., 39 (arguing that those who are "on the gay side" have a "shared history" that resembles the Israelites who were passed over in the Exodus narrative).

[24] See ibid., 144 (arguing that gay Christians need to reclaim the tradition of the Stonewall Rebellion with respect to revolutionary change).

how an ostensibly liberative theology might actually prevent many queer people—including queer people of color—from attaining true liberation or flourishing.

4. Summary

So what exactly is rainbow theology? Simply put, rainbow theology is a theology that is written by and for LGBTIQ people of color. It is a theology that fully embraces the beautiful hues of race and ethnicity in an LGBTIQ community that is predominantly white. It is also a theology that fully embraces the variety of sexualities and gender identities in communities of color that are predominantly straight and cisgender. And, as noted above, rainbow theology is a broader methodology and critique that can be applied to all forms of theological reflection.

Rainbow theology builds upon existing contextual theologies—for example, LGBTIQ theologies, as well as Black, Asian American, Latina/o, and Indigenous theologies—by specifically drawing upon and reflecting the experiences of LGBTIQ people of color. That is, rainbow theology weaves together the writings of queer theologians of color from the last two decades, as we have seen in Part I of this book. Although it cuts across different racial and ethnic groups, it also preserves the distinctive social locations for each group.

Rainbow theology does much more than just reflect the voices of queer people of color, however. It also reflects the unique positionality of LGBTIQ people of color vis-à-vis the larger marginalized communities in which they exist. LGBTIQ people of color are rejected twice-over. That is, they are not just overlooked or ignored, but they are explicitly told by the larger marginalized communities in which they are located that the very fact of their existence is anathema and that they should not even exist. This unique positionality manifests itself, theologically speaking, through three rainbow themes: (1) multiplicity, (2) middle spaces, and (3) mediation. Let us now turn to each of these themes.

Study Questions

1. How do rainbows reflect the experiences of LGBTIQ people of color, particularly with respect to issues of race, sexuality, and spirit?

2. What are some ways in which rainbows reflect the themes of multiplicity, middle spaces, and mediation?

3. How have you experienced the rainbow themes of multiplicity, middles spaces, and mediation in your own life?

4. Compare and contrast the three rainbow themes with the monochromatic themes of singularity, staying home, and selecting sides.

5. Define, in your own words, what constitutes rainbow theology. How might rainbow theology speak to your own life?

For Further Study

Rainbows
• Boyer, *The Rainbow*
• Conner, Sparks, and Sparks, *Cassell's Encyclopedia*, 278–79
• Lee and Fraser, *The Rainbow Bridge*
• Whelan, *The Book of Rainbows*

Rainbow Theology
• Cheng, *The Rainbow Connection*

Chapter 7

Multiplicity

One of the most amazing classes that I have ever taken in my life was the introduction to contemporary theology course at Union Theological Seminary in New York City. The class was taught by Dr. James Cone, the father of academic Black theology and my doctoral adviser and mentor. In the span of a single semester, we covered all of the major theological figures and movements of the twentieth century, ranging from liberalism to neo-orthodoxy to liberation theology. The course opened my eyes to the beautiful complexity of the theological enterprise, and it helped me to hear my calling as a systematic theologian.

As exciting as the course was—and it was my introduction to Black, feminist, womanist, African, Latin American, Asian, Asian American, Indigenous, gay and lesbian, ecofeminist, and other theologies—I wrestled with the problem of multiplicity. On the one hand, the course addressed questions of multiplicity because it covered so many different voices. On the other hand, however, the course was strangely silent with respect to multiplicity in that almost all of the theological voices we covered dealt with singular oppressions.

That is, virtually all of the theologies that we studied focused on a *single* oppression or identity, whether it was race, gender, or sexuality. Where did I fit in, as someone who was not just

Asian American, but *also* an openly gay man? I felt this issue acutely when the Asian American theologians we read were silent about LGBTIQ issues, and the LGBTIQ theologians we read were silent about race. Did the classical liberation paradigm work for queer people of color?

The one glimpse I had into a theology of multiplicity was when we covered womanist and Black feminist theologies (that is, theologies by African American women). These theologians wrestled with their multiple social location as (1) women in the male-dominated field of Black theology, and as (2) African Americans in the white-dominated field of feminist theology. It is to this question of multiplicity that we now turn.

1. Multiplicity and Queers of Color

a. Queer of Color Experience

The queer of color experience is marked by *multiplicity*. That is, queer people of color experience multiple oppressions based upon their identities as LGBTIQ people *and* as people of color. Unlike their white LGBTIQ siblings, queer people of color have to deal with the oppression of racism. And unlike their straight and cisgender siblings of color, queer people of color also have to deal with the oppression of queerphobia.

As Audre Lorde wrote in her essay "Age, Race, Class, and Sex: Women Redefining Difference," there is a "mythical norm" in the United States that is defined as "white, thin, male, young, heterosexual, Christian, and financially secure." Anyone who falls outside of this mythical norm often ends up choosing only a *single* way in which s/he differs from others. That is, s/he assumes that this singular marker of difference is the "primary cause of all oppression, forgetting other distortions around difference."[1] This is why Black women have criticized the white feminist movement for focusing on their oppression as women and ignoring issues of race and class.

---

[1] Lorde, *Sister Outsider*, 116.

It should be noted, of course, that even within queer communities of color, certain individuals experience more oppressions than others. For example, lesbians of color deal not just with issues of heterosexism and racism, but also with issues of sexism and often classism. Anu, who is a lesbian poet from India who came out in college in the United States, writes powerfully about the multiple layers of oppressive stereotypes that she faces as a queer woman of color: "WHO AM I? / I am Uncivilized, Barbaric, Heathen, Primitive, Oriental / I am Passive, Submissive, Self-Sacrificing, Obedient, Sati Savitri / I am Dyke, Deviant, Queer, Assimilated—Bitch-From-Hell."[2]

In addition to wrestling with multiple oppressions, queer people of color also deal with the multiplicity of specific identities within the larger categories of race, sexuality, and spirituality. For example, with respect to race, what does it mean to be a "person of color"? What do categories such as "Asian American" really mean? How much does a third-generation Japanese American professional who works in technology in Seattle really share with a first-generation Hmong immigrant woman in Minnesota? Should the umbrella category be "Asian Americans," "Asian Pacific Americans" (APAs), "Asian Pacific Islanders" (APIs), or some other term? Have we left out people of South Asian and Southeast Asian descent? What about mixed-heritage or multiracial persons?

This same tension between naming and erasure—that is, specific differences being erased as a result of using broader identity categories—is also present with terms relating to sexuality. For example, as we have noted above, the category of "queer" can be helpful as an umbrella term for those people who are marginalized on the basis of sexuality and gender identity. However, because "queer" includes many different identities such as "lesbian," "gay," "bisexual," "transgender," "intersex," "questioning," "ally," "Two-Spirit," "pansexual," and "asexual," the use of such a term can actually erase, rather than

---

[2] Anu, "Who Am I?," in *The Very Inside: An Anthology of Writing by Asian and Pacific Islander Lesbian and Bisexual Women*, ed. Sharon Lim-Hing (Toronto, ON: Sister Vision Press, 1994), 19.

honor, differences. That is why the use of acronyms such as "LGBTIQ2" is important, as unwieldy as they might be.

Finally, what does it mean to be a queer of color who is also "religious" or "spiritual"? When we use these words, are we talking about organized religion or more individualized experiences of ultimate reality? If we are talking about organized religion, are we only talking about Christianity and not all traditions? And if we do mean Christianity, what broad tradition are we talking about: Eastern Orthodox, Roman Catholic, or Protestant? If Protestant, which denomination? The issues of multiplicity go on and on.

Queer people of color are constantly being asked to choose among multiple identities of race, sexuality, and religion. It feels like they are always being asked: "Who am I right now?"[3] When they are within an LGBTIQ context (which is often predominantly white), they are often asked to suppress the racial and ethnic aspects of their lives. When they are within communities of color (which are often predominantly straight and cisgender), they are often asked to suppress the sexual and gender identity aspects of their lives. And when they are in communities of faith, they are often asked to suppress the racial, ethnic, sexual, and gender identity aspects of their lives. Thus, for many queer people of color, their multiplicity of identities and oppressions can lead to a profound sense of fragmentation. Paradoxically, it is often the acknowledgment of this fragmentation—as opposed to ignoring or suppressing it—that actually leads to wholeness on the part of LGBTIQ people of color.[4]

b. Queer of Color Critique

The themes of multiplicity and the co-constitutive nature of oppressions also appear in secular queer theory. In the last decade, we have seen a proliferation of works that fall under

---

[3] This recalls Judith Butler's argument about the performativity of gender. If gender reality is created through "sustained social performances," then racial reality can also be understood in the same way. Judith Butler, *Gender Trouble* (New York: Routledge, 1990), 192.

[4] See Cheng, "Multiplicity and Judges 19," 129–30.

the umbrella of the "queer of color critique" movement. This movement—which is a subset of the queer studies movement in academia—consists of writings by and about LGBTIQ people of color. Queer of color critique scholars include individuals such as Roderick A. Ferguson, José Esteban Muñoz, David L. Eng, Jasbir K. Puar, and others.

One of the key themes in queer of color critique is that of multiplicity. In *Strange Affinities: The Gender and Sexual Politics of Comparative Racialization*, Grace Kyungwon Hong and her co-editor Roderick A. Ferguson note how the intellectual roots of queer of color critique are located in women of color theory, which has long wrestled with issues of multiply-intersecting identities of race, gender, and other factors. According to Ferguson and Hong, it is important to avoid perpetuating the fallacy of essentialism in categorizing queer people of color as yet another "identity."

Rather, they argue that we should see how different groups can form coalitions on the basis of how they are similarly valued—or, more accurately, devalued—by the dominant culture. That is, instead of understanding queers of color as a monolithic blend of racial and sexual identities, the queer of color movement seeks to observe and honor both similarities and differences with respect to their multiple social locations. This "heterotopic mode of comparison" helps to preserve and not erase their multiple identities.[5]

Queer of color critique also addresses how racial and sexual identities are mutually co-constituted. That is, LGBTIQ people of color are not simply an amalgamation of race and sexuality. Rather, these categories are fluid and are inextricably inter-twined with the other. Take, for example, the category of "gay man." This ostensibly "sexual" category is actually profoundly shaped by racialization, whether or not we are consciously aware of this. That is, our imagined stereotypes of a "white gay man" (normal) differs greatly from that of a "black gay man" (hypersexual), an "Asian American gay man" (feminized

---

[5] Hong and Ferguson, "Introduction," 9.

bottom), a "Latino gay man" (sensual), and a "Native American gay man" (asexual).

In her book *Race, Ethnicity, and Sexuality*, Joane Nagel has written about the deep connections between the categories of race and sexuality as "ethnosexual frontiers." Nagel cites a number of these frontiers—including conquest, nationalism, war, tourism, and globalization—in which "ethnicity and sexuality join together to form a barrier to hold some people in and keep others out, to define who is pure and impure, . . . [and] to form sexualized perimeters around ethnic, racial, and national spaces."[6] It is precisely these ethnosexual frontiers that make the multiplicity of identities in LGBTIQ people of color so complicated.

Jasbir K. Puar, a lesbian South Asian professor of women's and gender studies at Rutgers University, has written in her book *Terrorist Assemblages: Homonationalism in Queer Times* about how the racialized bodies of South Asians in a post-9/11 world are signifiers for both political and sexual deviance. That is, in their desire to be accepted, white middle-class gays and lesbians subscribe to an ideology of homonationalism that ultimately marginalizes queer bodies of color as the terrorist "other." Puar's work uncovers the connections between queer-ness and themes of "patriotism, war, torture, security, death, terror, terrorism, detention, and deportation," which she notes is "usually imagined as devoid of connection to sexual politics in general and queer politics in particular."[7] Puar's work help-fully demonstrates that issues of sexuality cannot be separated from issues of race or politics.

In sum, multiplicity is an important issue for LGBTIQ people of color. Queer people of color experience multiplicity through the multiple oppressions of queerphobia and racism (and, for some, additional oppressions such as sexism, classism, body fascism, ableism, and ageism). However, queer people of color

---

[6] Nagel, *Race, Ethnicity, and Sexuality*, 1.

[7] Jasbir K. Puar, *Terrorist Assemblages: Homonationalism in Queer Times* (Durham, NC: Duke University Press, 2007), xii.

are often expected to ignore this experience of multiplicity in favor of singular oppressions. This is problematic because, as Jin Haritaworn of York University in Toronto, Canada, has written, "Queers of colour and other multiply minoritised queers have little interest in single-issue equations, which evade real power differences around gender, race, and sexuality."[8]

2. Multiplicity and Queer of Color Theologies

As we have seen in Part I of this book, multiplicity is an important theme in the work of LGBTIQ theologians of color. For example, the queer Black ethicist Roger Sneed has critiqued white gay men such as the syndicated columnist Dan Savage (who founded the "It Gets Better" project) for their one-dimensional characterization of communities of color. According to Sneed, Savage's view of Black people as uniformly homophobic in the aftermath of the California Proposition 8 vote in 2008 had the unfortunate result of minimizing and trivializing the experiences of Black gays and lesbians and making them "virtually invisible." In other words, Savage failed to acknowledge that "queer and black communities have members who occupy multiple subject positions."[9]

Indeed, the theme of multiplicity is central with respect to womanist and Black feminist reflections on sexuality. As noted above, Renée Hill critiqued the womanist movement in her 1993 essay "Who Are We for Each Other?" for failing to acknowledge and to accept the experience of Black lesbians, despite the movement's embracing of multiple issues relating to race, gender, and class.[10] Thirteen years later, in 2006, Monica Coleman, Irene Monroe, Traci West, and others raised similar issues in the "Must I Be Womanist?" roundtable in the

---

[8] Jin Haritaworn, "Shifting Positionalities: Empirical Reflections on a Queer/Trans of Colour Methodology," *Sociological Research Online* 13, no. 1.13 (March 21, 2008): 5.1, accessed January 3, 2013, http://bit.ly/ifbHzR.

[9] Sneed, *Representations of Homosexuality*, 193–94.

[10] See Hill, "Who Are We for Each Other?"

Journal of Feminist Studies in Religion.[11] For Coleman, Monroe, and West, Black feminist theologies might actually provide a more inclusive space than womanist theologies with respect to honoring the multiple identities of Black lesbians and bisexual women.

Multiplicity is also present in queer Asian American theologies. In "Multiplicity and Judges 19," I write about at least four ways in which LGBTIQ Asian Americans experience multiplicity as a result of their experiences: (1) multiple naming of their ethnic and sexual identities; (2) multiple silencing from the Asian American and LGBTIQ communities; (3) multiple oppression with respect to their racial, sexual, and religious identities; and (4) multiple fragmentation in terms of being forced to choose which part of their identities is operative in a given context. I argue that, paradoxically, it is important for LGBTIQ Asian Americans to acknowledge this multiplicity in order to experience wholeness.[12]

This experience of multiple oppression also extends to political and economic issues, as queer theologian Joseph Goh reminds us in his essays about the treatment of LGBTIQ people in his home country of Malaysia. In his essay "The Word Was *Not* Made Flesh," Goh writes about the Malaysian government's banning of the sexuality rights festival *Seksualiti Merdeka* in 2011 on the basis that the festival was "immoral" and "subversive." Goh critiques this governmental censorship from his Christian perspective, and he grounds his critique in the doctrines of the incarnation and the *imago Dei.*[13]

The theme of multiplicity is also present in queer Latina/o theologies. As Orlando Espín writes in *Grace and Humanness,* it is important to recognize that LGBTIQ Latina/os have a multiplicity of identities, and *all* of these identities must be addressed by Latina/o theologians. Queer Latina/os, he writes, are "gendered, raced, sexually oriented, classed, socially

---

[11] See Coleman, "Must I Be Womanist?"; Monroe, "Must I Be Womanist?"; West, "Must I Be Womanist?"

[12] See Cheng, "Multiplicity and Judges 19."

[13] See Goh, "The Word Was *Not* Made Flesh."

positioned, and so forth, just as everyone else." Just as straight Latina/o theologians have insisted to the broader theological academy that race (and other factors) cannot be ignored, they must also recognize sexual orientation with respect to their LGBTIQ siblings. That is, sexual orientation cannot be "bracketed or dismissed."[14]

For queer Latina/os, there is also the issue of multiplicity within the broader category of "Latina/o." Historically speaking, the category of "Hispanic" was invented in the mid-1970s by federal bureaucrats who wanted to group together all individuals with ancestral ties to the Spanish cultural diaspora. Although many people prefer the term "Latina/o" in order to avoid connotations of Spanish imperialism, that term is still problematic. This is because each of the subgroups (i.e., Mexicans, Puerto Ricans, Cubans, Central Americans, South Americans, and Dominicans) come from different cultural and socioeconomic contexts.[15]

Finally, multiplicity is present in Two-Spirit Indigenous writings. For example, the terms "Indigenous" and "Native" are not monolithic concepts. Rather, they include people from many different sovereign nations from North America and around the world. The essays in the anthology *Queer Indigenous Studies* draw upon multiple Indigenous sources, including Maori, Samoan, Mohawk, Navajo, Cherokee, and Cree voices.[16] The editors of the anthology also acknowledge that the individual essays embrace multiplicity in terms of methodology. In the volume's introduction, the authors note that the essays "model multiple queer theories as decolonial work in Native studies."[17]

---

[14] Espín, *Grace and Humanness*, 63.

[15] Joanne Rodríguez-Olmedo, "The U.S. Hispanic/Latino Landscape," in *Handbook of Latina/o Theologies*, ed. Edwin David Aponte and Miguel A. De La Torre (St. Louis, MO: Chalice Press, 2006). Indeed, Latina/os belong to multilingual, multiracial, multi-ethnic, and multireligious contexts.

[16] See Driskill et al., *Queer Indigenous Studies*.

[17] Driskill et al., "Introduction," 21.

3. Multiplicity and Rainbow Theology

The theme of multiplicity is significant for rainbow theology because it resists the fiction of a singular oppression. It also challenges the fiction that seemingly distinct oppressions—for example, race and sexuality—are separated and not in fact inextricably intertwined and imbricated. In constructing our rainbow theology, it is helpful to examine certain theoretical writings about multiplicity from the broader field of theology.

Laurel Schneider, the lesbian professor of theology at Chicago Theological Seminary and self-described "philosophical theologian working at the cutting edges of multiplicity theory,"[18] has argued in her recent books *Beyond Monotheism: A Theology of Multiplicity* and *Polydoxy: Theology of Multiplicity and Relation* (co-edited with Catherine Keller) that multiplicity—along with its attendant notions of fluidity, porosity, and interconnection[19]—is a critical idea to reclaim in theological discourse, notwithstanding the traditional focus on monotheism in Christianity.[20]

In addition to her work on multiplicity, Schneider has also examined how seemingly distinct oppressions—such as race and sex—are actually deeply interconnected. For example, in her essay "What Race Is Your Sex?," Schneider demonstrates that race and sex are co-constituted. As a result, Schneider argues that white supremacy is difficult to overcome because "the co-constitutive aspects of race, sex, and gender make the practice of whiteness very difficult to perceive in oneself, particularly when they also function as gender and sex."[21]

The work of the late bisexual Argentinian theologian Marcella Althaus-Reid is also instructive in the context of multiple oppressions. Althaus-Reid constructs an "indecent theology" to critique

---

[18] Catherine Keller and Laurel C. Schneider, *Polydoxy: Theology of Multiplicity and Relation* (Abingdon, UK: Routledge, 2011), i.

[19] See Laurel C. Schneider, *Beyond Monotheism: A Theology of Multiplicity* (Abingdon, UK: Routledge, 2008), 164.

[20] As noted above, Schneider will become a professor of religious studies, gender studies, and philosophy at Vanderbilt University as of the fall of 2013.

[21] Laurel C. Schneider, "What Race Is Your Sex?," in Boisvert and Johnson, *Queer Religion II*, 138.

the silences of Latin American and other liberation theologies with respect to sexuality. For Althaus-Reid, it is not enough for Latin American liberation theologians to challenge the economic and political status quo; they must also challenge the sexual status quo. That is, one cannot split off economic and political well-being from sexual well-being. Thus, by constructing her indecent theology, Althaus-Reid is in fact unmasking the highly ideological nature of non-indecent theologies.[22]

So where is God in all this? In my view, the queer of color experience of multiplicity is a direct reflection of a God who experiences multiplicity in God's own trinitarian self. God is not content to be simply one, but rather is three-in-one. God experiences multiplicity in the very depths of Godself. The lesbian theologian Elizabeth Stuart has used the classical theological concept of *perichōrēsis*—that is, a "dancing around"—in order to describe the multiple persons within the Godhead as having a "dynamic, non-hierarchical equal, mutual relationship, 'a beautiful intertwining, unending dance, whose movement flows to and fro between the dancers.'"[23] Multiplicity is at the very heart of God.

Indeed, we know that God is found in relationship, as we have seen in the relational and "erotic" theologies of lesbian theologians such as Carter Heyward, Mary Hunt, and Elizabeth Stuart.[24] A God who is found in relationship demands multiplicity (that is, the existence of the "other") and is never satisfied with mere singularity. That is why God engaged in the act of creation—so that God would have others with whom to share the divine love that constantly overflows with respect to the Trinity. Thus, the queer of color experience of multiplicity is a gift. Multiplicity is a constant reminder of the divine call to multiplicity and a window into the innermost—and, indeed,

---

[22] See Althaus-Reid, *Indecent Theology*.

[23] Elizabeth Stuart, *Just Good Friends: Towards a Lesbian and Gay Theology of Relationships* (London: Mowbray, 1995), 242.

[24] See Carter Heyward, *Touching Our Strength: The Erotic as Power and the Love of God* (New York: HarperSanFrancisco, 1989); Mary E. Hunt, *Fierce Tenderness: A Feminist Theology of Friendship* (New York: Crossroad, 1991); Stuart, *Just Good Friends*.

the most intimate—workings of the divine Godhead. LGBTIQ people of color are reminded that, in the multiplicity of their racial, sexual, and spiritual identities, they are created in the image and likeness of God.[25] And through the Holy Spirit, all of creation is constantly being drawn into the trinitarian dynamic of the Godhead, which ultimately remains an open—and not closed—system.

4. Summary

In sum, multiplicity is an important theme for LGBTIQ people of color. Not only do queer people of color experience multiple oppressions (for example, racism within the LGBTIQ community and homophobia and transphobia within communities of color), but they also experience multiplicity with respect to the naming of their racial, sexual, and spiritual identities. Not surprisingly, multiplicity is an important theme in the writings of secular queer of color theorists as well as LGBTIQ theologians of color. The rainbow theme of multiplicity is a gift from God. It is a window into the innermost workings of the trinitarian Godhead, which is overflowing with love and is in a constant state of dancing among the multiple persons of the Trinity. Having examined this theme, we now move to the second rainbow theme of middle spaces.

---

[25] See Cheng, "A Three-Part Sinfonia."

Study Questions

1. How have you experienced multiplicity in your own life? What multiple identities and social locations do you occupy simultaneously?

2. How do queer people of color experience multiplicity with respect to race, sexuality, and spirit?

3. What are some examples from queer Black, queer Asian American, queer Latina/o, and Two-Spirit Indigenous theologies that relate to multiplicity?

4. How is multiplicity manifested in contemporary theologies?

5. Describe how you might understand God in terms of multiplicity.

For Further Study

Multiplicity and Queers of Color
- Haritaworn, "Shifting Positionalities"
- Hong and Ferguson, *Strange Affinities*
- Lorde, *Sister Outsider*, 114–23
- Nagel, *Race, Ethnicity, and Sexuality*
- Puar, *Terrorist Assemblages*

Multiplicity and Queer of Color Theologies
- Cheng, "Multiplicity and Judges 19"
- Cheng, "A Three-Part Sinfonia"
- Coleman, "Roundtable Discussion: Must I Be Womanist?"
- Driskill et al., "Introduction," 21
- Espín, *Grace and Humanness*, 63
- Hill, "Who Are We for Each Other?"

Multiplicity and Rainbow Theology
- Althaus-Reid, *Indecent Theology*
- Heyward, *Touching Our Strength*
- Hunt, *Fierce Tenderness*
- Keller and Schneider, *Polydoxy*
- Schneider, *Beyond Monotheism*
- Schneider, "What Race Is Your Sex?"
- Stuart, *Just Good Friends*

Chapter 8

Middle Spaces

David Chung was a beloved member of the gay Asian community in Washington, D.C. As a bartender at Nellie's, a local gay sports bar, David was known for his infectious smile and caring for others. One of his coworkers said that "there was always a smile on his face," and one of his friends said that he was "full of love for everyone."[1] A photo in the *Washington Blade*, the local LGBTIQ newspaper, showed Chung with a big smile, waving to the camera.

In July of 2012, Chung—at the young age of twenty-six—committed suicide by hanging himself. Hundreds of people showed up at a memorial event at a local bar that paid tribute to Chung's life, and they toasted his memory with shots of Irish whiskey as photos of him were projected on television monitors around the bar. The proceeds from the memorial were donated to the Wanda Alston House, an organization for homeless LGBTIQ youth in Washington, D.C.

The news of Chung's death hit the queer Asian community hard in Washington, D.C. In addition to the fact that nobody had suspected that Chung was struggling with suicidal tendencies, it also reminded people in that community of the challenges of being a queer person of color.

---

[1] Michael K. Lavers, "Hundreds Pay Tribute to Nellie's Bartender," *Washington Blade* (July 16, 2012), accessed January 3, 2013, http://bit.ly/MBbwsL.

As someone who has ministered to LGBTIQ people of color for over a decade, I was incredibly saddened to read about Chung's story, not only because of his untimely death, but also because his story resonated with me deeply. In my own experience, many queer people of color seem to be extremely sociable and happy on the outside while at the same time experience intense loneliness and sadness inside. These feelings of loneliness and sadness are often magnified by an inability to reach out to other people about one's sense of "non-belonging." Indeed, many LGBTIQ people of color live in a middle space—that is, they are metaphorically "homeless"—and are caught between the predominantly white queer community on the one hand and the predominantly straight ethnic communities of origin on the other hand.[2]

This chapter will examine the theme of *middle spaces* in the lives of queer people of color and how this theme impacts queer theology and theological reflection in general. It concludes that, notwithstanding the pain of metaphorical homelessness that many queer people of color experience, the rainbow theme of middle spaces can be viewed as a window into the divine. In particular, Jesus Christ also was metaphorically homeless as a result of living in the middle space between the divine and the human; he had "nowhere to lay his head."[3] The rainbow theme of middle spaces is a reminder that our homes here on earth—no matter how comfortable—are illusory. Only in God can we find our true homes.

1. Middle Spaces and Queers of Color

The queer of color experience is one that is marked by *middle spaces*. That is, queer people of color never fully belong to the larger communities of which they are a part. Because

---

[2] Queer people of color also experience literal homelessness. For example, a recent study showed that 41 percent of Black transgender people have reported being homeless at some point in their lives, which is over five times the rate of the general population in the United States. See National Gay and Lesbian Task Force, "Injustice at Every Turn: A Look at Black Respondents."

[3] Matthew 8:20; Luke 9:58.

they are queer, LGBTIQ people of color do not belong fully to their racial and ethnic communities. And, because they are racial and ethnic minorities, LGBTIQ people of color do not belong fully to the queer community. In other words, queer people of color are metaphorically homeless. They live in a middle space between the binary of sexuality on the one hand, and race on the other hand.

Eric Wat, a gay Asian writer, has described this middle-space existence in his essay "Preserving the Paradox: Stories from a *Gay-Loh*." In that essay, Wat writes that many gay Asian men are "forever left in the middle of the road, unacceptable to those at either side of the street." In other words, gay Asian men are "run over at the intersection of racism and homophobia."[4] Similarly, Keith Boykin, a gay African American writer, has written about his search for a "home" from the standpoint of his middle-space existence: "I've spent a great deal of my time and energy as an openly gay black man shuttling back and forth between my two identities."[5]

The lesbian Latina writer Glora Anzaldúa has described this middle space as the "borderlands" or *la frontera*. For Anzaldúa, there is a psychological, sexual, and spiritual cost to this middle space, which occurs "wherever two or more cultures edge each other." She writes that the borderlands are "not a comfortable territory to live in, this place of contradictions." In fact, "hatred, anger and exploitation are the prominent features of this landscape."[6]

The theme of middle spaces also plays a prominent role in the queer of color critique movement. José Esteban Muñoz, a gay Latino professor of performance studies at New York University, has written about the strategy of "disidentification." In his book *Disidentifications: Queers of Color and the Performance of Politics*, Muñoz writes about how LGBTIQ performance artists have created a middle-space strategy of

---

[4] Eric C. Wat, "Preserving the Paradox: Stories from a Gay-Loh," in Leong, *Asian American Sexualities*, 79.

[5] Boykin, *One More River to Cross*, 26.

[6] Anzaldúa, *Borderlands, La Frontera*, 19.

disidentification. That is, instead of the outright acceptance or rejection of exclusionary ideas or discourses, such artists have found a third way of disidentification that allows them to transform such ideas or discourses for their own purposes. These artists are not forced into a binary structure of acceptance or rejection; they exist within a middle space of disidentification.[7]

One price paid by many LGBTIQ people of color who live in a middle space is a profound sense of disembodiment, or alienation from one's own body. This arises out of the fact that one's body is never completely at home; it is always a signifier of deviance. That is, one's black or brown body is constantly out of place in an LGBTIQ community that celebrates—and some would say is obsessed with—the beauty of whiteness. And one's queer body is constantly out of place in racial and ethnic communities that celebrate—and some would say are obsessed with—"family values" and heterosexuality.

For example, the gay Asian Canadian film critic Richard Fung has written about the absence of Asian bodies in mainstream gay pornography and the resulting "racial, cultural, *and* sexual alienation" that is experienced by gay Asian men.[8] In his celebrated essay "Looking for My Penis: The Eroticized Asian in Gay Video Porn," Fung writes about how East Asian and South Asian male bodies are seen as "undersexed" and "devoid of sexual connotation" in the context of gay porn.[9]

In sum, the queer of color experience is one of living in middle spaces, or being suspended between the binary poles of racial and sexual identities. It is an experience of being metaphorically homeless. And, as a result of this experience, many LGBTIQ people experience alienation from their bodies, which are seen as a marker of deviance from both the LGBTIQ community as well as communities of color.

---

[7] See José Esteban Muñoz, *Disidentifications: Queers of Color and the Performance of Politics* (Minneapolis: University of Minnesota Press, 1999).

[8] Richard Fung, "Looking for My Penis: The Eroticized Asian in Gay Video Porn," in Leong, *Asian American Sexualities*, 190.

[9] Ibid., 182. See also Nguyen Tan Hoang, "The Resurrection of Brandon Lee: The Making of a Gay Asian American Porn Star," in *Porn Studies*, ed. Linda Williams (Durham, NC: Duke University Press, 2004), 223–70.

2. Middle Spaces and Queer of Color Theologies

In this section, I will explore the role of middle spaces in the queer of color theologies that were discussed in the first part of this book. This theme is manifested in at least three ways: (1) racial and sexual homelessness; (2) spiritual homelessness; and (3) disembodiment. Although these experiences may on the surface seem rather bleak, I will argue in the next section that such experiences are actually windows into the divine homelessness of God. For now, however, let us examine how the theme of middle spaces manifests itself in queer of color theologies.

a. Racial and Sexual Homelessness

For many queer of color theologians, the theme of middle spaces is characterized by a sense of racial and sexual homelessness. For example, Irene Monroe, in her essay "Between a Rock and a Hard Place: Struggling with the Black Church's Heterosexism and the White Queer Community's Racism," discusses the challenging third space that LGBTIQ African Americans occupy between the binary of race on the one hand, and sexuality on the other hand.[10] According to Monroe, the sexual orientation of LGBTIQ African Americans "evicts" them from black communities, whereas their race marginalizes them with respect to LGBTIQ communities. This social location "dangles [their] lives precariously on a thin thread."[11]

I have written about middle spaces and gay Asian American men in my article "Gay Asian Masculinities and Christian Theologies." In that article, I note that, on the one hand, gay Asian American men are often seen as "sexually undesirable" by the white gay community. On the other hand, gay Asian American men are seen as "sexually dangerous" by the straight Asian American community because of their "deviance" from

---

[10] Irene Monroe, "Between a Rock and a Hard Place: Struggling with the Black Church's Heterosexism and the White Queer Community's Racism," in De La Torre, *Out of the Shadows*, 39–58.

[11] Ibid., 39–40.

heterosexual masculine norms. I suggest that, as a result of this middle-space existence, the "embattled gay Asian male body" might actually serve an atoning purpose by "decolonizing the racism and homophobia of contemporary Christian theologies."[12]

Middle spaces also play an important role in the writings of queer Latina/o theologians. As we have seen, the queer Latino biblical scholar Manuel Villalobos has used Gloria Anzaldúa's notion of the borderlands, or *la frontera*, to construct a queer Latino biblical hermeneutic. Villalobos writes that Anzaldúa's writings have become "sacred for all of us who struggle to maneuver daily in various 'borderlands,' living queer, living undocumented, living in poverty, living in the martyrized South, living in all kinds of ambiguity, and finally, living as a *Mexicano 'del otro lado.'*"[13]

Similarly, Michael Diaz, a gay Latino pastor with the Metropolitan Community Churches, has written about constructing a queer Latino biblical hermeneutic based upon the middle-space notion of *nepantla*. The word *nepantla* was coined by native Mesoamericans who found themselves engaging in both indigenous customs (including religious traditions) as well as the Christian faith of their Spanish colonizers.[14] Diaz uses the theme of *nepantla* to help "recall and retain memories of our queer indigenous ancestors" such as the *xochihua* (who were cross-dressers in ancient Meosoamerican societies) and to expand "our queer indigenous cultural memory."[15]

No discussion of middle spaces and metaphorical homelessness would be complete without noting the situation of Two-Spirit Indigenous people. As a result of settler colonialism, LGBTIQ2 Native people have literally lost their homelands due to "theft" and "continued occupation." In the words of the editors of the recent volume *Queer Indigenous Studies*: "Declaring

---

[12] Cheng, "Gay Asian Masculinities and Christian Theologies," 540.

[13] Villalobos, "Bodies *Del Otro Lado*," 191. The phrase "*Mexicano 'del otro lado'*" means "a Mexican person 'from the other side.'"

[14] Diaz, "*Nepantla* as Indigenous Middle Space," 21–22.

[15] Ibid., 71, 79.

'We're here and we're queer' does not mean we get our land back. It does not mean that we can be part of queer communities. The queer movement does not represent all of what queer Indigenous people desire." For many queer Indigenous people, coming out means "making a choice between being Indigenous" on the one hand, and "being queer" on the other.[16]

b. Spiritual Homelessness

In addition to the above experiences of racial and sexual homelessness, LGBTIQ people of color also experience a profound sense of spiritual homelessness. As noted previously, queer Black theologians such as Ibrahim Abdurrahman Farajajé[17] and Horace Griffin,[18] as well as Black allies such as Kelly Brown Douglas,[19] have written about how LGBTIQ African Americans are often rejected by their churches after they come out of the closet. Victor Anderson, a gay Black professor of ethics at Vanderbilt University Divinity School, has noted that a 1992 study showed that 79 percent of pastors in the Black Church were "categorically opposed" to homosexuality.[20] This has led many LGBTIQ African Americans to be estranged from the Black Church, including Anderson himself, who describes himself as a "radically estranged Black gay man from the Black Church."[21]

Similarly, many LGBTIQ Asian Americans have found themselves rejected by the Asian American churches in which they grew up. Michael Kim, a young gay Korean American man writing under a pseudonym,[22] has written about the pain of being alienated from the Korean church in his essay "Out

---

[16] Qwo-Li Driskill et al., "The Revolution Is for Everyone: Imagining an Emancipatory Future Through Queer Indigenous Critical Theories," in Driskill et al., *Queer Indigenous Studies*, 212.

[17] Farajajé-Jones, "Breaking Silence."

[18] Griffin, *Their Own Receive Them Not*.

[19] Douglas, *Sexuality and the Black Church*; Kelly Brown Douglas, "Black and Blues: God-Talk/Body-Talk for the Black Church," in Ellison and Douglas, *Sexuality and the Sacred*, 48–66.

[20] Victor Anderson, "African American Church Traditions," in Siker, *Homosexuality and Religion*, 48.

[21] Victor Anderson, "The Black Church and the Curious Body of the Black Homosexual," in Pinn and Hopkins, *Loving the Body*, 311.

[22] Kim writes that although he has "struggled somewhat endlessly" with the decision to use a pseudonym, he has concluded that anonymity is still "necessary at this stage in [his] life." Kim, "Out and About," 139.

and About: Coming of Age in a Straight White World." As Kim explains, the Korean church is the "locus of community-building and socialization."[23] For him to come out to his family and church community would be "quite literally, the ultimate failure—moral, social, and personal all at once." Coming out would "nullify everything good" that he has done, and it would be the "ultimate shame" upon his family.[24]

c. Disembodiment

Finally, many LGBTIQ people of color experience disembodiment, or a sense of bodily homelessness, as a result of their middle-space existence. On the one hand, queer bodies of color are often ignored—or fetishized—by the LGBTIQ community. On the other hand, queer bodies of color are often seen as deviant by racial and ethnic communities. As a result of this middle-space existence with respect to their bodies, many LGBTIQ people of color feel the need to reclaim and to affirm their embodied selves.

For example, in his essay "Holy Fuck," Ibrahim Abdurrahman Farajajé writes powerfully about the need for LGBTIQ African Americans to reclaim their bodies and to resist the erotophobia (that is, the fear of the erotic) that pervades the African American community.[25] Farajajé writes about the ways in which the queer body of color is "racialized, criminalized, and sexualized, all in potentially life-threatening ways."[26] One of the ways in which he reclaims his own body is through the

---

[23] Ibid., 146.

[24] Ibid., 147. Eunai Shrake, an Asian American professor at California State University Northridge and LGBTIQ ally, has written about the Korean church in her essay "Homosexuality and Korean Immigrant Protestant Churches." Shrake proposes three reasons for the rejection of homosexuality by such churches: (1) theological fundamentalism; (2) Confucian influences with respect to family roles; and (3) anxiety over American cultural liberalism. See Shrake, "Homosexuality and Korean Immigrant Protestant Churches," 147. To this I would add a fourth possible reason: the need for Asian American male pastors to assert their masculinity in the face of challenges to Asian manhood as "sexually deviant, asexual, effeminate, or dangerous." Christopher T. H. Liang et al., "Dealing with Gendered Racism and Racial Identity Among Asian American Men," in Liu, Iwamoto, and Chae, *Culturally Responsive Counseling*, 68.

[25] See farajajé-jones, "Holy Fuck."

[26] Ibid., 328.

practice of body piercing. For Farajajé, "piercing then becomes an act of resistance to physical erasure through creating sacred erotic rituals of inscription." Such piercings ultimately become "powerful reconfigurations of the body as icon."[27]

Black and womanist ethicists have also reflected upon the importance of embodiment issues for the LGBTIQ African American community. In her essay "The Dancing Mind: Queer Black Bodies in Academy and Church," Emilie M. Townes critiques how queer Black people—and African Americans in general—are seen as the "hypersexualized other / folk build legends around our imaged sexual prowess—lascivious hips, alluring breasts, big and bigger penises / that we know how to use better than others—or better than most / because we are a hot, black hot people, and we are only looking for the next lay, the next conquest, the next victim."[28] For Townes, the answer is "to try to refuse to be a part of this mess and be about the business of crafting moral thought that is . . . not terrified of my body, our bodies that carry our past, our present, our future."[29]

Queer Asian American theologians have also written about the spiritual need to affirm their bodies. I have written about how many gay Asian American men experience a profound sense of alienation with respect to their bodies as a result of the sexual racism within the gay male community. In my essay "'I Am Yellow and Beautiful': Reflections on Queer Asian Spirituality and Gay Male Cyberculture," I note that many gay Asian men are rendered invisible (or, on the other hand, fetishized) in the gay male online world. For example, the phrase "No fats, no femmes, no Asians" is "virtually a mantra in personal ads."[30] Indeed, David Eng, a gay Asian professor at the University of Pennsylvania, has written in his book *Racial Castration: Managing Masculinity in Asian America* about

---

[27] Ibid., 333–34.

[28] Townes, "The Dancing Mind," 7.

[29] Ibid., 12–13. Indeed, Kelly Brown Douglas has argued that Black homophobia is a function of white culture "equating blackness with sexual deviance." That is, the Black community has been eager to "sever the link between such deviance and blackness" and this has resulted in Black homophobia. Douglas, *Sexuality and the Black Church*, 97.

[30] Cheng, "'I Am Yellow and Beautiful,'" 5.

how Asian men are portrayed as the "antithesis of manhood, of masculinity." They are either "effeminate closet queens like Charlie Chan" or "homosexual menaces like Fu Manchu."[31]

In order to heal these experiences of sexual racism, the gay Asian American theologian Leng Lim has written about finding God through the exploration of his own body and those of others through erotic touch. For example, in "Webs of Betrayal, Webs of Blessings," Lim writes about finding a "community of brothers and sisters" at the Body Electric School of erotic massage.[32] Similarly, in his essay "Exploring Embodiment," Lim writes about his experiences with understanding the body as a temple. In that essay, Lim describes giving a lesbian a full-body massage as "sacramental erotic play." As a gay man, he was able to be fully present with her precisely because her body was so unfamiliar to him. For Lim, the "body is the vessel for experiencing/exploring God."[33]

Finally, the gay Latino theologian Vincent Cervantes has written about the need to affirm radical embodiment through the notion of promiscuous incarnation.[34] In his reading of the Mexican novel *El vampiro de la colonia Roma* by the writer Luis Zapata, which is about the adventures of an out, gay, and proud hustler in Mexico City, Cervantes affirms the importance of "excess, indiscriminate, and uninhibited sexuality" in the "reworking of the relationship of divinity to flesh." By viewing the gay hustler as a christological figure, Cervantes argues for the centrality of promiscuous incarnation—that is, an "excess and indiscriminate divine love"—for both God and for ourselves.[35]

---

[31] David L. Eng, *Racial Castration: Managing Masculinity in Asian America* (Durham, NC: Duke University Press, 2001), 1. Travis S. K. Kong has argued that "white men seem to express the norm and the ideal of 'masculinity,'" whereas Asian men "always seem inferior—poor imitations or undesireable [sic] deviations." Travis S. K. Kong, "Sexualizing Asian Male Bodies," in Seidman, Fischer, and Meeks, *Introducing the New Sexuality Studies*, 88.

[32] Lim, "Webs of Betrayal," 236.

[33] Leng Leroy Lim, "Exploring Embodiment," in Ragsdale, *Boundary Wars*, 70, 73.

[34] For more about Cervantes' discussion of "promiscuous incarnation" and the work of Laurel Schneider on this topic, see chapter four above.

[35] Cervantes, "Hustling the Divine," 1, 15.

3. Middle Spaces and Rainbow Theology

The idea of the "middle space" is important to rainbow theology. Middle spaces resist the monochromatic notion of "staying home." That is, they resist the fiction that there is ever a fixed "home" for LGBTIQ people of color. As we have seen in the previous section, LGBTIQ people of color often experience a deep sense of metaphorical homelessness with respect to race and sexuality, to spirituality, and to one's own body. They are, in effect, strangers in their own land and in their own bodies. Ironically, this notion of homelessness is actually a central theme in Christian theology.

For example, Jesus Christ, as one who is both fully divine and fully human, exists in a middle space. That is, he belongs neither solely to the divine world, nor solely to the human world. The incarnation, in which the Word became flesh, was a moment in which God dissolved the binary divide between divinity and humanity. Indeed, as Jesus mentions in the gospels, "the Son of Man has nowhere to lay his head."[36] He exists in a middle space, and he is metaphorically homeless.

The Greek word for homelessness, *astateō*, means to have "no fixed abode."[37] Paul uses this term in his first letter to the Corinthians to describe how he is "homeless" in the larger context of his physical sufferings for Christ. Paul and the other apostles are "fools for the sake of Christ," and yet they continue to bless, endure, and speak kindly to others.[38] (The opposite of *astateō* is *endēmeō*, which means to be "at home with the Lord," which Paul mentions in his second letter to the Corinthians.)[39]

Homelessness is an important theme in the Bible. Whether it is the homelessness of Noah and his family during the flood, or the wanderings of Abraham and Sarah, or the wilderness and exile experiences of the ancient Israelites, the middle-space

---

[36] Matthew 8:20; Luke 9:58.

[37] Gerhard Kittel, ed., *Theological Dictionary of the New Testament*, vol. 1, trans. Geoffrey W. Bromiley (Grand Rapids, MI: Wm. B. Eerdmans, 1964), 503 ("*astateō*").

[38] 1 Corinthians 4:11–13.

[39] 2 Corinthians 5:8.

condition of homelessness is central to the biblical experience. In fact, within the larger narrative of Christian theology, all human being are homeless. That is, we are not yet truly home with God; we currently exist in a middle space of being caught between the Fall and the Second Coming. We are in this world, but not of it.

The theme of middle spaces also appears in contemporary theological reflections. For example, a number of contemporary Asian American theologians have written about the middle-space social location of Asian Americans as being neither fully Asian, nor fully American. For example, the Korean American theologian Sang Hyun Lee, a professor emeritus at Princeton Theological Seminary, has written *From a Liminal Place: An Asian American Theology*, which focuses on the notion of liminality. According to Lee, Asian Americans are located in the "peripheral location" of "liminal space." The central task for those who occupy this space is to resist demoralization and to instead "exercise the creative potentials of liminality in spite of marginalization."[40]

Similarly, the late Korean American theologian Jung Young Lee from Drew University Theological School has written about the theme of marginality. In his book *Marginality: The Key to Multicultural Theology*, Lee writes about the middle-space notions of in-between, in-both, and in-beyond, and how these notions reflect the experience of Asian Americans.[41]

The notion of middle space is also at the heart of queer theology. As I have argued in my book *Radical Love*, queer theology centers around the dissolution of binaries, particularly with respect to sexuality and gender identity (that is, bisexuality as a dissolution of straight/gay boundaries; transgender as

---

[40] Lee, *From a Liminal Place*, 181.

[41] See Lee, *Marginality*. An Yountae, a Korean Argentinian doctoral student at Drew University, has published an article from a Deleuzian perspective that "re-envision[s] 'home' for twenty-first century nomadic subjects who inhabit an ambiguous space of interstitiality." An Yountae, "Decolonizing Home: Re-Envisioning Nomadic Identities at the Border of Globalization," *Apuntes* 31, no. 2 (2011): 68–77. For a queer reading of Gilles Deleuze's work, see Chrysanthi Nigianni and Merl Storr, eds., *Deleuze and Queer Theory* (Edinburgh, UK: Edinburgh University Press, 2009).

a dissolution of male/female boundaries; intersex as a dissolution of men/women boundaries).[42] Thus, the queer categories of bisexuality, transgender, and intersex occupy middle spaces. As we have seen, LGBTIQ people of color also occupy middle spaces, but this time with respect to the binary poles of race and sexuality.

So where is God in all this? How can we understand the queer of color experience of middle spaces to be a divine blessing and not a curse? One of the gifts of middle-space existence—no matter how painful it might feel—is that it helps us to recognize that only in God can we find our true homes. As Christians, we are called to look toward the horizon of last things, and thus we are *all* sojourners on this earth. Although we may think we have found "home" in a given community or with particular people, in fact we exist in a middle space, eschatologically speaking. To think otherwise—for example, as the religious right has done with elevating so-called "family values" above all other values—is in fact idolatry.

Thus, in their experience of middle spaces, queer people of color are gifted with a constant reminder that they are still awaiting their true home in God. Often, when we think of "home," we think of being with others who are just like us. Ironically, this can close us off from the rest of the world. Such a limited notion of "home" actually inhibits our ability to reach out to those who are radically—or even not so radically—different from us. The experience of metaphorical homelessness can be a helpful corrective that can help us to venture outside of our safety zones of conformity and engage with the richness that is the world.[43] That is the gift of middle spaces, and that is the gift of rainbow theology.

---

[42] See Cheng, *Radical Love*, 9–11.

[43] As Roger Sneed has written, the Black queer body exists in a place of "betwixt and betweeness" that is a "new way of being that has not yet been defined or described." For Sneed, this liminal place is ultimately "a joy, not a burden." See Sneed, "Dark Matter."

4. Summary

In sum, the theme of middle spaces is central not only for LGBTIQ people of color, but also with respect to queer theory and Christian theology. Because they are caught in between the binary of race and sexuality, queer people of color experience a profound sense of metaphorical homelessness with respect to their social location, their spirituality, as well as their bodies. But this experience, as painful as it may seem, is in fact a window into the divine nature of God.

By focusing on the experiences of LGBTIQ people of color, rainbow theology helps to enrich Christian theological reflection as a whole. Specifically, the rainbow theme of middle spaces—and the notion of metaphorical homelessness—removes us from our comfort zones and helps us to reach out to those who are different from us. Rainbow theology reminds all of us that only in God can we find our true homes.

Study Questions

1. How have you experienced middle spaces in your own life? What middle spaces do you occupy?

2. How do queer people of color experience middle spaces with respect to the binaries of race and sexuality?

3. What are some examples from queer Black, queer Asian American, queer Latina/o, and Two-Spirit Indigenous theologies that relate to middle spaces? What is the relationship between embodiment and middle spaces?

4. What role does homelessness play in Christian theology? How are middle spaces—that is, places of metaphorical homelessness—manifested in contemporary theologies?

5. Describe how God is working in your own life with respect to the rainbow theme of middle spaces.

For Further Study

Middle Spaces and Queers of Color
- Anzaldúa, *Borderlands/La Frontera*
- Boykin, *One More River to Cross*
- Fung, "Looking for My Penis"
- Hoang, "The Resurrection of Brandon Lee"
- Muñoz, *Disidentifications*
- Wat, "Preserving the Paradox"

Middle Spaces and Queer of Color Theologies
- Cheng, "Gay Asian Masculinities and Christian Theologies"
- Diaz, "*Nepantla* as Indigenous Middle Space"
- Driskill et al., "The Revolution Is for Everyone"
- Monroe, "Between a Rock and a Hard Place"
- Villalobos, "Bodies *Del Otro Lado*"

Spiritual Homelessness
- Anderson, "The Black Church and the Curious Body of the Black Homosexual"
- Douglas, *Sexuality and the Black Church*
- Farajaje-Jones, "Breaking Silence"
- Griffin, *Their Own Receive Them Not*
- Kim, "Out and About"

Disembodiment
- Cervantes, "Hustling the Divine"
- Cheng, "'I Am Yellow and Beautiful'"
- farajajé-jones, "Holy Fuck"
- Lim, "Exploring Embodiment"
- Lim, "Webs of Betrayal"
- Townes, "The Dancing Mind"

Middle Spaces and Rainbow Theology
- An, "Decolonizing Home"
- Cheng, *Radical Love*
- Lee, *From a Liminal Space*
- Lee, *Marginality*
- Sneed, "Dark Matter"

Chapter 9

Mediation

In July of 2012, I attended a national conference of LGBTIQ Asian Americans in Washington, D.C. The conference was an amazing experience. It spanned three days, and some 350 LGBTIQ Asian Americans and allies from across the country attended dozens of events, ranging from workshops to plenary panels to a spoken word performing arts festival to a festive banquet that was emceed by the Asian American actress Tamlyn Tomita.

In addition to the conference events, there were also separate gatherings of interest groups, such as parents of queer Asian Americans and queer South Asians. There was also a visit to the White House for a briefing by Obama administration officials on issues of interest to the LGBTIQ Asian community, including immigration, international human rights, bullying, and HIV/AIDS.[1]

What impressed me deeply about this conference was the way in which it brought together so many people from around the country and created a space in which LGBTIQ Asian Americans could simply be themselves. For me, the conference was a powerful witness to the ways in which queer people of color served as mediators by gathering together people from

---

[1] See Cheng, "A Unicorn at the White House."

different contexts—the arts, social services, academia, campus activism, law, politics, and ministry—and, in the words of the prophet Isaiah, by creating a "new thing."[2]

One of the highlights of my time at the conference was a half-day gathering of queer Asians Americans of faith that took place before the conference events officially began. There were around a dozen of us at the gathering, and we were not only Christians, but also Hindus and Muslims. It was a powerful experience to hear similar stories from people of different faith traditions who were trying to reconciling their racial, sexual, and spiritual identities.

During the conference itself, there was also a workshop on LGBTIQ issues and Christian churches. Like the pre-conference interfaith gathering, this workshop was an amazing experience of mediation that brought together a broad spectrum of queer Asian American Christians and their family members. Some participants were deeply spiritual; others were deeply alienated from organized religion and even spirituality. What was special about the workshop, however, was that it provided a mediating space in which connections could be made across lines of difference.

For me, these two gatherings of queer Asian Americans of faith were wonderful examples of the third and final rainbow theme of mediation. The gatherings allowed the participants to reach outside of their own specific contexts and experience similarities as well as differences with other queer Asian Americans of faith. This chapter will examine how, more broadly speaking, the theme of mediation is manifested in the lives and theological reflections of LGBTIQ people of color.

1. Mediation and Queers of Color

The queer of color experience is marked by *mediation*. That is, queer people of color are constantly gathering—that is, bringing together—disparate strands in their lives, whether it might be different languages, different forms of expression,

---

[2] Isaiah 43:19.

transnational experiences, and/or other LGBTIQ people of color. Perhaps this mediation is a byproduct of LGBTIQ people of color constantly living with multiplicity (that is, with multiply co-constituted oppressions) or in middle spaces (that is, in a state of metaphorical homelessness with respect to race and sexuality, spirituality, and their bodies). Regardless of the rationales or reasons for this mediation, however, LGBTIQ people of color often end up being agents of creative transformation.

The theme of mediation with respect to different languages can literally be seen, for example, in the writings of the lesbian Latina writer Gloria Anzaldúa. In her writings, Anzaldúa fuses together Spanish and English to create a new language. She writes that "change, *evolución, enriquecimiento de palabras nuevas por invención o adopción* have created variants of Chicano Spanish, *un Nuevo lenguaje.*"[3] For her, "Chicano Spanish is not incorrect, it is a living language."[4] This fusing together of languages can also be seen in the writings of the Two-Spirit Indigenous scholar Qwo-Li Driskill, who uses non-transliterated Cherokee words in the essay "*Asegi Ayetl.*"[5]

Queer of color discourse also involves mediation through the weaving together of different forms of expression beyond that of prose. For example, the queer Asian Canadian anthology *Rice: Explorations into Gay Asian Culture and Politics* includes not just essays, but also photographs, short stories, poetry, drawings, personal ads, an interview, and the transcript of a roundtable discussion.[6] One of the leading scholars of the queer of color critique movement, José Esteban Muñoz of New York University, brings together various examples of performance—from drag shows to reality TV to strip clubs—as examples for his scholarship.[7]

---

[3] Anzaldúa, *Borderlands, La Frontera,* 77. That is, "change, evolution, enrichment of new words for invention or adoption have created variants of Chicano Spanish, a new language."

[4] Ibid.

[5] Qwo-Li Driskill, "*Asegi Ayetl*: Cherokee Two-Spirit People Reimaging Nation," in Driskill et al., *Queer Indigenous Studies,* 97–112.

[6] See Song Cho, ed., *Rice: Explorations into Gay Asian Culture and Politics* (Toronto, ON: Queer Press, 1998).

[7] See Muñoz, *Disidentifications*; José Esteban Muñoz, *Cruising Utopia: The Then and There of Queer Futurity* (New York: New York University Press, 2009).

This kind of rhetorical mediation—that is, the weaving together of different forms of expression—also occurred during the July 2012 national LGBTIQ Asian American conference that I described above. There were many different kinds of expression at the conference beyond the typical conference panels and talks. These forms of expression included art, photography, dance, music, and stand-up comedy. Furthermore, the substantive content of the presentations at the conference were extremely diverse, and they included academic, religious, political, artistic, and activist discourses.

Mediation also happens when LGBTIQ people of color gather across transnational borders. This has been made possible with technological advances that allow people to gather together through cyberspace in the privacy and safety of their own homes. For example, for over a decade I have coordinated the Queer Asian Spirit (QAS) network, an email listserv of over 150 LGBTIQ people of Asian descent and allies from around the world who are interested in issues of religion and spirituality.[8] One of the strengths of the QAS listserv is that it serves as a resource for people who need referrals or help no matter where they may be geographically. QAS is, quite literally, a space of mediation.

Finally, the theme of mediation can also be seen whenever LGBTIQ people of color come together to form their own gatherings and organizations. The act of mediation—that is, coming together, despite differences, in order to form relationships and to create change—is an extremely powerful experience. For example, the gay Black activist Keith Boykin writes: "In the black gay community I found a support group, if not a family, willing to love me and accept my love for them regardless of our differences."[9]

Boykin's experience is echoed in the writings of Ann Yuri Uyeda, an Asian American lesbian, who documents her transformative experience of being in a space with some 170

[8] Queer Asian Spirit, accessed January 3, 2013, http://www.queerasianspirit.org.

[9] Boykin, *One More River to Cross*, 28.

other Asian American lesbians for the first time in 1989 at a retreat of the Asian Pacific Lesbian Network. Uyeda writes about how gathering with her queer Asian sisters literally allowed herself to come into existence: "We created ourselves as queer API women in a culture that otherwise would ignore or erase our contributions, identities, and our very presence."[10]

Indeed, themes of mediation and coalition-building are central to the queer of color critique movement. In their recent book, *Strange Affinities: The Gender and Sexual Politics of Comparative Racialization*, Grace Kyungwon Hong and Roderick A. Ferguson propose a strategy of "comparative racialization" that allows for mediation and coalition building, but without falling into the traps of essentialism.[11] That is, Hong and Ferguson argue that LGBTIQ people of color are able to come together across differences of race, gender, and sexuality without reinforcing essentialist categories. Rather than relying upon fixed notions of identity, they suggest that queer people of color can organize around similarities and differences in how they are valued or devalued. This allows different groups to build coalitions, consistent with the notion of mediation, but without perpetuating the illusion of fixed categories.[12]

The gift of mediation—particularly in terms of coming together and creating queer of color spaces—ultimately allows LGBTIQ people of color to bridge the multiplicities and middle spaces in which they exist. In the words of Eric Wat, queer people of color are called to "find that third side of the street where we can grow, find our voices, learn about ourselves, and educate others about who we are." Queer people of color need to find this "third side of the street" so that they can eventually join the LGBTIQ community as well as communities of color

---

[10] Ann Yuri Uyeda, "All at Once, All Together: One Asian American Lesbian's Account of the 1989 Asian Pacific Lesbian Network Retreat," in Lim-Hing, *The Very Inside*, 119.

[11] See Hong and Ferguson, *Strange Affinities*.

[12] See Hong and Ferguson, "Introduction." For an example of theological dialogue between the LGBTIQ Asian American and Black communities, see Patrick S. Cheng, "From a 'Far East Coast Cousin': Queer Asian Reflections on Roger A. Sneed's *Representations of Homosexuality*," *Black Theology: An International Journal* 10, no. 3 (2012): 292–300.

on "both sides of the street."[13] Through mediation, LGBTIQ people of color become agents of transformation and change.

2. Mediation and Queer of Color Theologies

The rainbow theme of mediation—that is, gathering together disparate sources that would normally not be seen as belonging together—appears throughout the writings of the LGBTIQ theologians of color who were discussed in the first part of this book. These writings can be organized into at least three categories of mediation: (1) interdisciplinary mediation; (2) transnational mediation; and (3) interfaith mediation. In each of these three categories, queer of color theologians have woven together disparate sources that are not normally associated with the theological enterprise. Although some may use the derogatory term "syncretism" to characterize this weaving together of sources,[14] I prefer to use the term mediation, which, as we will see in the following section, recalls God's mediating work of reconciliation in salvation history.

a. Interdisciplinary Mediation

First, queer of color theologians have used interdisciplinary sources in their work. Emilie Townes, the Black lesbian ethicist and newly-appointed dean of Vanderbilt University Divinity School, draws extensively from literature in her work. In her 2011 lecture, "The Dancing Mind," she reflects upon Toni Morrison's notion of the "dancing mind" (that is, a peaceful state of "an open mind when it engages another equally open one") as a form of mediation. According to Townes, it is often through the dancing mind of "books and essays and lectures and sermons and papers" that people meet "for the first, if not the only time and way."[15] Thus, the dancing mind of scholarship is often a form of mediation for queer people of color and our allies.

---

[13] Wat, "Preserving the Paradox," 80.

[14] For a positive view of syncretism in the context of Asian feminist theologies, see Chung Hyun Kyung, *Struggle to Be the Sun Again: Introducing Asian Women's Theology* (Maryknoll, NY: Orbis Books, 1990), 113.

[15] Townes, "The Dancing Mind," 6.

Townes' language dances on the page; she uses flowing language as a way of mediating between the normally rigid categories of theology, ethics, and poetry. For example, Townes urges scholars to reject the "scholarship of death and destruction that is so terrified of the complexity of existence that it shapes answers before even hearing the questions." She urges scholars to embrace "the curve of our hips / the arch of our backs / the slow swing in our walks / the glide of our fingers / the fire in our eyes / the coil of our hair / the deep moans and shouts of our ecstasies / the bottomless welling cries of our sorrows / the slow bend of our smiles / the precision of our minds / the sass of our talk."[16]

Other queer of color theologians have also used interdisciplinary sources in their work. For example, Roger Sneed, the gay Black ethicist at Furman University, has not only drawn upon gay Black men's literature in his work, but he also quotes from gay men's internet hook-up ads to illustrate the construction of Black gay masculinities. In his book *Representations of Homosexuality*, Sneed has excerpted "snapshots" of profiles from Manhunt.net and BGCLive.com to illustrate how some gay Black men "embrace their alternative constructions of black gay male identity."[17]

I have also drawn upon interdisciplinary sources from the online world in my work on sexual racism in the gay male community and how it impacts Asian American men of color. For example, in my essay "'I Am Yellow and Beautiful,'" I cite posts from Grindr, the online hookup app, as well as the work of Richard Fung, the gay Asian Canadian film theorist, on the absence of Asian American bodies in gay pornography.[18]

Vincent Cervantes, the gay Latino theologian and doctoral student at the University of Southern California, has used

---

[16] Ibid., 12.

[17] Sneed, *Representations of Homosexuality*, 166, 172. One such profile reads: "WWE1981 / Agenda: . . . / Men with meaty calf muscles and masculine looking hands, definitely say hi :-) / Be emotionally mature, in decent shape, and reasonably intelligent please. Thanks. I can be shy, so say hello :-) / Please note. If you measure your self-worth by the size of your dick, I don't want to know you in any capacity. / 27 | Athletic | Brown / Dark Brown | Bottom/Vers." Sneed, *Representations of Homosexuality*, 168.

[18] See Cheng, "'I Am Yellow and Beautiful.'"

literature as a source for his theological reflection. In his essay "Hustling the Divine," Cervantes engages in a reading of a gay novel from 1979 about the adventures of a young gay hustler in Mexico City to construct a theology of promiscuous incarnation from a "seemingly non-theological novel."[19] Cervantes also has a blog, *jot(e)ología*, which uses multimedia sources in his reflections on a Latino queer postcolonial theology.[20]

Finally, as noted above, Qwo-Li Driskill, a Cherokee Two-Spirit professor of English at Texas A&M University, uses interdisciplinary sources in her/his work. In her/his essay *"Asegi Ayetl,"* Driskill uses the Cherokee language as well as specialized language fonts. S/he does this work of "reimagining and reclaiming our cultural memories" in order to "uncover . . . stories that have been forgotten or ignored."[21]

b. Transnational Mediation

Second, queer of color theologians have used transnational sources as a form of geographical mediation in their work. By contrast with most white queer theologians, these theologians do not limit themselves to the experiences of LGBTIQ people in the United States or Western Europe. Rather, they draw from the experiences of queer people of color from around the world.

We see this, for example, in the work of Jojo, a queer Black religious scholar who is also known as Kenneth Hamilton. In his search for an authentic "African queer ancestry,"[22] Jojo draws upon nineteenth-century narratives about same-sex acts in precolonial East Africa as well as contemporary African scholarship about LGBTIQ issues. Jojo concludes that anti-LGBTIQ discourse in Africa was actually imported by Western Christian missionaries and was not indigenous to Africa. Indeed, more work needs to be done about the transnational connections between the United States and Africa, particularly in light of

---

[19] Cervantes, "Hustling the Divine," 1.

[20] *jot(e)ología*, accessed on January 3, 2013, http://joteologia.blogspot.com.

[21] Driskill, *"Asegi Ayetl,"* 111.

[22] Jojo, "Searching for Gender-Variant East African Spiritual Leaders," 127.

the antigay legislation that is being proposed in countries such as Uganda, as well as the resistance by many African Christians to LGBTIQ issues. The anthology *Other Voices, Other Worlds: The Global Church Speaks Out on Homosexuality* is a helpful resource for pro-LGBTIQ perspectives from Kenya, Nigeria, Uganda, and South Africa.[23]

We also see transnational mediation in the work of queer Asian American theologians. As noted above, Michael Campos, the gay Filipino American theologian, has used transnational sources such as Tagalog film as well as Roman Catholic religious processions in the Philippines in his work.[24] Similarly, Lai-shan Yip, the queer doctoral student from Hong Kong at the Graduate Theological Union, has drawn upon voices of Catholic lesbians from Hong Kong (that is, *nu-tongzhi*) in her scholarship.[25] Joseph Goh and Yuenmei Wong, who are both queer scholars from Malaysia and who have done graduate work in the United States, draw extensively upon the experiences of LGBTIQ Malaysians in their work.[26] In December 2012, the Queer Asian Spirit website published the inaugural issue of its online journal, the *Queer Asian Spirit E-Zine*, which featured contributions from LGBTIQ people of Asian descent from Australia, Malaysia, the Philippines, Singapore, and the United States.[27]

Queer Latin American theologians such as Marcella Althaus-Reid, Hugo Córdova Quero, and André Musskopf also use transnational sources as a form of mediation in their scholarship. Althaus-Reid famously begins her book *Indecent Theology* by describing the scent of women lemon vendors from the streets of Buenos Aires who do not wear underwear.[28] Córdova Quero

---

[23] Brown, *Other Voices, Other Worlds*.

[24] Campos, "The *Baklâ*," 167.

[25] See Yip, "Listening to the Passion."

[26] See Goh, "*Mak Nyah* Bodies as Sacred Sites"; Goh, "The Word Was *Not* Made Flesh"; Wong, "Islam, Sexuality, and the Marginal Positioning of *Pengkids*."

[27] See *Queer Asian Spirit E-Zine* 1 (December 2012), accessed January 3, 2013, http://bit.ly/YeGNM7.

[28] Althaus-Reid, *Indecent Theology*, 1–4.

cites the work of international non-governmental organizations such as the National Union of Sex Workers of Argentina in his scholarship.[29] And Musskopf has used popular culture—including popular music—from Brazil to construct his queer Brazilian theology.[30] (It should be noted that the very existence of queer Latin American theologians challenges the categories set out in Part I of this book. Because they live and work outside of the borders of the United States, they are not technically Latina/o. Nevertheless, their work is highly relevant to rainbow theology.)

Finally, Two-Spirit Indigenous scholarship also draws upon transnational sources in its work. The anthology *Queer Indigenous Studies* includes not just perspectives from North America, but also perspectives from New Zealand[31] and Samoa.[32] Such works aside, it might actually be argued that *all* Two-Spirit Indigenous studies are transnational because, by definition, they deal with the cross-border relationships between settler colonizers (such as the United States) and Indigenous nation-states that had existed on this land prior to the arrival of such colonizers.

Thus, instead of limiting their sources only to United States voices on the one hand, or only to international voices on the other hand, LGBTIQ theologians of color and religious studies scholars of color have crossed national borders in their theological reflection.

c. Interfaith Mediation

Third, queer of color theologians have engaged in interfaith mediation in their work. For example, the lesbian womanist theologian Renée Hill has argued for the importance of a "multireligious, multidialogical" approach for doing theologies. In her essay, "Disrupted/Disruptive Movements," Hill

---

[29] See Córdova Quero, "The Prostitutes Also Go into the Kingdom of God."

[30] See André S. Musskopf, "Ungraceful God: Masculinity and Images of God in Brazilian Popular Culture," *Theology and Sexuality* 15, no. 2 (2009): 145–57.

[31] Michelle Erai, "A Queer Caste: Mixing Race and Sexuality in Colonial New Zealand," in Driskill et al., *Queer Indigenous Studies*, 66–80.

[32] Dan Taulapapa McMullin, "*Fa'afafine* Notes: On Tagaloa, Jesus, and Nafanua," in Driskill et al., *Queer Indigenous Studies*, 81–94.

writes that "Black Christian theologies cannot afford *not* to be in dialogue with other religious traditions"—that is, traditions such as "Islam, African-derived traditional religions (including Santeria, Akan, Yoruba, and Vodun), Buddhism, Judaism, and Humanism." In particular, Hill argues that Black Christian theologies should be "knocked off-center," even if it means calling our "theological foundations into question."[33]

I, too, have written about the importance of non-Christian religious traditions in the lives of many LGBTIQ Asian Americans. In my essay "Reclaiming Our Traditions, Rituals, and Spaces," I have argued for the importance of "reclaiming the Asian spiritual traditions of our ancestors," whether this takes the form of meditating, reading sacred philosophical texts, practicing yoga, or performing sacred drum rituals. For me, these acts of mediating across religious traditions constitute a recognition of the "diversity of the Body of Christ."[34]

Queer Latina/o religious scholars have also written about the ways in which LGBTIQ people of color have reclaimed non-Christian faith traditions in their lives. For example, Salvador Vidal-Ortiz, the gay Latino professor at American University, has written an essay about the practice of Santería in the lives of LGBTIQ Latina/os in New York City. His essay, "Sexuality and Gender in Santería," addresses a number of different ethnic groups, including queer people of Puerto Rican, Cuban, and Mexican American descent.[35]

Finally, the Indigenous scholar Andrea Smith—who has written about the intersections of queer theory and Native studies—has engaged in interfaith mediation in her book *Native Americans and the Christian Right*. In that book, Smith writes about her involvement with both Native activism and evangelical Christianity and how surprising new alliances may arise out of these two communities.[36]

---

[33] Hill, "Disrupted/Disruptive Movements," 147.

[34] Cheng, "Reclaiming Our Traditions, Rituals, and Spaces," 236–37.

[35] See Vidal-Ortiz, "Sexuality and Gender in Santería."

[36] See Smith, *Native Americans and the Christian Right*, 272.

In sum, interfaith mediation is an important theme for queer theologians of color. The mediating work of such theologians can be summarized in a powerful prayer written by the queer Black theologian Ibrahim Abdurrahman Farajajé. In that poem, "Invocation of Remembrance, Healing, and Empowerment in a Time of AIDS," Farajajé recalls the devastation of genocide and disease, and he makes connections between Two-Spirit Indigenous, queer Black, queer Asian American, and queer Latina/o communities of color. He begins by making a sacred space "in honor of our Mother Earth" and by inviting "our ancestors to be present with us, bringing their spirit of resistance." He then recalls the sufferings of various communities of color and asks for healing through the mediation of their queer ancestors of color.

Farajajé closes with the following prayer: "May they walk with us and bring us new strength for the struggle. May they tenderly wipe the tears from our eyes. May they guide us to see that, as lesbian, gay, bisexual, and transgendered people of color, our walk is together. May they remind us that we are the tribes of the moon, a sacred people."[37]

3. Mediation and Rainbow Theology

The rainbow theme of mediation—that is, bringing together sources, voices, and perspectives that are normally not seen as belonging together—is an important one for rainbow theology. Some people might criticize the theme of mediation (particularly with respect to interfaith mediation) as a form of syncretism that threatens the integrity of Christian theology. As the Korean feminist theologian Chung Hyun Kyung has argued, however, we must "move away from our imposed fear of losing Christian identity" and focus on what really matters: the survival and liberation of our communities.[38]

---

[37] Elias Farajaje-Jonez, "Invocation of Remembrance, Healing, and Empowerment in a Time of AIDS," in Cherry and Sherwood, *Equal Rites*, 25–27.

[38] Chung, *Struggle to Be the Sun Again*, 113.

Indeed, mediation can help us to resist the monochromatic theme of "selecting sides," or stubbornly aligning oneself with a particular position and refusing to reach out to others who might have a different position. It may be that the first two rainbow themes—multiplicity and middle spaces—inevitably lead queer people of color to a place of mediation (as opposed to a place of selecting sides). That is, perhaps the experience of constantly living in a place of fragmentation and meta-phorical homelessness (that is, multiplicity and middle spaces) ultimately requires a reaching out across differences (that is, mediation) for the sake of one's own survival and liberation.[39]

Mediation is a key theme in Christian theology. Jesus Christ, who brought together both the divine and the human in the incarnation, is the mediator *par excellence*. That is, in the act of the Word becoming flesh, God broke down the boundaries of divine vs. human and gathered together the two realms that, prior to the incarnation, had not been brought together. In fact, the theme of covenant—which is so central to both the Hebrew scriptures and the Christian Bible—centers around the notion of mediation. As a result of a covenant, God mediates between Godself and humanity. God reaches out beyond Godself and, as a result, we reach out beyond ourselves. Both God and humanity are transformed.

The Greek word for mediator is *mesitēs*. Jesus Christ is described in the First Letter to Timothy as the *"eis mesitēs,"* or the "one mediator between God and humankind."[40] And drawing upon the notion of covenant, Jesus Christ is described in the Letter to the Hebrews not just as a mediator of a new

---

[39] From a postcolonial perspective, the theme of mediation is closely connected with the theme of middle spaces. Take, for example, the postcolonial theorist Homi Bhabha's notion of middle space as the stairwell in between two floors. Mediation occurs in this hybrid space when both the upper floor (the colonizer) and the lower floor (the colonized) meet and are mutually transformed. See Homi K. Bhabha, *The Location of Culture* (London: Routledge, 1994), 5. In the queer Asian context, Chong Kee Tan has written about how hybridity has allowed for a "creative renegotiation of local cultural norms" by the Taiwanese gay and lesbian movement. Chong Kee Tan, "Transcending Sexual Nationalism and Colonialism," in *Post-Colonial, Queer: Theoretical Intersections*, ed. John C. Hawley (Albany: State University of New York Press, 2001), 124.

[40] 1 Timothy 2:5.

covenant (that is, *"diathēkēs kainēs mesitēs estin"*), but rather the mediator of a better covenant (that is *"kreittonos estin diathēkēs mesitēs"*).[41]

Despite the fact that this word appears only a few times in the New Testament, it has a rich history of usage in Hellenistic culture as well as in Christian theology.[42] For example, Jon M. Robertson, a professor of historical theology at Multnomah University in Portland, Oregon, has traced the theme of Christ as mediator in the early church from Origen to Eusebius of Caesarea to Athanasius of Alexandria.[43] Similarly, Byung-Ho Moon, a professor of theology at Chongshin University in Seoul, South Korea, has written about the theme of Christ as a mediator of the law in John Calvin's writings.[44]

So where is God in all this? How is the rainbow theme of mediation a gift for LGBTIQ people of color? For those of us who walk the Christian path, we are called to a life of reconciliation. That is, we are called to model ourselves after the reconciling work of God in Jesus Christ. Through the incarnation, God reconciled the divine with the human. Queer people of color engage in a similar act of reconciliation whenever they live out the rainbow theme of mediation and bring together interdisciplinary, transnational, and interfaith concerns.

Rainbow theology is, at its core, a mediating concept. That is, it recognizes the "strange affinities" among LGBTIQ people of color without reinforcing essentialist notions of race, sexuality, and spirit. In other words, rainbow theology serves a mediating function by creating a space in which LGBTIQ people of color can bring together their races, sexualities, and spiritualities, and

---

[41] Hebrews 9:15, 8:6.

[42] Gerhard Kittel, ed., *Theological Dictionary of the New Testament*, vol. 4, trans. Geoffrey W. Bromiley (Grand Rapids, MI: Wm. B. Eerdmans, 1967), 598–624 ("*mesitēs*").

[43] See Jon M. Robertson, *Christ as Mediator: A Study of the Theologies of Eusebius of Caesarea, Marcellus of Ancyra and Athanasius of Alexandria* (Oxford, UK: Oxford University Press, 2007).

[44] See Byung-Ho Moon, *Christ the Mediator of the Law: Calvin's Christological Understanding of the Law as the Rule of Living and Life-Giving* (Bletchley, UK: Paternoster, 2006).

yet still honor their individual differences.[45] By living authentically as mediators in this rainbow space, queer people of color can live out their divine calling to transform the world.

4. Summary

In sum, the rainbow theme of mediation—like those of multiplicity and middle spaces—is a window into the divine. Queer people of color engage in mediation by bringing together different languages, different forms of expression, transnational experiences, and other LGBTIQ people of color. And, as we have seen, queer of color theologians engage in mediation through interdisciplinary, transnational, and interfaith reflections. Mediation can be understood as a reflection of the divine imperative for reconciliation. By mediating across all kinds of differences—including, but not limited to, differences arising out of race, sexuality, and spirit—LGBTIQ people of color serve as divine reconcilers, which is at the heart of the gospel message.

---

[45] There are a number of ecclesial spaces that allow for this bridging. The Unity Fellowship Church is one such space. Several works have been written about the power of this space for LGBTIQ people of color. See, for example, Aryana Bates, "Liberation in Truth: African American Lesbians Reflect on Religion, Spirituality, and Their Church," in Thumma and Gray, *Gay Religion*, 221–37; and Tonyia M. Rawls, "Yes, Jesus Loves Me: The Liberating Power of Spiritual Acceptance for Black Lesbian, Gay, Bisexual, and Transgender Christians," in *Black Sexualities: Probing Powers, Passions, Practices, and Policies*, ed. Juan Battle and Sandra L. Barnes (New Brunswick, NJ: Rutgers University Press, 2010), 327–52.

Study Questions

1. How have you experienced mediation in your own life? Define, in your own words, what mediation means to you.

2. How do queer people of color experience mediation with respect to bringing together different languages, forms of discourse, people, and/or transnational geographies?

3. What are some examples from queer Black, queer Asian American, queer Latina/o, and Two-Spirit Indigenous theologies that relate to mediation?

4. How is mediation manifested in contemporary theologies?

5. Describe how you might understand God in terms of mediation.

For Further Study

Mediation and Queers of Color
- Anzaldúa, *Borderlands/La Frontera*, 77
- Boykin, *One More River to Cross*, 28
- Cho, *Rice*
- Hong and Ferguson, "Introduction"
- Muñoz, *Cruising Utopia*
- Muñoz, *Disidentifications*
- Tan, "Transcending Sexual Nationalism and Colonialism"
- Uyeda, "All at Once, All Together"
- Wat, "Preserving the Paradox"

Interdisciplinary Mediation
- Cervantes, "Hustling the Divine"
- Cheng, "'I Am Yellow and Beautiful'"
- Driskill, "*Asegi Ayetl*"
- Sneed, *Representations of Homosexuality*
- Townes, "The Dancing Mind"
- Villalobos, "Bodies *Del Otro Lado*"

Transnational Mediation
- Brown, *Other Voices, Other Worlds*
- Campos, "The *Baklâ*"
- Erai, "A Queer Caste"
- Goh, "*Mak Nyah* Bodies as Sacred Sites"
- Goh, "The Word Was *Not* Made Flesh"
- Jojo, "Searching for Gender-Variant East African Spiritual Leaders"
- McMullin, "*Fa'afafine* Notes"
- Yip, "Listening to the Passion of Catholic *nu-tongzhi*"

Interfaith Mediation
- Cheng, "Reclaiming Our Traditions, Rituals, and Spaces"
- Farajaje-Jonez, "Invocation of Remembrance"
- Hill, "Disrupted/Disruptive Movements"
- Vidal-Ortiz, "Sexuality and Gender in Santería"
- Wong, "Islam, Sexuality, and the Marginal Positioning of *Pengkids*"

Mediation and Rainbow Theology
- Bantum, *Redeeming Mulatto*
- Moon, *Christ the Mediator of the Law*
- Robertson, *Christ as Mediator*

Chapter 10

Example: Rainbow Christology

W hat would a concrete example of rainbow theology look like? In Part I of this book, we examined queer of color theologies, including the writings of queer Black, queer Asian American, queer Latina/o, and Two-Spirit Indigenous theologians and religion scholars from the last twenty years. In Part II, we brought together these theologies under the notion of rainbow theology. In particular, we examined three themes of rainbow theology: (1) multiplicity; (2) middle spaces; (3) and mediation.

This chapter will close Part II of this book by constructing a *rainbow christology*—that is, a queer of color theological reflection on the preexistence, lifespan, and second coming of Jesus Christ—and by demonstrating how such a christology might enrich the theological world. It is my hope that this chapter on rainbow christology can serve as a model for future incarnations of rainbow theology.

As an initial matter, let us begin with the "Rainbow Christ." Both the rainbow and Jesus Christ are symbols of God's covenant with humanity. In Genesis 9, God places the rainbow in the sky as a sign of God's promise never again to destroy all living creatures through flooding.[1] This covenant binds God

---

[1] See Genesis 9:8–17.

and humanity together. Similarly, Jesus Christ—at least for those of us who walk the Christian path—is the covenant *par excellence* between God and humanity. The incarnation of the Word reverses the Fall, and it also binds together the divine and human realms in a new way. Thus, the rainbow and Jesus Christ are closely connected through the concept of the covenant.

Assuming that it makes sense to talk about the Rainbow Christ, what would it look like to draw upon other faith traditions and their uses of the rainbow to deepen our understanding of Jesus Christ? For example, what if we used the Buddhist notion of the rainbow body—that is, a person who has reached enlightenment and thus dissolves into light—to think about the Rainbow Christ's ascension into heaven?[2] Or what if we used the Yoruba deity of Oxumaré—the divine rainbow serpent who is the "patron of gender-variant, homosexual, and bisexual persons"—to think about the Rainbow Christ as an "androgynous deity" who is a divine protector of LGBTIQ people of color?[3] These two examples are just some of the exciting possibilities for a rainbow christology that draws upon other faith traditions.

Let us now look more closely at the three rainbow themes of (1) multiplicity, (2) middle spaces, and (3) mediation from the perspective of a rainbow christology. Recall that rainbow theology is not just a theology about queer people of color, but rather it is also a more expansive way of thinking about theology from the unique social location of LGBTIQ people of color.

1. Multiplicity

The first rainbow theme is that of *multiplicity*. A rainbow christology emphasizes the many ways in which Jesus Christ is a symbol of multiplicity—and not singularity—in the Bible and in Christian theology. The fact that there are not one, but four, canonical gospels—and many more apocryphal gospels— reminds us that the Rainbow Christ cannot be reduced to a

---

[2] See Whelan, *Book of Rainbows*, 120.

[3] Randy P. Conner, *Blossom of Bone: Reclaiming the Connections Between Homoeroticism and the Sacred* (New York: HarperSanFrancisco, 1993), 245–46.

singular narrative. The fact that there are multiple gospels about the events of Jesus Christ's life highlights the importance of interpretation and multiple perspectives. And the fact that the four canonical gospels simply do not agree on many points shows that there are multiple ways of constructing a rainbow christology.[4]

Multiplicity is also an important theme from the Pauline perspective. In his First Letter to the Corinthians, Paul describes the Body of Christ as having many (that is, *"polus"* in the Greek) members.[5] What are the implications with respect to the multiplicity of the Body of Christ? Assuming that there are queer persons who are members of this body—and we do know that queer Christians exist—then the body of Jesus Christ is also queer. Furthermore, assuming that there are queers of color who are members of this body (and there are), then Jesus Christ is also a queer person of color. This point is highlighted by the womanist theologian M. Shawn Copeland in her book *Enfleshing Freedom*, in which she claims that "the only body capable of taking us *all* in as we are with all our different body marks—certainly including the mark of homosexuality—is the body of Christ."[6]

In fact, we know that Jesus Christ is a queer person of color because he appears to us in a multiplicity of ways. In the parable of the sheep and the goats in Matthew 25, Jesus Christ says that he takes the form of the least among us: the hungry, the thirsty, the stranger, the naked, the sick, and the imprisoned. That is, we minister to Jesus whenever we have ministered to the "least of these."[7] And we fail to minister to Jesus whenever we do not minister to the least of these, which includes homeless trans youth of color, queer sex workers of color, and others. According to the recent report "The State of

---

[4] For the differences among the gospel narratives, see Kurt Aland, ed., *Synopsis of the Four Gospels* (New York: United Bible Societies, 1982).

[5] 1 Corinthians 12:14 ("Indeed, the body does not consist of one member but of many.").

[6] Copeland, *Enfleshing Freedom*, 83.

[7] Matthew 25:40: "And the king will answer them, 'Truly I tell you, just as you did it to one of the least of these who are members of my family, you did it to me.'"

Gay and Transgender Communities of Color in 2012," LGBTIQ people of color "face high rates of unemployment or underemployment, overall lower rates of pay, higher rates of poverty, and a greater likelihood of being uninsured."[8] Indeed, Jesus Christ is a queer person of color.

Jesus Christ's own question to his disciples—"Who do you say that I am?"[9]—shows that Jesus *anticipated* a multiplicity of christologies from his followers. Indeed, the twentieth century has seen a proliferation of contextual christologies from around the world, including feminist, Black, womanist, African, Asian American, Asian, Latina/o, Latin American, and Indigenous christologies. Furthermore, these christologies are not limited to racial and ethnic perspectives; there are also christologies that reflect upon Jesus in the context of non-Christian religious traditions such as Islam, Buddhism, Hinduism, Shamanism, and African traditional religions.[10]

These contextual christologies also include LGBTIQ perspectives. Robert E. Shore-Goss, a queer theologian and ordained minister in the Metropolitan Community Churches, has published two important queer christologies: *Jesus Acted Up: A Gay and Lesbian Manifesto* and *Queering Christ: Beyond Jesus Acted Up.*[11] Thomas Bohache, also an ordained MCC minister, has published his own queer christology, *Christology from the Margins.*[12] Theodore W. Jennings, a bisexual biblical scholar and theologian at Chicago Theological Seminary, has published *The Man Jesus Loved: Homoerotic Narratives from the New Testament.*[13]

The task for a rainbow christology is to take this multiplicity of christologies—racial/ethnic and sexual—and bring them together.

---

[8] Dunn and Moodie-Mills, "The State of Gay and Transgender Communities of Color in 2012," 1.

[9] Mark 8:29; Matthew 16:15.

[10] See Martien E. Brinkman, *The Non-Western Jesus: Jesus as* Bodhisattva, Avatara, Guru, *Prophet, Ancestor or Healer?* (London: Equinox, 2009).

[11] See Robert Goss, *Jesus Acted Up: A Gay and Lesbian Manifesto* (New York: HarperSanFrancisco, 1993); Robert E. Goss, *Queering Christ: Beyond Jesus Acted Up* (Cleveland, OH: Pilgrim Press, 2002).

[12] See Thomas Bohache, *Christology from the Margins* (London: SCM Press, 2008).

[13] See Theodore W. Jennings, *The Man Jesus Loved: Homoerotic Narratives from the New Testament* (Cleveland, OH: Pilgrim Press, 2003).

That is, rather than seeing these categories of christologies as separate or mutually exclusive works, LGBTIQ theologians of color are called to juxtapose racial/ethnic christologies with sexual christologies and have them interrogate each other. That is, queer theologians must ask: how does a racial/ethnic christology silence—or lift up—queer issues? Conversely, how does a sexual christology silence—or lift up—racial or ethnic issues?

One example of the juxtaposition of racial/ethnic and sexual issues can be found in my rainbow christology, *From Sin to Amazing Grace: Discovering the Queer Christ.*[14] In that book, I propose seven models of the queer Christ for LGBTIQ people and our allies. (These models are the Erotic Christ, the Out Christ, the Liberator Christ, the Transgressive Christ, the Self-Loving Christ, the Interconnected Christ, and the Hybrid Christ.) At the end of each of the seven christological chapters, I use the voices of queer Asian Americans to illustrate each model.

I have also explored the theme of religious multiplicity in my queer theological work. For example, I have argued that the Chinese Buddhist bodhisattva Kuan Yin can be understood as a reflection of the queer Asian Christ. That is, Kuan Yin is *queer* because s/he changes gender as a male in India to a female in China. S/he is *Asian* because of his/her roots in Asian spirituality. And s/he is *Christ*-like because s/he serves a soteriological function by helping others reach enlightenment. Thus, Kuan Yin can be seen as a reflection of the queer Asian Christ.[15]

2. Middle Spaces

The second rainbow theme is that of *middle spaces*. A rainbow christology emphasizes the ways in which Jesus Christ—like LGBTIQ people of color—occupies a middle space, such as the middle space between the divine and human realms. Like queer people of color, who are often "caught" in between the racism of the LGBTIQ community and the queerphobia of communities

---

[14] See Cheng, *From Sin to Amazing Grace.*
[15] See Cheng, "Kuan Yin."

of color, Jesus Christ is metaphorically homeless. He has "no place to lay his head."[16] Akin to the situation of queer people of color, Jesus Christ proclaimed that "prophets are not without honor except in their own country and in their own house."[17] In other words, prophets are honored everywhere except in their own homes.

To be in a middle space is to experience homelessness. A rainbow christology acknowledges how Jesus Christ literally takes the form of the homeless in the parable of the sheep and the goats.[18] That is, Jesus Christ is found wherever there are the hungry, thirsty, stranger, naked, sick, or imprisoned—all marks of those who are homeless. Sadly, there is an overwhelming need for shelters that serve LGBTIQ youth—many of whom are queer people of color—such as Sylvia's Place in New York City.[19]

As a recent series of reports has noted, transgender people of color experience homelessness at a much higher rate than the general population. For example, 14 percent of transgender Asian Americans (nearly twice the rate of the general population) have experienced homelessness at some point in their lives—as have 41 percent of transgender African Americans (over five times), 27 percent of transgender Latina/os (nearly four times), and 40 percent of transgender American Indians and Alaskan Natives (nearly six times).[20] There is also the experience of Two-Spirit Indigenous people, who have noted that settler colonialism resulted in the theft of their ancestral lands and has left them literally without a sovereign homeland.[21]

---

[16] Matthew 8:20; Luke 9:58.

[17] Matthew 13:57; see also Mark 6:4: "Prophets are not without honor, except in their hometown, and among their own kin, and in their own house."

[18] See Matthew 25:31–46.

[19] Sylvia's Place is a ministry of the Metropolitan Community Church of New York.

[20] See National Gay and Lesbian Task Force, "Injustice at Every Turn: A Look at Asian American, South Asian, Southeast Asian, and Pacific Islander Respondents"; National Gay and Lesbian Task Force, "Injustice at Every Turn: A Look at Black Respondents"; National Gay and Lesbian Task Force, "Injustice at Every Turn: A Look at Latino/a Respondents"; and National Gay and Lesbian Task Force, "Injustice at Every Turn: A Look at American Indian and Alaskan Native Respondents."

[21] Driskill et al., "The Revolution Is for Everyone," 212.

A rainbow christology would also focus on bisexual, transgender, and intersex christologies. These three christologies focus on middle-space identities, which are the letters of the queer alphabet (that is, the "BTI") that are often forgotten or ignored. As we have seen, bisexuals occupy a middle space with respect to sexual orientation, transgender people occupy a middle space with respect to gender identity, and intersex people occupy a middle space between biological sex. There have been a number of such middle-space christologies written, including Laurel Dykstra's "Jesus, Bread, Wine and Roses: A Bisexual Feminist at the Catholic Worker" (bisexual);[22] Justin Tanis' *Trans-Gendered: Theology, Ministry, and Communities of Faith* (transgender);[23] and Susannah Cornwall's *Sex and Uncertainty in the Body of Christ: Intersex Conditions and Christian Theology* (intersex).[24]

The challenge of rainbow christologies—as with the case of the queer christologies mentioned in the previous section—is to hold these bisexual, transgender, and intersex christologies in tension with racial/ethnic minority christologies. That is, a rainbow christology must highlight how bisexual, transgender, and intersex people of color occupy yet another additional middle space in light of their complex racial, sexual, and gender identities.[25]

Finally, a rainbow christology of middle spaces would focus on the theme of disembodiment and the need for queer people of color to reclaim their own bodies. Many LGBTIQ people of color experience a great sense of alienation about their bodies.

---

[22] Laurel Dykstra, "Jesus, Bread, Wine and Roses: A Bisexual Feminist at the Catholic Worker," in *Blessed Bi Spirit: Bisexual People of Faith*, ed. Debra R. Kolodny (New York: Continuum, 2000), 78–88.

[23] Justin Tanis, *Trans-Gendered: Theology, Ministry, and Communities of Faith* (Cleveland, OH: Pilgrim Press, 2003), 138–43.

[24] Susannah Cornwall, *Sex and Uncertainty in the Body of Christ: Intersex Conditions and Christian Theology* (London: Equinox, 2010).

[25] For a discussion about recognizing the "colors" of bisexual, pansexual, and polysexual perspectives in religious studies, see Ibrahim Abdurrahman Farajajé, "Foreword," in *Sexuality, Religion, and the Sacred: Bisexual, Pansexual and Polysexual Perspectives*, ed. Loraine Hutchins and H. Sharif Williams (Abingdon, UK: Routledge, 2012), x–xi.

Because they exist in the middle space between white queer communities and straight and cisgender communities of color, queer people of color often need to find ways to affirm their beauty and desirability. For example, I have written about the challenges faced by gay Asian men with sexual racism in cyberspace.[26] From a christological perspective, I have argued that the gay Asian male body—"like the bruised and battered corpus of Jesus Christ on the cross"—might serve an "atoning purpose" by "decolonizing the racism and homophobia of contemporary Christian theologies."[27]

In the same way that Jesus Christ exercised hospitality with the outsiders of his day, a rainbow christology would find ways in which queer people might exercise sexual hospitality with queer people of color by welcoming them into spaces in which they would otherwise be excluded. For example, Kathy Rudy, in her book *Sex and the Church*, has proposed a sexual ethic of hospitality that would affirm the goodness of practices such as sex with strangers as well as communal sex.[28] Perhaps Rudy's sexual ethic of hospitality can be the basis upon which LGBTIQ people of color are welcomed into the arms of the Rainbow Christ.

3. Mediation

The third and final rainbow theme is that of *mediation*. As discussed previously, mediation is about bringing together disparate sources that normally do not belong together, whether that relates to interdisciplinary, transnational, interfaith, or other issues. In the same way that Jesus Christ serves as a mediator between the divine and the human realms, the queer person of color becomes a manifestation of the incarnate Word through the act of mediation.

A rainbow christology of mediation not only focuses on how

---

[26] Cheng, "Gay Asian Masculinities and Christian Theologies," 542.

[27] Ibid., 540.

[28] Kathy Rudy, *Sex and the Church: Gender, Homosexuality, and the Transformation of Christian Ethics* (Boston, MA: Beacon Press, 1997), 126, 128.

Jesus Christ brought together God and humanity through the incarnation, but it also focuses on how Jesus Christ brought together both clean and unclean people through his ministry. That is, Jesus Christ served as a mediator by drawing to himself people who were considered to be outsiders under the Levitical laws (for example, lepers, bleeding women, people possessed with demons, and so on). In today's world, LGBTIQ people of color are often seen as outsiders because of their racial and sexual identities.

As discussed earlier, the rainbow theme of mediation involves the weaving together of theological reflection with unconventional means of expression, such as photographs or film. A rainbow christology would do this by drawing upon theological sources that involve images instead of words. One such source is the photography of the gay Spanish photographer Fernando Bayona González. González created a series of fourteen photographs called *Circus Christi*, or Circle of Christ, that focuses on a gay Hispanic Christ.

Many of the photographs in the *Circus Christi* series have homoerotic undertones. For example, a photograph called "The Doubt of Thomas" shows a young man putting his fingers into the bloody side wound of a handsome shirtless Jesus while a third man watches. Another photograph called "Crucifixion" shows a man of color lying unconscious, with his shirt open and unbuttoned, in the middle of a street with his arms extended as if he were crucified.

González received death threats as a result of his exhibit, and the exhibit was forced to close early because of protests from Roman Catholic and other groups.[29] Perhaps it was the mediating function of Gonzalez's art—that is, bringing together theology with homoerotic photography—that created the fury about this exhibit. Other examples of this kind of mediating art might include the gay Latino artist Andres Serrano's *Piss Christ*, a photograph of a crucifix immersed in urine, that created a

---

[29] Kitt Cherry, "Protests End Gay Jesus Exhibit in Spain," *Jesus in Love Blog* (November 6, 2010), accessed January 3, 2013, http://bit.ly/Seyhro.

furor when it was originally exhibited and was destroyed in April 2011 by an assailant in France.[30]

Other sources for a rainbow christology of mediation might include the work of the gay Latino poet Emanuel Xavier. In his collection of poems entitled *If Jesus Were Gay*, Xavier writes about wanting to be "Just Like Jesus": "Just like Jesus, / I want to be nestled half-naked against your chest / Sanctified, / even after my time spent with over a dozen lovers / Claiming your spirit when I come / Baptize you with the promise of salvation / Just like Jesus, / I simply want to live before I die."[31] Timothy Liu is another queer poet of color who has written about christological themes; he has written poems entitled "His Body Like Christ Passed In and Out of My Life" and "On Hearing the Seven Last Words of Christ."[32]

Finally, a rainbow christology could also draw upon comedic language as a possible theological source. The queer Asian American comedian Margaret Cho has imagined Jesus Christ coming back and responding to the queerphobia of the religious right. She writes: "I want Jesus to come back and say, 'That's not what I meant!' Where's the kindness? Where's the compassion? Where's the charity? . . . . They need to read Matthew 6:5, where it says, 'Shut the fuck up.' (That's the King James Version, by the way.)"[33]

All of these sources manifest the rainbow theme of mediation to the extent that they are works by LGBTIQ people of color who bring together theological ideas about Jesus Christ with unconventional forms of theological expression, whether through photography, poetry, or comedy.[34]

---

[30] Cecile Brisson, "Andres Serrano's Controversial Photograph 'Piss Christ' Destroyed In France," *Huffington Post* (April 18, 2011), accessed January 3, 2013, http://huff.to/ie8DY5.

[31] Emanuel Xavier, "Just Like Jesus," in Xavier, *If Jesus Were Gay*, 2.

[32] Timothy Liu, "His Body Like Christ Passed In and Out of My Life," in Timothy Liu, *Vox Angelica* (Cambridge, MA: Alice James Books, 1992), 15; Timothy Liu, "On Hearing the Seven Last Words of Christ," in Timothy Liu, *For Dust Thou Art* (Carbondale: Southern Illinois University Press, 2005), 50.

[33] Margaret Cho, *I Have Chosen to Stay and Fight* (New York: Riverhead Books, 2005), 185.

[34] As noted in chapter two above, the Black queer ethicist Roger A. Sneed has used music and science fiction in his recent works. See Sneed, "Dark Matter."

4. Rainbow Christ Prayer

I close this chapter with a prayer to the Rainbow Christ. In 2012, I collaborated with my friend Kitt Cherry, a lesbian minister with the Metropolitan Community Churches, to write this prayer. It is based upon the seven models of the queer Christ in my book *From Sin to Amazing Grace: Discovering the Queer Christ.*[35] In this prayer, each christological model is assigned a color of the rainbow, and the prayer can be used in a variety of liturgical and devotional contexts.

This prayer is an example of rainbow christology because it manifests each of the three rainbow themes. First, the prayer manifests *multiplicity* because it provides seven different models of the Rainbow Christ. Each christological model focuses on a different—yet equally valid—aspect of the Rainbow Christ. Second, the prayer manifests *middle spaces* because it refuses to locate the Rainbow Christ within a single model. That is, the Rainbow Christ is metaphorically homeless in this prayer because there is no one model that is "home." Third, the prayer manifests *mediation* because it weaves together traditional theological concepts with liturgical and poetic language.

Here is the Rainbow Christ prayer:

> *Rainbow Christ, you embody all the colors of the world. Rainbows serve as bridges between different realms: heaven and earth, east and west, queer and non-queer. Inspire us to remember the values expressed in the rainbow flag of the lesbian, gay, bisexual, transgender, and queer community.*
>
> • *Red is for life, the root of spirit. Living and Self-Loving Christ, you are our Root. Free us from shame and grant us the grace of healthy pride so we can follow our own inner light. With the red stripe in the rainbow, we give thanks that God created us just the way we are.*
>
> • *Orange is for sexuality, the fire of spirit. Erotic Christ, you are our Fire, the Word made flesh. Free us from exploitation and*

---

[35] Cheng, *From Sin to Amazing Grace*, 67–145.

grant us the grace of mutual relationships. With the orange stripe in the rainbow, kindle a fire of passion in us.

- *Yellow is for self-esteem, the core of spirit. Out Christ, you are our Core. Free us from closets of secrecy and give us the guts and grace to come out. With the yellow stripe in the rainbow, build our confidence.*

- *Green is for love, the heart of spirit. Transgressive Outlaw Christ, you are our Heart, breaking rules out of love. In a world obsessed with purity, you touch the sick and eat with outcasts. Free us from conformity and grant us the grace of deviance. With the green stripe in the rainbow, fill our hearts with untamed compassion for all beings.*

- *Blue is for self-expression, the voice of spirit. Liberator Christ, you are our Voice, speaking out against all forms of oppression. Free us from apathy and grant us the grace of activism. With the blue stripe in the rainbow, motivate us to call for justice.*

- *Violet is for vision, the wisdom of spirit. Interconnected Christ, you are our Wisdom, creating and sustaining the universe. Free us from isolation and grant us the grace of interdependence. With the violet stripe in the rainbow, connect us with others and with the whole creation.*

- *Rainbow colors come together to make one light, the crown of universal consciousness. Hybrid and All-Encompassing Christ, you are our Crown, both human and divine. Free us from rigid categories and grant us the grace of interwoven identities. With the rainbow, lead us beyond black-and-white thinking to experience the whole spectrum of life.*

Rainbow Christ, you light up the world. You make rainbows as a promise to support all life on earth. In the rainbow space, we can see all the hidden connections between sexualities, genders, and races. Like the rainbow, may we embody all the colors of the world! Amen.

Summary

A rainbow christology focuses on the themes of multiplicity, multiple spaces, and mediation. Although a rainbow christology arises out of the social location and embodied experiences of queer people of color, it does not speak only to LGBTIQ people of color. Ultimately, a rainbow christology must speak to—and engage in dialogue with—*all* people. Although it starts in a place of particularity, a rainbow christology ultimately morphs into the realm of universality. It is my hope that the outlines of a rainbow christology described in this chapter will encourage others to engage in future work in rainbow theology.

Study Questions

1. What is your christology? That is, who do you say that Jesus Christ is for you and/or your communities?

2. Name some ways in which the theme of multiplicity is reflected in rainbow christology. What has your experience been with multiple christologies?

3. Name some ways in which the theme of middle spaces is reflected in rainbow christology. How can Jesus Christ be understood as being literally and/or metaphorically homeless?

4. Name some ways in which the theme of mediation is reflected in rainbow christology. How might you bring together unconventional theological sources with your reflection upon Jesus Christ?

5. Which colors of the Rainbow Christ prayer speak the most to you? The least? Why or why not?

For Further Study

Rainbow Theology and Multiplicity

- Cheng, *From Sin to Amazing Grace*, 135
- Cheng, "Kuan Yin"
- Conner, *Blossom of Bone*, 245–46
- Copeland, *Enfleshing Freedom*
- Goss, *Queering Christ*, 253

Rainbow Theology and Middle Spaces

- Cheng, "Gay Asian Masculinities and Christian Theologies"
- Cornwall, *Sex and Uncertainty*
- Driskill et al., "The Revolution Is for Everyone"
- Dykstra, "Jesus, Bread, Wine and Roses"
- Farajajé, "Foreword"
- Rudy, *Sex and the Church*
- Tanis, *Trans-Gendered*

Rainbow Theology and Mediation

- Cho, *I Have Chosen to Stay and Fight*, 185
- Gonzalez, *"Circus Christi"*
- Liu, "His Body Like Christ Passed In and Out of My Life"
- Liu, "On Hearing the Seven Last Words of Christ"
- Serrano, "Piss Christ"
- Sneed, "Dark Matter"
- Xavier, "Just Like Jesus"

Conclusion

As I mentioned at the beginning of this book, I have had the privilege of serving as a mentor for the last three summers at the Human Rights Campaign Summer Institute. The HRC Summer Institute is a week-long gathering of fifteen doctoral and advanced masters' students who are doing work in LGBTIQ theology and/or religious studies. The program is run by Rebecca Alpert of Temple University, Ken Stone of the Chicago Theological Seminary, and Sharon Groves of the HRC Religion and Faith Program.

As a mentor at the HRC Summer Institute, I am responsible each year for facilitating a small group of five students.[1] The small group meets several times during the week as a time for checking in, for providing mutual support, and for teaching the ins and outs of academia to future scholars who will be doing work on LGBTIQ issues. It is also a space in which the participants can share their scholarly research with others and get encouragement and feedback.

During the summer of 2012, I was fortunate to experience my small group as a "rainbow space." Specifically, all six of us—that is, the five students and myself—self-identified as LGBTIQ/allied people of color, and all of us had scholarly interests that involved issues of race, sexuality, and spirituality to one degree or another. It was a wonderful way to experience our "strange affinities."[2] That is, we all shared a number of similarities in

---

[1] In 2012 and 2011, I served as a mentor at the HRC Summer Institute along with Kent L. Brintnall of the University of North Carolina at Charlotte and Heather White of the New College of Florida. In 2010, the three of us also served with Noach Dzmura, currently of the Star King School for the Ministry.

[2] See Hong and Ferguson, *Strange Affinities*.

terms of our identities as queers/allies of color, but we also had very different backgrounds and research interests.

For me, the small group was a great example of doing the work of rainbow theology. First, our small group experienced the rainbow theme of *multiplicity* in that we were from a variety of racial and ethnic backgrounds—African American, Asian American, and Latina/o—and we also had a variety of sexualities and gender identities. Second, we experienced the rainbow theme of *middle spaces* in that most of us straddled predominantly straight communities of color on the one hand and predominantly white LGBTIQ communities on the other. Finally, we experienced the rainbow theme of *mediation* in that we brought together a variety of interdisciplinary, transnational, and interfaith interests.

This book has been an attempt to articulate a rainbow theology based upon the experiences of LGBTIQ people of color. In Part I of the book, we looked systematically at four different strands of queer of color theologies. First, we looked at queer Black theologies with its themes of Black Church exclusion, reclaiming Black lesbian voices, and challenging Black liberation theologies. Second, we looked at queer Asian American theologies with its themes of Asian and Asian American church exclusion, critiquing LGBTIQ racism, and highlighting transnational perspectives. Third, we looked at queer Latina/o theologies with its themes of living on the borderlands, challenging machismo, and crossing literary and religious borders. Fourth, we looked at Two-Spirit Indigenous scholarship with its themes of resisting settler colonialism, recognizing Two-Spirit identities, and doing the work of allies.

In Part II of the book, we turned to the broader question of constructing a rainbow theology. That is, how might we rethink the broader enterprise of theology from the perspective of LGBTIQ people of color? What would happen if queers of color were at the center of theological reflection instead of at the margins? What if rainbow theology was not just about the theological experiences of LGBTIQ people of color, but it was actually a new way of doing theology? Accordingly, Part II of the book explored the three rainbow themes of (1) multiplicity, (2) middle spaces, and (3) mediation, and contrasted them with the monochromatic themes of (1) singularity, (2) staying home, and (3) selecting sides.

There is still much work to be done. For example, although we have tried to examine systematically the disparate strands of queer Black, queer Asian American, queer Latina/o, and Two-Spirit Indigenous theology and scholarship in Part I of the book, there are still many voices that are left out, such as LGBTIQ people of color who trace their heritage from the Caribbean, the Middle East, South and Southeast Asia, and the Pacific Islands. Other voices are also missing, such as queer people of color with disabilities, as well as mixed-heritage and multiracial queer people. And there is much more work to be done with respect to interfaith dialogue—not just from an Abrahamic perspective, but also with Eastern religions and philosophies—as well as ecotheological issues.

That being said, it is my hope that this book is simply the beginning of an extended conversation about the contributions of queer of color theologies to the broader theological discourse. It has been over a quarter of a century since I first came out of the closet as a gay Asian American man, and I feel that we may be finally moving—theologically speaking—from the monochromatic shades of Dorothy's and Toto's Kansas home into the Technicolor hues of Munchkinland and the Land of Oz. Perhaps the words of "Somewhere Over the Rainbow" will in fact be realized: "Somewhere over the rainbow / Skies are blue, / And the dreams that you dare to dream / Really do come true."[3]

---

[3] Harold Arlen and E.Y. Harburg, "Somewhere Over the Rainbow," 1939.

Bibliography

Adam, A. K. M., ed. *Handbook of Postmodern Biblical Interpretation*. St. Louis, MO: Chalice Press, 2000.

Adams, Carol J., and Marie M. Fortune, eds. *Violence Against Women and Children: A Christian Theological Sourcebook*. New York: Continuum, 1995.

Aizumi, Marsha, with Aiden Aizumi. *Two Spirits, One Heart: A Mother, Her Transgender Son, and Their Journey to Love and Acceptance*. Arcadia, CA: Peony Press, 2012.

Aland, Kurt, ed. *Synopsis of the Four Gospels*. New York: United Bible Societies, 1982.

Aldrich, Robert, ed. *Gay Life and Culture: A World History*. New York: Universe Publishing, 2006.

Althaus-Reid, Marcella. *Indecent Theology: Theological Perversions in Sex, Gender and Politics*. London: Routledge, 2000.

_____. "'Let Them Talk . . .!': Doing Liberation Theology from Latin American Closets." In Althaus-Reid, *Liberation Theology*, 5-17.

_____, ed. *Liberation Theology and Sexuality*. Aldershot, UK: Ashgate, 2006.

_____. *The Queer God*. London: Routledge, 2003.

_____. "Queer I Stand: Lifting the Skirts of God." In Althaus-Reid and Isherwood, *The Sexual Theologian*, 99-109.

Althaus-Reid, Marcella, and Lisa Isherwood, eds. *The Sexual Theologian: Essays on Sex, God, and Politics*. London: T&T Clark, 2004.

An Yountae. "Decolonizing Home: Re-Envisioning Nomadic Identities at the Border of Globalization." *Apuntes* 31, no. 2 (2011): 68-77.

Anderson, Lisa Ann. "Desiring to Be Together: A Theological Reflection on Friendship Between Black Lesbians and Gay Men." *Theology and Sexuality* no. 9 (September 1998): 59-63.

Anderson, Victor. "African American Church Traditions." In Siker, *Homosexuality and Religion*, 48-50.

_____. "The Black Church and the Curious Body of the Black Homosexual." In Pinn and Hopkins, *Loving the Body*, 297-312.

_____. "Deadly Silence: Reflections on Homosexuality and Human Rights." In Olyan and Nussbaum, *Sexual Orientation and Human Rights*, 185-200.

Anu. "Who Am I?" In Lim-Hing, *The Very Inside*, 19-21.

Anzaldúa, Gloria. *Borderlands/La Frontera: The New Mestiza*. 3rd ed. San Francisco, CA: Aunt Lute Books, 2007.

_____. *The Gloria Anzaldúa Reader*. Edited by AnaLouise Keating. Durham, NC: Duke University Press, 2009.

Aponte, Edwin David, and Miguel A. De La Torre, eds. *Handbook of Latina/o Theologies*. St. Louis, MO: Chalice Press, 2006.

Asanti, Ifalde Ta'shia. "Living with Dual Spirits: Spirituality, Sexuality and Healing in the African Diaspora." In Hutchins and Williams, *Sexuality, Religion and the Sacred*, 54-62.

Asencio, Marysol, ed. *Latina/o Sexualities: Probing Powers, Passions, Practices, and Policies*. New Brunswick, NJ: Rutgers University Press, 2010.

Ashcroft, Bill, Gareth Griffiths, and Helen Tiffin, eds. *Post-Colonial Studies: The Key Concepts*. London: Routledge, 2000.

"Asian Americans in the Marriage Equality Debate." *Amerasia Journal* 32, no. 1 (2006).

Bailey, Randall C., Tat-siong Benny Liew, and Fernando F. Segovia, eds. *They Were All Together in One Place?: Toward Minority Biblical Criticism.* Atlanta, GA: Society of Biblical Literature, 2009.

Baldwin, James. *The Cross of Redemption: Uncollected Writings.* Edited by Randall Kenan. New York: Vintage International, 2010.

_____. "To Crush a Serpent." In Baldwin, *Cross of Redemption,* 195–204.

Bantum, Brian. *Redeeming Mulatto: A Theology of Race and Christian Hybridity.* Waco, TX: Baylor University Press, 2010.

Barnard, Ian. *Queer Race: Cultural Interventions in the Racial Politics of Queer Theory.* New York: Peter Lang, 2004.

Bates, Aryana. "Liberation in Truth: African American Lesbians Reflect on Religion, Spirituality, and Their Church." In Thumma and Gray, *Gay Religion,* 221–37.

Battle, Juan, and Sandra L. Barnes. *Black Sexualities: Probing Powers, Passions, Practices, and Policies.* New Brunswick, NJ: Rutgers University Press, 2010.

Bay-Cheng, Laina Y. "The Social Construction of Sexuality: Religion, Medicine, Media, Schools, and Families." In McAnulty and Burnette, *Sex and Sexuality,* Volume 1, 203–28.

Beckford, Robert. "Does Jesus Have a Penis?: Black Male Sexual Representation and Christology." *Theology and Sexuality* 5 (September 1996): 10–21.

Beemyn, Brett Genny. "The Americas: From Colonial Times to the 20th Century." In Aldrich, *Gay Life and Culture,* 145–65.

Bérubé, Allan. *My Desire for History: Essays in Gay, Community, and Labor History.* Chapel Hill: University of North Carolina Press, 2011.

Bhabha, Homi K. *The Location of Culture.* London: Routledge, 1994.

Bohache, Thomas. *Christology from the Margins.* London: SCM Press, 2008.

Boisvert, Donald L., and Jay Emerson Johnson, eds. *Queer Religion: Volume I, Homosexuality in Modern Religious History.* Santa Barbara, CA: Praeger, 2012.

_____, eds. *Queer Religion: Volume II, LGBT Movements and Queering Religion.* Santa Barbara, CA: Praeger, 2012.

Boyer, Carl B. *The Rainbow: From Myth to Mathematics.* Princeton, NJ: Princeton University Press, 1987.

Boykin, Keith, ed. *For Colored Boys Who Have Considered Suicide When the Rainbow Is Still Not Enough: Coming of Age, Coming Out, and Coming Home.* New York: Magnus Books, 2012.

_____. *One More River to Cross: Black and Gay in America.* New York: Anchor Books, 1996.

Brinkman, Martien E. *The Non-Western Jesus: Jesus as Bodhisattva, Avatara, Guru, Prophet, Ancestor or Healer?* London: Equinox, 2009.

Brock, Rita Nakashima, Jung Ha Kim, Kwok Pui-lan, and Seung Ai Yang, eds. *Off the Menu: Asian and Asian North American Women's Religion and Theology.* Louisville, KY: Westminster John Knox Press, 2007.

Bronski, Michael. *A Queer History of the United States.* Boston, MA: Beacon Press, 2011.

Brown, Terry. *Other Voices, Other Worlds: The Global Church Speaks Out on Homosexuality.* New York: Church Publishing, 2006.

Busto, Rudy V. "Normally Queer?: An Asian American Religious Studies Response." Paper presented at the Human Rights Campaign Summer Institute, Vanderbilt University Divinity School, August 8, 2012.

Butler, Judith. *Gender Trouble.* New York: Routledge, 1990.

Campos, Michael Sepidoza. "The *Baklâ*: Gendered Religious Performance in Filipino Cultural Spaces." In Boisvert and Johnson, *Queer Religion II,* 167–91.

Carbado, Devon W., Dwight A. McBride, and Donald Weise, eds. *Black Like Us: A Century of Lesbian, Gay, and Bisexual African American Fiction.* Berkeley, CA: Cleis Press, 2002.

Carlin, Deborah, and Jennifer DiGrazia, eds. *Queer Cultures.* Upper Saddle River, NJ: Pearson Prentice Hall, 2004.

Carrette, Jeremy, and Mary Keller. "Religions, Orientation and Critical Theory: Race, Gender and Sexuality at the 1998 Lambeth Conference." *Theology and Sexuality* 11 (September 1999): 21–43.

Carton, Adrian. "Desire and Same-Sex Intimacies in Asia." In Aldrich, *Gay Life and Culture*, 303–31.

Castellanos, Mari E. "Barriers Not Withstanding: A Lesbianista Perspective." In Ragsdale, *Boundary Wars*, 197–207.

Cecil, Leslie, ed. *New Frontiers in Latin American Borderlands*. Newcastle upon Tyne, UK: Cambridge Scholars Publishing, 2012.

Cervantes, Vincent D. "Evolving Theologies: Rethinking Progressive Theology Along the Lines of Jotería Studies." Unpublished paper, 2012.

_____. "Hustling the Divine: Promiscuously Rethinking Sex, Flesh, and Incarnation in Luis Zapata's *El vampiro de la colonia Roma*." Unpublished paper, 2012.

Cheng, Patrick S. "From a 'Far East Coast Cousin': Queer Asian Reflections on Roger A. Sneed's Representations of Homosexuality." *Black Theology: An International Journal* 10, no. 3 (2012): 292–300.

_____. *From Sin to Amazing Grace: Discovering the Queer Christ*. New York: Seabury Books, 2012.

_____. "Galatians." In Guest et al., *Queer Bible Commentary*, 624–29.

_____. "Gay Asian Masculinities and Christian Theologies." *CrossCurrents* 61, no. 4 (December 2011): 540–48.

_____. "Hybridity and the Decolonization of Asian American and Queer Theologies." Postcolonial Theology Network, October 17, 2009. Accessed January 3, 2013. http://bit.ly/P8mLNi.

_____. "'I Am Yellow and Beautiful': Reflections on Queer Asian Spirituality and Gay Male Cyberculture." *Journal of Technology, Theology, and Religion* 2, no. 3 (June 2011): 1–21. Accessed January 3, 2013. http://bit.ly/jOCltG.

_____. "Kuan Yin: Mirror of the Queer Asian Christ." Unpublished paper, 2003. Accessed January 3, 2013. http://bit.ly/qyvGtk.

_____. "'Mr. Wong's Dong Emporium': Racism and the Gay Community." *Huffington Post,* September 28, 2011. Accessed January 3, 2013. http://huff.to/rlrTuG.

_____. "Multiplicity and Judges 19: Constructing a Queer Asian Pacific American Biblical Hermeneutic." *Semeia* 90/91 (2002): 119–33.

_____. *Radical Love: An Introduction to Queer Theology*. New York: Seabury Books, 2011.

_____. *The Rainbow Connection: Bridging Asian American and Queer Theologies*. Berkeley, CA: Center for Lesbian and Gay Studies in Religion and Ministry, 2011.

_____. "Reclaiming Our Traditions, Rituals, and Spaces: Spirituality and the Queer Asian Pacific American Experience." *Spiritus* 6, no. 2 (Fall 2006): 234–40.

_____. "Rethinking Sin and Grace for LGBT People Today." In Ellison and Douglas, *Sexuality and the Sacred*, 105–18.

_____. "Roundtable Discussion: Same-Sex Marriage." *Journal of Feminist Studies in Religion* 20, no. 2 (Fall 2004): 103–7.

_____. "A Three-Part Sinfonia: Queer Asian Reflections on the Trinity." In Fernandez, *New Overtures*, 173–91.

_____. "A Unicorn at the White House." *Huffington Post* (July 30, 2012). Accessed January 3, 2013. http://huff.to/Phq3d2.

Cherry, Kittredge, and Zalmon Sherwood, eds. *Equal Rites: Lesbian and Gay Worship, Ceremonies, and Celebrations*. Louisville, KY: Westminster John Knox Press, 1995.

Cho, Margaret. *I Have Chosen to Stay and Fight*. New York: Riverhead Books, 2005.

Cho, Song, ed. *Rice: Explorations into Gay Asian Culture and Politics*. Toronto, ON: Queer Press, 1998.

Chung Hyun Kyung. *Struggle to Be the Sun Again: Introducing Asian Women's Theology*. Maryknoll, NY: Orbis Books, 1990.

Cleaver, Richard. *Know My Name: A Gay Liberation Theology*. Louisville, KY: Westminster John Knox Press, 1995.

Coleman, Monica A, ed. *Ain't I a Womanist, Too?: Third Wave Womanist Religious Thought*. Minneapolis, MN: Fortress Press, forthcoming.

_____. "Invoking Oya: Practicing a Polydox Soteriology Through a Postmodern Womanist Reading of Tananarive Due's *The Living Blood*." In Keller and Schneider, Polydoxy, 186–202.

_____. *Making a Way Out of No Way: A Womanist Theology*. Minneapolis, MN: Fortress Press, 2008.

_____. "Roundtable Discussion: Must I Be Womanist?" *Journal of Feminist Studies in Religion* 22, no. 1 (Spring 2006): 85–96.

Comstock, Gary David. *A Whosoever Church: Welcoming Lesbians and Gay Men into African American Congregations*. Louisville, KY: Westminster John Knox Press, 2001.

Comstock, Gary David, and Susan E. Henking, eds. *Que(e)rying Religion: A Critical Anthology*. New York: Continuum, 1997.

Cone, James H., and Gayraud S. Wilmore, eds. *Black Theology: A Documentary History, Volume II, 1980–1992*. Maryknoll, NY: Orbis Books, 1993.

Conner, Randy P. *Blossom of Bone: Reclaiming the Connections Between Homoeroticism and the Sacred*. New York: HarperSanFrancisco, 1993.

Conner, Randy P., David Hatfield Sparks, and Mariya Sparks. *Cassell's Encyclopedia of Queer Myth, Symbol and Spirit*. London: Cassell, 1997.

Consolacion, Teddy. "Where I Am Today." In Kumashiro, *Troubling Intersections*, 83–85.

Constantine-Simms, Delroy. *The Greatest Taboo: Homosexuality in Black Communities*. Los Angeles, CA: Alyson Books, 2000.

Copeland, M. Shawn. *Enfleshing Freedom: Body, Race, and Being*. Minneapolis, MN: Fortress Press, 2010.

Corber, Robert J., and Stephen Valocchi, eds. *Queer Studies: An Interdisciplinary Reader*. Malden, MA: Blackwell, 2003.

Córdova Quero, Hugo. "Risky Affairs: Marcella Althaus-Reid Indecently Queering Juan Luis Segundo's Hermeneutical Circle Propositions." In Isherwood and Jordan, *Dancing Theology*, 207–18.

Córdova Quero, Martín Hugo. "Friendship with Benefits: A Queer Reading of Aelred of Rievaulx and His Theology of Friendship." In Althaus-Reid and Isherwood, *The Sexual Theologian*, 26–46.

_____. "The Prostitutes Also Go into the Kingdom of God: A Queer Reading of Mary of Magdala." In Althaus-Reid, *Liberation Theology*, 81–110.

Cornell, Michiyo. "Living in Asian America: An Asian American Lesbian's Address Before the Washington Monument (1979)." In Leong, *Asian American Sexualities*, 83–84.

Cornwall, Susannah. *Controversies in Queer Theology*. London: SCM Press, 2011.

_____. *Sex and Uncertainty in the Body of Christ: Intersex Conditions and Christian Theology*. London: Equinox, 2010.

Crawley, Ashon T. "Circum-Religious Performance: Queer(ed) Black Bodies and the Black Church." *Theology and Sexuality* 14, no. 2 (January 2008): 201–22.

Crowley, Paul. "An Ancient Catholic: An Interview with Richard Rodriguez." In Comstock and Henking, *Que(e)rying Religion*, 338–42.

Cruz-Malavé, Arnaldo, and Martin F. Manalansan. *Queer Globalizations: Citizenship and the Afterlife of Colonialism*. New York: New York University Press, 2002.

Daniels, Roger. *Coming to America: A History of Immigration and Ethnicity in American Life*. 2nd ed. New York: Harper Perennial, 2002.

de la Huerta, Christian. *Coming Out Spiritually: The Next Step*. New York: Jeremy P. Tarcher/Putnam, 1999.

De La Torre, Miguel A. "Beyond Machismo: A Cuban Case Study." In Ellison and Douglas, *Sexuality and the Sacred*, 221–38.

_____. "Confessions of a Latino Macho: From Gay Basher to Gay Ally." In De La Torre, *Out of the Shadows*, 59–75.

_____. *A Lily Among the Thorns: Imagining a New Christian Sexuality*. San Francisco, CA: Jossey-Bass, 2007.

_____, ed. *Out of the Shadows into the Light: Christianity and Homosexuality*. St. Louis, MO: Chalice Press, 2009.

De La Torre, Miguel A., Ignacio Castuera, and Lisbeth Meléndez Rivera. *A La Familia: Conversation About Our Families, the Bible, Sexual Orientation and Gender Identity*. Edited by Sharon Groves and

Rebecca Voelkel. Washington, DC: Human Rights Campaign Foundation, 2010.

Diaz, Michael A. "*Nepantla* as Indigenous Middle Space: Developing Biblical Reading Strategies for Queer Latina/os." DMin thesis, Episcopal Divinity School, 2012.

Díaz, Rafael M. *Latino Gay Men and HIV: Culture, Sexuality, and Risk Behavior.* New York: Routledge, 1998.

Douglas, Kelly Brown. "Black and Blues: God-Talk/Body-Talk for the Black Church." In Ellison and Douglas, *Sexuality and the Sacred*, 48–66.

_____. "The Black Church and the Politics of Sexuality." In Pinn and Hopkins, *Loving the Body*, 347–62.

_____. *Sexuality and the Black Church: A Womanist Perspective.* Maryknoll, NY: Orbis Books, 1999.

Driskill, Qwo-Li. "*Asegi Ayetl*: Cherokee Two-Spirit People Reimaging Nation." In Driskill et al., *Queer Indigenous Studies*, 97–112.

Driskill, Qwo-Li, Chris Finley, Brian Joseph Gilley, and Scott Lauria Morgensen. "Introduction." In Driskill et al., *Queer Indigenous Studies*, 1–28.

_____, eds. *Queer Indigenous Studies: Critical Interventions in Theory, Politics, and Literature.* Tuscon: University of Arizona Press, 2011.

_____. "The Revolution Is for Everyone: Imagining an Emancipatory Future Through Queer Indigenous Critical Theories." In Driskill et al., *Queer Indigenous Studies*, 211–21.

Duberman, Martin. *Stonewall.* New York: Plume, 1993.

Dunn, Melissa, and Aisha Moodie-Mills. "The State of Gay and Transgender Communities of Color in 2012" (April 13, 2012). Center for American Progress. Accessed January 3, 2013. http://bit.ly/IhiwY6.

Dykstra, Laurel. "Jesus, Bread, Wine and Roses: A Bisexual Feminist at the Catholic Worker." In Kolodny, *Blessed Bi Spirit*, 78–88.

Dynes, Wayne R., and Stephen Donaldson. *Asian Homosexuality.* New York: Garland Publishing, 1992.

Eaklor, Vicki L. *Queer America: A People's GLBT History of the United States.* New York: New Press, 2008.

Ellison, Marvin M., and Kelly Brown Douglas, eds. *Sexuality and the Sacred: Sources for Theological Reflection.* 2nd ed. Louisville, KY: Westminster John Knox Press, 2010.

Ellison, Marvin M., and Judith Plaskow, eds. *Heterosexism in Contemporary World Religion: Problem and Prospect.* Cleveland, OH: Pilgrim Press, 2007.

Eng, David L. *Racial Castration: Managing Masculinity in Asian America.* Durham, NC: Duke University Press, 2001.

Eng, David L., Judith Halberstam, and José Esteban Muñoz. "What's Queer About Queer Studies Now?" *Social Text* nos. 84–85 (2005): 1–17.

Eng, David L., and Alice Y. Hom. *Q&A: Queer in Asian America.* Philadelphia, PA: Temple University Press, 1998.

Erai, Michelle. "A Queer Caste: Mixing Race and Sexuality in Colonial New Zealand." In Driskill et al., *Queer Indigenous Studies*, 66–80.

Espín, Orlando O. *Grace and Humanness: Theological Reflections Because of Culture.* Maryknoll, NY: Orbis Books, 2007.

Fackre, Gabriel. *The Rainbow Sign: Christian Futurity.* Grand Rapids, MI: Wm. B. Eerdmans Publishing, 1969.

Farajajé, Ibrahim Abdurrahman. "Foreword." In Hutchins and Williams, *Sexuality, Religion and the Sacred*, x–xi.

Farajaje-Jones, Elias. "Breaking Silence: Toward an In-the-Life Theology." In Cone and Wilmore, *Black Theology II*, 139–59.

_____. "Invocation of Remembrance, Healing, and Empowerment in a Time of AIDS." In Cherry and Sherwood, *Equal Rites*, 25–27.

farajajé-jones, elias "Holy Fuck." In Kay, Nagle, and Gould, *Male Lust*, 327–35.

Farajaje-Jonez, Elias "Loving 'Queer': We're All a Big Mix of Possibilities of Desire Just Waiting to Happen," *In the Family* 6, no. 1 (Summer 2000): 14–21.

Fernandez, Eleazar S., ed. *New Overtures: Asian North American Theology in the 21st Century.* Upland, CA: Sopher Press, 2012.

Finley, Chris. "Decolonizing the Queer Native Body (and Recovering the Native Bull-Dyke): Bringing 'Sexy Back' and Out of Native Studies' Closet." In Driskill et al., *Queer Indigenous Studies*, 31–42.

Foster, David William, ed. *Chicano/Latino Homoerotic Identities*. New York: Garland Publishing, 1999.

Foulke, Mary L. "Coming Out as White/ Becoming White: Racial Identity Development as a Spiritual Journey." *Theology and Sexuality* 3, no. 5 (September 1996): 22–36.

Foulke, Mary L., and Renee L. Hill. "We Are Not Your Hope for the Future: Being an Interracial Lesbian Family Living in the Present." In Goss and Strongheart, *Our Families, Our Values*, 243–49.

Fung, Richard. "Looking for My Penis: The Eroticized Asian in Gay Video Porn." In Leong, *Asian American Sexualities*, 181–98.

Gamson, Joshua. "Must Identity Movements Self-Destruct?: A Queer Dilemma." In Carlin and DiGrazia, *Queer Cultures*, 279–303.

García, Ramón. "Priests." In Evans and Healey, *Queer and Catholic*, 129–32.

Garner, Darlene. "A Sample Service of Holy Union Based on the Tradition of Kwanzaa." In Cherry and Sherwood, *Equal Rites*, 94–100.

Girman, Chris. *Mucho Macho: Seduction, Desire, and the Homoerotic Lives of Latin Men*. Binghamton, NY: Harrington Park Press, 2004.

Goh, Joseph N. "*Mak Nyah* Bodies as Sacred Sites: Uncovering the Queer Body-Sacramentality of Malaysian Male-to-Female Transsexuals." *CrossCurrents* 62, no. 4 (December 2012): 512–21.

_____. "The Word Was *Not* Made Flesh: Theological Reflections on the Banning of *Seksualiti Merdeka* 2011." *Dialog: A Journal of Theology* 51, no. 2 (Summer 2012): 145–54.

Goss, Robert. *Jesus Acted Up: A Gay and Lesbian Manifesto*. New York: HarperSanFrancisco, 1993.

Goss, Robert E. *Queering Christ: Beyond Jesus Acted Up*. Cleveland, OH: Pilgrim Press, 2002.

Goss, Robert E., and Amy Adams Squire Strongheart. *Our Families, Our Values: Snapshots of Queer Kinship*. Binghamton, NY: Harrington Park Press, 1997.

Gregory, Steven, and Roger Sanjek, eds. *Race*. New Brunswick, NJ: Rutgers University Press, 1994.

Griffin, Horace. "Toward a True Black Liberation Theology: Affirming Homoeroticism, Black Gay Christians, and Their Love Relationships." In Pinn and Hopkins, *Loving the Body*, 133–53.

Griffin, Horace L. *Their Own Receive Them Not: African American Lesbians and Gays in Black Churches*. Cleveland, OH: Pilgrim Press, 2006.

_____. "Their Own Received Them Not: Lesbians and Gays in Black Churches." *Theology and Sexuality* no. 12 (March 2000): 88–100.

Guest, Deryn, Robert E. Goss, Mona West, and Thomas Bohache, eds. *The Queer Bible Commentary*. London: SCM Press, 2006.

Guitiérrez, Ramón A., ed. "Further Desire: Asian and Asian American Sexualities." *Amerasia Journal* 37, no. 2 (2011).

Hames-García, Michael. "Queer Theory Revisited." In Hames-García and Martínez, *Gay Latino Studies*, 19–45.

Hames-García, Michael, and Ernesto Javier Martínez. "Introduction: Re-membering Gay Latino Studies." In Hames-García and Martínez, *Gay Latino Studies*, 1–18.

_____, eds. *Gay Latino Studies: A Critical Reader*. Durham, NC: Duke University Press, 2011.

Hamilton, Kenneth. "Colonial Legacies, Decolonized Spirits: Balboa, Ugandan Martyrs and AIDS Solidarity Today." In Hutchins and Williams, *Sexuality, Religion and the Sacred*, 78–93.

_____. "'The Flames of Namugongo': Postcoloniality Meets Queer on African Soil?" *Journal of Commonwealth and Postcolonial Studies* 10, no. 1 (2003): 183–208.

Han, Arar, and John Hsu, eds. *Asian American X: An Intersection of 21st Century Asian American Voices*. Ann Arbor: University of Michigan Press, 2004.

Hanks, Tom. *The Subversive Gospel: A New Testament Commentary of Liberation*.

Translated by John P. Doner. Cleveland, OH: Pilgrim Press, 2000.

Haritaworn, Jin. "Shifting Positionalities: Empirical Reflections on a Queer/Trans of Colour Methodology." *Sociological Research Online* 13, no. 1.13 (March 21, 2008): 5.1. Accessed January 3, 2013. http://bit.ly/ifbHzR.

Harper, Indie. "No Asians, Blacks, Fats, or Femmes." In Boykin, *For Colored Boys*, 129–35.

Hassett, Miranda K. *Anglican Communion in Crisis: How Episcopal Dissidents and Their African Allies Are Reshaping Anglicanism*. Princeton, NJ: Princeton University Press, 2007.

Hawley, John C., ed. *Post-Colonial, Queer: Theoretical Intersections*. Albany: State University of New York Press, 2001.

Henderson-Espinoza, Robyn. "*El Cuerpo Como (un) Espacio de Frontera*: The Body as (a) Borderland Space." In Cecil, *New Frontiers*, 41–48.

Hernandez, Lydia. "And So It Was." In Thorson-Smith et al., *Called Out With*, 85–91.

Hernández-Gutiérrez, Manuel de Jesús. "Building a Research Agenda on U.S. Latino Lesbigay Literature and Cultural Production: Texts, Writers, Performance Artists, and Critics." In Foster, *Chicano/Latino Homoerotic Identities*, 287–304.

Herrero-Brasas, Juan A. "Whitman's Church of Comradeship: Same-Sex Love, Religion, and the Marginality of Friendship." In Boisvert and Johnson, *Queer Religion I*, 169–89.

Heyward, Carter. *Touching Our Strength: The Erotic as Power and the Love of God*. New York: HarperSanFrancisco, 1989.

Hick, John. *A Christian Theology of Religions: The Rainbow of Faiths*. Louisville, KY: Westminster John Knox Press, 1995.

Highleyman, Liz. "Kiyoshi Kuromiya: Integrating the Issues." In Mecca, *Smash the Church*, 17–21.

Hill, Renee L. "Who Are We for Each Other?: Sexism, Sexuality and Womanist Theology." In Cone and Wilmore, *Black Theology II*, 345–51.

Hill, Renée Leslie. "Disrupted/Disruptive Movements: Black Theology and Black Power 1969/1999." In Hopkins, *Black Faith and Public Talk*, 138–49.

Hinze, Christine Firer, J. Patrick Hornbeck, and Michael A. Norko. *More Than a Monologue: Sexual Diversity in the Catholic Church*. Bronx, NY: Fordham University Press, forthcoming.

Hoang, Nguyen Tan. "The Resurrection of Brandon Lee: The Making of a Gay Asian American Porn Star." In Williams, *Porn Studies*, 223–70.

Hong, Grace Kyungwon, and Roderick A. Ferguson. "Introduction." In Hong and Ferguson, *Strange Affinities*, 1–22.

_____, eds. *Strange Affinities: The Gender and Sexual Politics of Comparative Racialization*. Durham, NC: Duke University Press, 2011.

Hopkins, Dwight N., ed. *Black Faith and Public Talk: Critical Essays on James H. Cone's* Black Theology and Black Power. Maryknoll, NY: Orbis Books, 1999.

Hopkins, Julian, and Julian C.H. Lee, eds. *Thinking Through Malaysia: Culture and Identity in the 21st Century*. Petaling Jaya, Malaysia: Strategic Information and Research Development Centre, 2012.

Hornsby, Teresa J., and Ken Stone, eds. *Bible Trouble: Queer Reading at the Boundaries of Biblical Scholarship*. Atlanta, GA: Society of Biblical Literature, 2011.

HoSang, Daniel Martinez, Oneka LaBennett, and Laura Pulido, eds. *Racial Formation in the Twenty-First Century*. Berkeley: University of California Press, 2012.

Hsiung, Ann-Marie. "Gender and Same-Sex Relations in Confucianism and Taoism." In Ellison and Plaskow, *Heterosexism in Contemporary World Religion*, 99–34.

Hunt, Mary E. *Fierce Tenderness: A Feminist Theology of Friendship*. New York: Crossroad, 1991.

Hutchins, Loraine, and H. Sharif Williams. *Sexuality, Religion, and the Sacred: Bisexual, Pansexual and Polysexual Perspectives*. Abingdon, UK: Routledge, 2012.

Isherwood, Lisa, and Mark D. Jordan, eds. *Dancing Theology in Fetish Boots: Essays in Honour of Marcella Althaus-Reid*. London: SCM Press, 2010.

Jacobs, Sue-Ellen, Wesley Thomas, and Sabine Lang, eds. *Two-Spirit People: Native American Gender Identity, Sexuality, and Spirituality*. Urbana: University of Illinois Press, 1997.

James, G. Winston, and Lisa C. Moore, eds. *Spirited: Affirming the Soul and Black Gay/Lesbian Identity.* Washington, DC: RedBone Press, 2006.

Jennings, Theodore W. *The Man Jesus Loved: Homoerotic Narratives from the New Testament.* Cleveland, OH: Pilgrim Press, 2003.

Johnson, E. Patrick. "Feeling the Spirit in the Dark: Expanding Notions of the Sacred in the African American Gay Community." In Constantine-Simms, *The Greatest Taboo*, 88–109.

Jojo (Kenneth Hamilton). "Searching for Gender-Variant East African Spiritual Leaders, From Missionary Discourse to Middle Course." In Boisvert and Johnson, *Queer Religion I*, 127–45.

Jones, Serene. *Feminist Theory and Christian Theology: Cartographies of Grace.* Minneapolis, MN: Fortress Press, 2000.

Justice, Daniel Heath, Mark Rifkin, and Bethany Schneider, eds. "Sexuality, Nationality, Indigeneity." *GLQ: A Journal of Lesbian and Gay Studies* 16, nos. 1–2 (2010).

Kamitsuka, Margaret D., ed. *The Embrace of Eros: Bodies, Desires, and Sexuality in Christianity.* Minneapolis, MN: Fortress Press, 2010.

Kay, Kerwin, Jill Nagle, and Baruch Gould, eds. *Male Lust: Pleasure, Power, and Transformation.* Binghamton, NY: Harrington Park Press, 2000.

Keller, Catherine, and Laurel C. Schneider. *Polydoxy: Theology of Multiplicity and Relation.* Abingdon, UK: Routledge, 2011.

Kim, Michael. "Out and About: Coming of Age in a Straight White World." In Han and Hsu, *Asian American X*, 139–48.

Kittel, Gerhard, ed. *Theological Dictionary of the New Testament.* Volume 1. Translated by Geoffrey W. Bromiley. Grand Rapids, MI: Wm. B. Eerdmans, 1964.

_____, ed. *Theological Dictionary of the New Testament.* Volume 4. Translated by Geoffrey W. Bromiley. Grand Rapids, MI: Wm. B. Eerdmans, 1967.

Kolodny, Debra R., ed. *Blessed Bi Spirit: Bisexual People of Faith.* New York: Continuum, 2000.

Kong, Travis S.K. *Chinese Male Homosexualities: Memba, Tongzhi and Golden Boy.* London: Routledge, 2011.

_____. "Sexualizing Asian Male Bodies." In Seidman, Fischer, and Meeks, *Introducing the New Sexuality Studies*, 84–88.

Kornegay, EL. "Queering Black Homophobia: Black Theology as a Sexual Discourse of Transformation." *Theology and Sexuality* 11, no. 1 (September 2004): 29–51.

Krondorfer, Björn, ed. *Men and Masculinities in Christianity and Judaism: A Critical Reader.* London: SCM Press, 2009.

Kumashiro, Kevin K. *Restored Selves: Autobiographies of Queer Asian/Pacific American Activists.* Binghamton, NY: Harrington Park Press, 2004.

_____. *Troubling Intersections of Race and Sexuality: Queer Students of Color and Anti-Oppressive Education.* Lanham, MD: Rowman and Littlefield, 2001.

Kwok Pui-lan. "Asian and Asian American Churches." In Siker, *Homosexuality and Religion*, 59–61.

_____. "Body and Pleasure in Postcoloniality." In Isherwood and Jordan, *Dancing Theology*, 31–43.

_____. *Postcolonial Imagination and Feminist Theology.* Louisville, KY: Westminster John Knox Press, 2005.

_____. "Touching the Taboo: On the Sexuality of Jesus." In Ellison and Douglas, *Sexuality and the Sacred*, 119–34.

Law, Eric H.F. "A Litany for Dialogue Among People with Different Sexual Orientations." In Cherry and Sherwood, *Equal Rites*, 32–34.

_____. "A Spirituality of Creative Marginality." In Comstock and Henking, *Que(e)rying Religion*, 343–46.

_____. "A True WOW Experience: A Dialogue." Allies Gather (website). Accessed January 3, 2013. http://bit.ly/NuZ0xa.

_____. *The Word at the Crossings: Living the Good News in a Multicontextual Community.* St. Louis, MO: Chalice Press, 2004.

Lee, Jeanette Mei Gim. "Queerly a Good Friday." In Kumashiro, *Restoried Selves*, 81–86.

Lee, Jung Young. *Marginality: The Key to Multicultural Theology.* Minneapolis, MN: Fortress Press, 1995.

Lee, Raymond L., and Alistair B. Fraser. *The Rainbow Bridge: Rainbows in Art, Myth, and Science.* University Park: Pennsylvania State University Press, 2001.

Lee, Sang Hyun. *From a Liminal Place: An Asian American Theology.* Minneapolis, MN: Fortress Press, 2010.

Leong, Russell, ed. *Asian American Sexualities: Dimensions of the Gay and Lesbian Experience.* New York: Routledge, 1996.

Lewis, Linwood J. "Sexuality, Race, and Ethnicity." In McAnulty and Burnette, *Sex and Sexuality, Volume 1,* 229–64.

Li, Yu-chen. "Reconstructing Buddhist Perspectives on Homosexuality: Enlightenment from the Study of the Body." In Ellison and Plaskow, *Heterosexism in Contemporary World Religion,* 135–53.

Liang, Christopher T.H., Amanda L.Y. Rivera, Anisha Nathwani, Phillip Dang, and Ashley N. Douroux. "Dealing with Gendered Racism and Racial Identity Among Asian American Men." In Liu, Iwamoto, and Chae, *Culturally Responsive Counseling,* 63–81.

Liew, Tat-siong Benny. "(Cor)Responding: A Letter to the Editor." In Stone, *Queer Commentary and the Hebrew Bible,* 182–92.

————. "Queering Closets and Perverting Desires: Cross-Examining John's Engendering and Transgendering Word Across Different Worlds." In Bailey, Liew, and Segovia, *They Were All Together in One Place?,* 251–88.

Lightsey, Pamela R. "The Eddie Long Scandal: It *Is* About Anti-Homosexuality." *Religion Dispatches* (September 29, 2010). Accessed January 3, 2013. http://bit.ly/SRiuNQ.

————. "Methodist Clergy Pledge to Defy Church in Blessing LGBT Unions," *Religion Dispatches* (June 11, 2011). Accessed January 3, 2013. http://bit.ly/ksYH9j.

Lim, Leng, with Kim-Hao Yap and Tuck-Leong Lee. "The Mythic-Literalists in the Province of Southeast Asia." In Brown, *Other Voices,* 58–76.

Lim, Leng Leroy. "'The Bible Tells Me to Hate Myself': The Crisis in Asian American Spiritual Leadership." *Semeia* 90/91 (2002): 315–22.

————. "Exploring Embodiment." In Ragsdale, *Boundary Wars,* 58–77.

————. "The Gay Erotics of My Stuttering Mother Tongue." *Amerasia Journal* 22, no. 1 (1996): 172–77.

————. "Webs of Betrayal, Webs of Blessings." In Goss and Strongheart, *Our Families, Our Values,* 227–41.

Lim-Hing, Sharon, ed. *The Very Inside: An Anthology of Writing by Asian and Pacific Islander Lesbian and Bisexual Women.* Toronto, ON: Sister Vision Press, 1994.

Liu, Timothy. *For Dust Thou Art.* Carbondale: Southern Illinois University Press, 2005.

————. "His Body Like Christ Passed In and Out of My Life." In Liu, *Vox Angelica,* 15.

————. "On Hearing the Seven Last Words of Christ." In Liu, *For Dust Thou Art,* 50.

————. *Vox Angelica.* Cambridge, MA: Alice James Books, 1992.

Liu, William Ming, and William R. Concepcion. "Redefining Asian American Identity and Masculinity." In Liu, Iwamoto, and Chae, *Culturally Responsive Counseling,* 127–44.

Liu, William Ming, Derek Kenji Iwamoto, and Mark H. Chae, eds. *Culturally Responsive Counseling with Asian American Men.* New York: Routledge, 2010.

Long, Michael G. *Martin Luther King Jr., Homosexuality, and the Early Gay Rights Movement: Keeping the Dream Straight?* New York: Palgrave Macmillan, 2012.

Lorde, Audre. *Sister Outsider: Essays and Speeches.* Rev. ed. Berkeley, CA: Crossing Press, 2007.

Loughlin, Gerard, ed. *Queer Theology: Rethinking the Western Body.* Malden, MA: Blackwell Publishing, 2007.

Lowe, Mary Elise. "Gay, Lesbian, and Queer Theologies: Origins, Contributions, and Challenges." *Dialog: A Journal of Theology* 48, no. 1 (Spring 2009): 49–61.

Maiztegui, Humberto. "Homosexuality and the Bible in the Anglican Church of the Southern Cone of America." In Brown, *Other Voices, Other Worlds,* 236–48.

Manalansan, Martin F. *Global Divas: Filipino Gay Men in the Diaspora.* Durham, NC: Duke University Press, 2003.

Marcus, Eric. *Making Gay History: The Half-Century Fight for Lesbian and Gay Equal Rights.* New York: Harper, 2002.

Martin, Fran, Peter A. Jackson, Mark McLelland, and Audrey Yue, eds. *AsiaPacifiQueer: Rethinking Genders and Sexualities.* Urbana: University of Illinois Press, 2008.

Martin, Joan M. "What I Don't Know About Brittney Griner, NCAA Women's Basketball Champion." *99 Brattle* (April 4, 2012). Accessed January 3, 2013. http://bit.ly/HO9btF.

———. "Yes, There Is a God!" *99 Brattle* (May 11, 2011). Accessed January 3, 2013. http://bit.ly/MnGPZF.

Masequesmay, Gina, and Sean Metzger, eds. *Embodying Asian/American Sexualities.* Lanham, MD: Lexington Books, 2009.

McAnulty, Richard D., and M. Michele Burnette, eds. *Sex and Sexuality, Volume 1: Sexuality Today—Trends and Controversies.* Westport, CT: Praeger, 2006.

McMullin, Dan Taulapapa. "*Fa'afafine* Notes: On Tagaloa, Jesus, and Nafanua." In Driskill et al., *Queer Indigenous Studies,* 81–94.

Mecca, Tommi Avicolli, ed. *Smash the Church, Smash the State!: The Early Years of Gay Liberation.* San Francisco, CA: City Lights Books, 2009.

Messmer, Marietta. "Transformations of the Sacred in Contemporary Chicana Culture." *Theology and Sexuality* 14, no. 3 (May 2008): 259–78.

Miller, Neil. *Out of the Past: Gay and Lesbian History from 1869 to the Present.* Rev. and updated ed. New York: Alyson Books, 2006.

Misa, Cristina M. "Where Have All the Queer Students of Color Gone?: Negotiated Identity of Queer Chicana/o Students." In Kumashiro, *Troubling Intersections,* 67–80.

Monroe, Irene. "Between a Rock and a Hard Place: Struggling with the Black Church's Heterosexism and the White Queer Community's Racism." In De La Torre, *Out of the Shadows,* 39–58.

———. "Lifting Our Voices." In James and Moore, *Spirited,* xi–xiv.

———. "Racism Haunts Queer and Christian Communities." Reverend Irene Monroe. Accessed January 3, 2013. http://bit.ly/PZYX0J.

———. "Roundtable Discussion: Must I Be Womanist?" *Journal of Feminist Studies in Religion* 22, no. 1 (Spring 2006): 107–13.

———. "When and Where I Enter, Then the Whole Race Enters with Me: Que(e)rying Exodus." In Pinn and Hopkins, *Loving the Body,* 121–31.

Moon, Byung-Ho. *Christ the Mediator of the Law: Calvin's Christological Understanding of the Law as the Rule of Living and Life-Giving.* Bletchley, UK: Paternoster, 2006.

Moore, Darnell L. "Theorizing the 'Black Body' as a Site of Trauma: Implications for Theologies of Embodiment." *Theology and Sexuality* 15, no. 2 (May 2009): 175–88.

Moraga, Cherríe, and Gloria Anzaldúa, eds. *This Bridge Called My Back: Writings by Radical Women of Color.* New York: Kitchen Table: Women of Color Press, 1981.

Morgensen, Scott Lauria. *Spaces Between Us: Queer Settler Colonialism and Indigenous Decolonization.* Minneapolis: University of Minnesota Press, 2011.

———. "Unsettling Queer Politics: What Can Non-Natives Learn from Two-Spirit Organizing?" In Driskill et al., *Queer Indigenous Studies,* 132–52.

Moya, Paula M.L. "Comment: Dancing with the Devil—When the Devil Is Gay." In Hames-García and Martínez, *Gay Latino Studies,* 250–58.

Muñoz, José Esteban. *Cruising Utopia: The Then and There of Queer Futurity.* New York: New York University Press, 2009.

———. *Disidentifications: Queers of Color and the Performance of Politics.* Minneapolis: University of Minnesota Press, 1999.

Muñoz, Manuel. "Zizgagger." In Muñoz, *Zigzagger,* 5–19.

———. *Zigzagger.* Evanston, IL: Northwestern University Press, 2003.

Murray, Stephen O. *Latin American Male Homosexualities.* Albuquerque: University of New Mexico Press, 1995.

Musskopf, André S. "Cruising (with) Marcella." In Isherwood and Jordan, *Dancing Theology*, 228–39.

_____. "A Gap in the Closet: Gay Theology in the Latin American Context." In Krondorfer, *Men and Masculinities in Christianity and Judaism*, 460–71.

_____. "Ungraceful God: Masculinity and Images of God in Brazilian Popular Culture." *Theology and Sexuality* 15, no. 2 (2009): 145–57.

Nagel, Joane. *Race, Ethnicity, and Sexuality: Intimate Intersections, Forbidden Frontiers.* New York: Oxford University Press, 2003.

Nardi, Peter, ed. *Gay Masculinities.* Thousand Oaks, CA: Sage Publications, 2000.

National Gay and Lesbian Task Force. "Injustice at Every Turn: A Look at American Indian and Alaskan Native Respondents in the National Transgender Discrimination Survey" (October 8, 2012). Accessed January 3, 2013. http://bit.ly/RM31A6.

_____. "Injustice at Every Turn: A Look at Asian American, South Asian, Southeast Asian, and Pacific Islander Respondents in the National Transgender Discrimination Survey" (July 19, 2011). Accessed January 3, 2013. http://bit.ly/MRTpT

_____. "Injustice at Every Turn: A Look at Black Respondents in the National Transgender Discrimination Survey" (September 15, 2011). Accessed January 3, 2013. http://bit.ly/nLZBHX.

_____. "Injustice at Every Turn: A Look at Latino/a Respondents in the National Transgender Discrimination Survey" (April 18, 2011). Accessed January 3, 2013. http://bit.ly/QPEBGU.

Nickoloff, James B. "Sexuality: A Queer Omission in U.S. Latino/a Theology." *Journal of Hispanic/Latino Theology* 10, no. 3 (2003): 31–51.

Nigianni, Chrysanthi, and Merl Storr, eds. *Deleuze and Queer Theory.* Edinburgh, UK: Edinburgh University Press, 2009.

Okihiro, Gary Y. *The Columbia Guide to Asian American History.* New York: Columbia University Press, 2001.

Oliveto, Karen P., Kelly D. Turney, and Traci C. West. *Talking About Homosexuality: A Congregational Resource.* Cleveland, OH: Pilgrim Press, 2005.

Oliver, Juan. "Why Gay Marriage?" *Journal of Men's Studies* 4, no. 3 (1996): 209–24.

Olyan, Saul M., and Martha C. Nussbaum. *Sexual Orientation and Human Rights in American Religious Discourse.* New York: Oxford University Press, 1998.

Omi, Michael, and Howard Winant. *Racial Formation in the United States: From the 1960s to the 1990s.* 2nd ed. New York: Routledge, 1994.

Palmer, Timothy, and Debra W. Haffner. *A Time to Seek: Study Guide on Sexual and Gender Diversity.* Westport, CT: Religious Institute, 2006.

Pérez, Laura E. "Decolonizing Sexuality and Spirituality in Chicana Feminist and Queer Art." *Tikkun Magazine* (July/August 2010). Accessed January 3, 2013. http://bit.ly/ahPJiW.

Petrella, Ivan. "Queer Eye for the Straight Guy: The Making Over of Liberation Theology, A Queer Discursive Approach." In Althaus-Reid, *Liberation Theology*, 33–49.

Pinn, Anthony B., and Dwight N. Hopkins, eds. *Loving the Body: Black Religious Studies and the Erotic.* New York: Palgrave Macmillan, 2004.

Puar, Jasbir K. *Terrorist Assemblages: Homonationalism in Queer Times.* Durham, NC: Duke University Press, 2007.

Ragsdale, Katherine Hancock, ed. *Boundary Wars: Intimacy and Distance in Healing Relationships.* Cleveland, OH: Pilgrim Press, 1996.

Ramirez-Valles, Jesus. *Compañeros: Latino Activists in the Face of AIDS.* Urbana: University of Illinois Press, 2011.

Rawls, Tonyia M. "Yes, Jesus Loves Me: The Liberating Power of Spiritual Acceptance for Black Lesbian, Gay, Bisexual, and Transgender Christians." In Battle and Barnes, *Black Sexualities*, 327–52.

Rhee, Margaret. "Towards Community: *KoreAm Journal* and Korean American Cultural Attitudes on Same-Sex Marriage." *Amerasia Journal* 32, no. 1 (2006): 75–88.

Ribas, Mario. "Practising Sexual Theology: Undressing Sex, Pleasure, Sin and Guilt in Colonised Mentalities." In Brown, *Other Voices, Other Worlds,* 221–35.

Richardson, Alan, and John Bowden, eds. *The Westminster Dictionary of Christian Theology.* Philadelphia, PA: Westminster Press, 1983.

Rifkin, Mark. *The Erotics of Sovereignty: Queer Native Writing in the Era of Self-Determination.* Minneapolis: University of Minnesota Press, 2012.

_____. *When Did Indians Become Straight?: Kinship, the History of Sexuality, and Native Sovereignty.* New York: Oxford University Press, 2011.

Robertson, Jon M. *Christ as Mediator: A Study of the Theologies of Eusebius of Caesarea, Marcellus of Ancyra and Athanasius of Alexandria.* Oxford, UK: Oxford University Press, 2007.

Robinson, Gene. *In the Eye of the Storm: Swept to the Center by God.* New York: Seabury Books, 2008.

Rodriguez, Eric M., and Suzanne C. Ouellette. "Religion and Masculinity in Latino Gay Lives." In Nardi, *Gay Masculinities,* 101–29.

Rodriguez, Richard. *Hunger of Memory: The Education of Richard Rodriguez.* New York: Dial Press, 1982.

Rodríguez-Olmedo, Joanne. "The U.S. Hispanic/Latino Landscape." In Aponte and De La Torre, *Handbook of Latina/o Theologies,* 123–29.

Roland Guzmán, Carla E. "Sexuality." In Aponte and De La Torre, *Handbook of Latina/o Theologies,* 257–64.

Roque Ramírez, Horacio N. "Borderlands, Diasporas, and Transnational Crossings: Teaching LGBT Latina and Latino Histories." *OAH Magazine of History* (March 2006): 39–42.

"Roundtable Discussion: Must I Be Womanist?" *Journal of Feminist Studies in Religion* 22, no. 1 (Spring 2006): 85–134.

"Roundtable Discussion: Same-Sex Marriage." *Journal of Feminist Studies in Religion* 20, no. 2 (Fall 2004): 83–117.

Rudy, Kathy. *Sex and the Church: Gender, Homosexuality, and the Transformation of Christian Ethics.* Boston, MA: Beacon Press, 1997.

_____. "Subjectivity and Belief." In Loughlin, *Queer Theology,* 37–49.

Sanjek, Roger. "The Enduring Inequalities of Race." In Gregory and Sanjek, *Race,* 1–17.

Schippert, Claudia. "Implications of Queer Theory for the Study of Religion and Gender: Entering the Third Decade." *Religion and Gender* 1, no. 1 (2011): 66–84.

_____. "Queer Theory and the Study of Religion." *Rever: Revista de Estudos da Religião* 5, no. 4 (2005): 90–99.

Schexnayder, James A. *Setting the Table: Preparing Catholic Parishes to Welcome Lesbian, Gay, Bisexual, and Transgender People and Their Families.* 2011.

Schneider, Laurel C. *Beyond Monotheism: A Theology of Multiplicity.* Abingdon, UK: Routledge, 2008.

_____. "Promiscuous Incarnation." In Kamitsuka, *The Embrace of Eros,* 231–34.

_____. "Queer Theory." In Adam, *Handbook of Postmodern Biblical Interpretation,* 206–12.

_____. "What Race Is Your Sex?" In Boisvert and Johnson, *Queer Religion II,* 125–41.

Seerveld, Calvin G. *Rainbows for the Fallen World: Aesthetic Life and Artistic Task.* Toronto, ON: Toronto Tuppence Press, 2005.

Seidman, Steven, Nancy Fischer, and Chet Meeks, eds. *Introducing the New Sexuality Studies.* 2nd ed. Abingdon, UK: Routledge, 2011.

Shah, Nayan. "Perversity, Contamination, and the Dangers of Queer Domesticity." In Corber and Valocchi, *Queer Studies,* 121–41.

Showalter, Elaine, ed. *The New Feminist Criticism: Essays on Women, Literature, and Theory.* New York: Pantheon Books, 1985.

Shrake, Eunai. "Homosexuality and Korean Immigrant Protestant Churches." In Masequesmay and Metzger, *Embodying Asian/American Sexualities,* 145–56.

Siker, Jeffrey S., ed. *Homosexuality and Religion: An Encyclopedia*. Westport, CT: Greenwood Press, 2007.

_____. "Latin@ Church Traditions." In Siker, *Homosexuality and Religion*, 145–46.

Smith, Andrea. *Conquest: Sexual Violence and American Indian Genocide*. Cambridge, MA: South End Press, 2005.

_____. *Native Americans and the Christian Right: The Gendered Politics of Unlikely Alliances*. Durham, NC: Duke University Press, 2008.

_____. "Queer Theory and Native Studies: The Heteronormativity of Settler Colonialism." In Driskill et al., *Queer Indigenous Studies*, 43–65.

Smith, Barbara. "Toward a Black Feminist Criticism." In Showalter, *The New Feminist Criticism*, 168–85.

Sneed, Roger A. "Dark Matter: Liminality and Black Queer Bodies." In Coleman, *Ain't I a Womanist, Too?*

_____. "Like Fire Shut Up in Our Bones: Religion and Spirituality in Black Gay Men's Literature." *Black Theology: An International Journal* 6, no. 2 (2008): 241–61.

_____. *Representations of Homosexuality: Black Liberation Theology and Cultural Criticism*. New York: Palgrave Macmillan, 2010.

Stone, Ken, ed. *Queer Commentary and the Hebrew Bible*. Cleveland, OH: Pilgrim Press, 2001.

Stringfellow, Roland. "Soul Work: Developing a Black LGBT Liberation Theology." In Boisvert and Johnson, *Queer Religion I*, 113–25.

Strongman, Roberto. "Syncretic Religion and Dissident Sexualities." In Cruz-Malavé and Manalansan, *Queer Globalizations*, 176–92.

Stuart, Elizabeth. *Just Good Friends: Towards a Lesbian and Gay Theology of Relationships*. London: Mowbray, 1995.

Suárez, Margarita. "Reflections on Being Latina and Lesbian." In Comstock and Henking, *Que(e)rying Religion*, 347–50.

Sueyoshi, Amy. *Queer Compulsions: Race, Nation, and Sexuality in the Affairs of Yone Noguchi*. Honolulu: University of Hawai'i Press, 2012.

Takaki, Ronald. *A Different Mirror: A History of Multicultural America*. Rev. ed. New York: Back Bay Books, 2008.

_____. *Strangers from a Different Shore: A History of Asian Americans*. Updated and rev. ed. New York: Back Bay Books, 1998.

Tan, Chong Kee. "Transcending Sexual Nationalism and Colonialism." In Hawley, *Post-Colonial, Queer*, 123–37.

Tanis, Justin. *Trans-Gendered: Theology, Ministry, and Communities of Faith*. Cleveland, OH: Pilgrim Press, 2003.

Tejedor, Chon. *Starting with Wittgenstein*. London: Continuum, 2011.

Thadani, Giti. *Sakhiyani: Lesbian Desire in Ancient and Modern India*. London: Cassell, 1996.

Thorson-Smith, Sylvia, Johanna W.H. van Wijk-Bos, Norm Pott, and William P. Thompson, eds. *Called Out With: Stories of Solidarity in Support of Lesbian, Gay, Bisexual, and Transgendered Persons*. Louisville, KY: Westminster John Knox Press, 1997.

Thumma, Scott, and Edward R. Gray, eds. *Gay Religion*. Walnut Creek, CA: AltaMira Press, 2005.

Townes, Emilie M. "The Dancing Mind: Queer Black Bodies in Academy and Church." 2011 Gilberto Castañeda Lecture, Chicago Theological Seminary, Chicago, IL, May 20, 2011.

_____. "Marcella Althaus-Reid's Indecent Theology: A Response." In Isherwood and Jordan, *Dancing Theology*, 61–67.

_____. "Roundtable Discussion: Same-Sex Marriage." *Journal of Feminist Studies in Religion* 20, no. 2 (Fall 2004): 100–103.

_____. "Washed in the Grace of God." In Adams and Fortune, *Violence Against Women and Children*, 60–70.

_____. *Womanist Ethics and the Cultural Production of Evil*. New York: Palgrave Macmillan, 2006.

Triana, Pedro. "Do Not Judge . . . Only Comprehend: The Anglican Communion and Human Sexuality." In Brown, *Other Voices, Other Worlds*, 208–20.

Tuaolo, Esera, with John Rosengren. *Alone in the Trenches: My Life as a Gay Man in the NFL*. Naperville, IL: Sourcebooks, 2006.

Tutu, Desmond. *The Rainbow People of God: The Making of a Peaceful Revolution*. Edited by John Allen. New York: Image Books, 1994.

Uyeda, Ann Yuri. "All at Once, All Together: One Asian American Lesbian's Account of the 1989 Asian Pacific Lesbian Network Retreat." In Lim-Hing, *The Very Inside*, 109–21.

Vallescorbo, Heriberto. "Latino Gay Men's Experiences of Spiritual Reintegration: A Heuristic Study." PsyD diss., California Institute of Integral Studies, 2010. UMI (No. 3432452).

Valentín, Benjamín. "Introduction." In Valentín, *New Horizons in Hispanic/Latino(a) Theology*, 1–9.

_____, ed. *New Horizons in Hispanic/Latino(a) Theology*. Cleveland, OH: Pilgrim Press, 2003.

Vanita, Ruth. "Hinduism and Homosexuality." In Boisvert and Johnson, *Queer Religion I*, 1–23.

Vazquez, Charlie. "Presión Bajo Gracia." In Evans and Healey, *Queer and Catholic*, 105–13.

Vázquez, Jared. "Queer Tongues Confess, I Know That I Know That I Know: A Queer Reading of James K.A. Smith's *Thinking in Tongues*." MDiv thesis, Phillips Theological Seminary, 2012.

Vidal-Ortiz, Salvador. "Religion/Spirituality, U.S. Latina/o Communities, and Sexuality Scholarship: A Thread of Current Works." In Asencio, *Latina/o Sexualities*, 173–87.

_____. "Sexuality and Gender in Santería: LGBT Identities at the Crossroads of Santería Religious Practices and Beliefs." In Thumma and Gray, *Gay Religion*, 115–37.

Villalobos, Manuel. "Bodies *Del Otro Lado* Finding Life and Hope in the Borderland: Gloria Anzaldúa, the Ethiopian Eunuch of Acts 8:26–40, y Yo." In Hornsby and Stone, *Bible Trouble*, 191–221.

Vitiello, Giovanni. *The Libertine's Friend: Homosexuality and Masculinity in Late Imperial China*. Chicago, IL: University of Chicago Press, 2011.

Wakefield, Gordon S. "Spirituality." In Richardson and Bowden, *Westminster Dictionary of Christian Theology*, 549–50.

Wat, Eric C. *The Making of a Gay Asian Community: An Oral History of Pre-AIDS Los Angeles*. Lanham, MD: Rowman and Littlefield, 2002.

_____. "Preserving the Paradox: Stories from a Gay-Loh." In Leong, *Asian American Sexualities*, 71–80.

Watanabe, Tsuneo, and Jun'ichi Iwata. *The Love of the Samurai: A Thousand Years of Japanese Homosexuality*. London: GMP Publishers, 1989.

Weeks, Jeffrey. "The Social Construction of Sexuality." In Seidman, Fischer, and Meeks, *Introducing the New Sexuality Studies*, 13–19.

West, Traci C. *Defending Same-Sex Marriage*. Volume 2 of *Our Family Values: Same-Sex Marriage and Religion*. Westport, CT: Greenwood-Praeger, 2006.

_____. *Disruptive Christian Ethics: When Racism and Women's Lives Matter*. Louisville, KY: Westminster John Knox Press, 2006.

_____. "Race and Gender Oppression Can Really Get in the Way: Ethical Concerns in the Counseling of African American Women." In Ragsdale, *Boundary Wars*, 44–57.

_____. "Roundtable Discussion: Must I Be Womanist?" *Journal of Feminist Studies in Religion* 22, no. 1 (Spring 2006): 128–34.

_____. "A Space for Faith, Sexual Desire, and Ethical Black Ministerial Practices." In Pinn and Hopkins, *Loving the Body*, 31–50.

Whelan, Richard. *The Book of Rainbows: Art, Literature, Science, and Mythology*. Cobb, CA: First Glance Books, 1997.

Wilcox, Melissa M. "Queer Theory and the Study of Religion." In Boisvert and Johnson, *Queer Religion II*, 227–51.

Williams, Linda. *Porn Studies*. Durham, NC: Duke University Press, 2004.

Wong, Yuenmei. "Islam, Sexuality, and the Marginal Positioning of *Pengkids* and Their Girlfriends in Malaysia." *Journal of Lesbian Studies* 16 (2012): 1–14.

Wu, Rose, ed. "Beyond Right and Wrong: Doing Queer Theology in Hong Kong." In *God's Image* 29, no. 3 (September 2010).

_____. *Liberating the Church from Fear: The Story of Hong Kong's Sexual Minorities.* Kowloon, Hong Kong: Hong Kong Women Christian Council, 2000.

_____. "A Story of Its Own Name: Hong Kong's *Tongzhi* Culture and Movement." In Brock et al., *Off the Menu*, 275–92.

_____. "A Story of Its Own Name: Hong Kong's *Tongzhi* Culture and Movement." In Brown, *Other Voices, Other Worlds*, 40–57.

Xavier, Emanuel. *If Jesus Were Gay and Other Poems.* Bar Harbor, ME: Queer Mojo, 2010.

_____. "Just Like Jesus." In Xavier, *If Jesus Were Gay*, 1–2.

_____. "The Mexican." In Xavier, *If Jesus Were Gay*, 21.

Yip, Lai-shan. "Listening to the Passion of Catholic *nu-tongzhi*: Developing a Catholic Lesbian Feminist Theology in Hong Kong." In Boisvert and Johnson, *Queer Religion II*, 63–80.

_____. "A Proposal for Catholic Lesbian Feminist Theology in Hong Kong." In *God's Image* 29, no. 3 (September 2010): 21–32.

Yomekpe, Kuukua Dzigbordi. "Not Just a Phase: Single Black Women in the Black Church." In Boisvert and Johnson, *Queer Religion II*, 109–23.

Young, Thelathia "Nikki." "De-Centering Religion as Queer Pedagogical Practice." *Bulletin for the Study of Religion* 39, no. 4 (November 2010): 13–18.

_____. "Queering 'The Human Situation.'" *Journal of Feminist Studies in Religion* 28, no. 1 (Spring 2012): 126–31.

_____. "'Uses of the Erotic' for Teaching Queer Studies." *WSQ* 40, nos. 3–4 (Fall/Winter 2012): 297–301.

Index

179

About the Author

Patrick S. Cheng is the Associate Professor of Historical and Systematic Theology at the Episcopal Divinity School in Cambridge, Massachusetts. He is the author of *Rainbow Theology: Bridging Race, Sexuality, and Spirit* (2013); *From Sin to Amazing Grace: Discovering the Queer Christ* (2012); and *Radical Love: An Introduction to Queer Theology* (2011). Cheng holds a Ph.D., M.Phil., and M.A. from Union Theological Seminary in the City of New York, a J.D. from Harvard Law School, and a B.A. from Yale College. He is an ordained minister with the Metropolitan Community Churches, and he contributes to the *Huffington Post*. For more information, please see his website at http://www.patrickcheng.net.

CPSIA information can be obtained
at www.ICGtesting.com
Printed in the USA
BVHW031949210222
629710BV00014B/96

9 781596 272415